W9-AHT-138

THE TROUBLES

THE TROUBLES

Richard Broad   Taylor Downing   Caroline Elliston
Isobel Hinshelwood   Annie Kossoff   Sarah Manwaring-White
Ian Stuttard   Adrian Wood

EDITOR
Taylor Downing

PICTURE EDITOR
Isobel Hinshelwood

THAMES/MACDONALD FUTURA

CONTENTS

First published in Great Britain in 1980 by

THAMES TELEVISION LTD
in association with
MACDONALD FUTURA PUBLISHERS LTD

Copyright © 1980 by the authors

All rights reserved. No part of this publication may be
reproduced by any means without prior permission.
This book is sold subject to the condition that it shall not, by way
of trade or otherwise, be lent, re-sold, hired out or otherwise
circulated without the publishers' prior consent in form of binding
other than that in which it is published and without a similar
condition including this condition being imposed on the subsequent
purchaser.

ISBN (hardback): 0 354 04608 X
ISBN (paperback): 0 7088 1966 4

Thames Television Ltd
306 Euston Road
London NW1 3BB

Macdonald Futura Publishers Ltd
Paulton House
8 Shepherdess Walk
London N1 7LW

Typesetting by Bookmag, Inverness, Scotland.

Printed and bound by Butler and Tanner Ltd, Frome, Somerset.

PREFACE

This is not a conventional history book and it is perhaps necessary to explain its unusual lay-out. The book comes out of the Thames Television series of the same name, and each of the five chapters corresponds with one of the five programmes of the television series. But a book, obviously, communicates information in a different way to a television programme. Each chapter has been constructed out of two closely related components. The text comprises a general survey of the history of Anglo–Irish affairs from the Reformation to the present day. The picture boxes of each chapter are intended to supplement the text. They consist of illustrations and extended captions which follow up in detail some of the points made in the text. The captions provide a little of the background to the history to complement the text, a selection from some of the key documents, and an analysis of the images themselves. They are intended to provide a visual but reflective coverage of some of the key episodes in the history. The text can be read from start to finish, and the captions can be read separately or along with the text.

The first chapter, 'Conquest', analyses the nature of the colonial relationship between England and Ireland. It looks at the history of Irish resistance to British rule from the sixteenth century onwards which culminated in the 1916 Easter Rising.

The second chapter, 'Partition', goes back over some of the same history, to follow events from an Ulster perspective. The chapter begins with the Act of Union and shows how, for the Ulster Protestants, defence of the Union became the centrepiece of their policy. The chapter ends with the Anglo–Irish War of 1919–21, the partition of the country and the creation of a six-county province of Northern Ireland.

Chapter three, 'Legacy', provides an historical analysis of the Northern Ireland province from its formation in 1921 to the revival of violence at the end of the 1960s.

Chapter four, 'Rebellion', is a detailed narrative of the Catholic Rebellion against the Northern Ireland state. Beginning with the violence of the early 1960s, it traces the development of the Civil Rights movement and the gradual transition from peaceful protest to armed resistance. The chapter ends with the collapse of the Northern Ireland state and the introduction of Direct Rule in 1972.

Chapter five, 'Deadlock', looks briefly at events from 1972 to 1980, and then ends with a survey of the history from the Reformation to the present, examining the common patterns that emerge over and over again through the centuries. It concludes with an assessment of the different possible solutions to the problem of Northern Ireland today and discusses whether or not any solution is politically acceptable.

Chapters four and five pose great problems for the writing of what claims to be a work of history. Events of the last few years are usually thought to be unworthy of the attention of historians, being so recent that they defy the clear analysis that can be given to earlier periods. We do not agree. We have set out in this book to provide a background to what is going on in Northern Ireland today and to understand events of the last few years in the context of the history. Although many of the documents usually essential to historical research, like government records, are unavailable for the recent past, the last few decades have been the age of information and communication. There is, therefore, enough material available to make a survey of the history possible in the last two chapters, despite the closeness of the events. And even for distant events, like the Anglo–Irish War of 1919–21, some government records are still under a 100-year embargo. This does not prevent histories from being written.

During the making of *The Troubles* series, we have met and talked with literally hundreds of people whose ideas, opinions and experiences have informed this book throughout. We are grateful to them all for the time they have given us and interest they have shown. We are especially indebted to Professor F.S.L. Lyons, Provost of Trinity College, Dublin, who although not directly connected with the book, has been the historical adviser to the television series. We have included, at the end, a list of the books and films which we have found the most useful in studying the history.

This book is a collective work. It is written by the group of people who are making the television series. It has all the advantages and disadvantages of a collectively written piece. Almost every line has been argued over and if, at times, this has affected the style of the writing, then we apologise. We still believe that in something as long and as complex as Irish history over the last three and a half centuries, several heads are better than one. Finally, it must be said that any opinions expressed in this book are entirely those of the authors and in no sense represent the attitudes of Thames Television or, indeed, anyone else.

1: CONQUEST

England's conquest and colonisation of Ireland began in the twelfth century with Henry II's invasion, and culminated in the middle of the seventeenth century with Cromwell's land confiscation. It was resented by the Irish from the beginning. Much of Ireland's history in the succeeding centuries is the story of Irish resistance to and rebellion against British rule.

In 1500, Ireland had an identity, language, culture and social order distinct from English society. They were the amalgam of the influences and ideas of the conquerors and adventurers — Celts, Gauls, Vikings and Normans — which combined with Ireland's distinctive tradition of Catholicism to produce its own unique culture. A similar process, though with very different results, had produced English society.

The medieval conquest of Ireland had never penetrated far beyond the area around Dublin, called the Pale, but in the sixteenth and seventeenth centuries, English rule in Ireland became far more effective. This Tudor and Stuart conquest was made possible by the new techniques of statecraft; an increasingly sophisticated bureaucracy, the deployment of standing armies, and the capacity to collect taxes and administer justice efficiently. In the sixteenth century this transformed kingdoms, from loose associations of semi-autonomous nobles swearing fealty to kings, into modern nation-states where authority was centralised in a governmental bureaucracy. But it was the timing of this conquest, the fact that it was during the Reformation and Counter-Reformation, which was a period of profound religious and political upheaval and passion, that most deeply complicated and disturbed Anglo-Irish relations throughout the succeeding centuries and into the present day. Catholic Ireland was conquered by Protestant England.

The Reformation had grown from small beginnings in the early sixteenth century into a momentous force for change in society. By the eve of the Reformation, the Roman Catholic Church had become wealthy and corrupt. The Pope was not only the Vicar of God but, as ruler of the territory around Rome he was also an Italian prince who had to administer matters both sacred and secular. Similarly, many of his bishops were more like feudal lords than spiritual leaders. Offices throughout the Church were often sold to the highest bidder or given away to relatives. The monasteries had ceased to be places of learning and had become opulent centres of decadent living.

Luther's revolution was that, in providing a more rigorous, self-searching religious code, he also offered the opportunity for political reform. When he emphasised the need for inner religious faith rather than outward conformity to the rituals of the Church, Luther was in fact unleashing something far more fundamental than just a spiritual rejuvenation. In medieval society, the Church and the state were inseparable; all political activity was supposed to be directed towards religious ends; politics and religion were one and the same thing. So, if Luther challenged the authority of the Church, he challenged the structure of society. By establishing a 'reformed' religion, Luther was legitimising revolt against the established order. All the tensions that were generated by the shift from the medieval to the modern world became caught up with this religious upheaval. Princes could now use religion to justify rebellion against their overlords. Governments could demand the obedience of their citizens out of a desire for religious uniformity. Nations could declare themselves independent from the international authority of the Church of Rome by proclaiming their adherence to the reformed religions. The new faith became known as 'Protestantism' as it was a 'Protest' against the existing order of things. So a whole host of political ambitions became caught up in a religious revival, leading to a dramatic realignment of political divisions in Europe.

These ideas caught the imagination of many millions throughout Europe. The Catholic Church responded to the theological onslaught of the Reformation with the self-examination of the Counter-Reformation, and this further fuelled the religious debate, leaving Europe deeply divided. Now, both Protestant and Catholic were determined to champion their faith. The intensity with which both sides fought for their cause could not be contained. Religious violence became a feature of political life.

By the 1560s, Norway, Denmark, Sweden, Prussia, England and most of Germany and the Netherlands had joined the Protestant revolution. Italy, Spain, France and Ireland remained staunchly Catholic. As a result, there was a series of civil and national religious wars which further intensified the hatred between Catholic and Protestant.

It was in this context of the sectarianism of post-Reformation Europe that the Tudor monarchs turned their attention to Ireland. Their interest was primarily strategic. If the natural enemies of the Tudors, Catholic France or Spain, made an alliance with Catholic Ireland, Protestant England would be threatened from two sides (see map on page 198). The threat was more menacing at a time when improved sailing techniques much enhanced the military potential of navies. Ireland held the key to the backdoor of England. The Tudors and their advisers feared the use of Ireland as a base for an invasion of England, as have successive governments over the centuries, so Henry VIII, Edward, Mary and Elizabeth successively sought to bring Ireland under English control.

From 1530, Henry VIII's new breed of bureaucrats began to press English interests in Dublin in an attempt to bring the Gaelic chieftains of Ireland into line as vassals of the English Crown. This provoked a rebellion in the area around Dublin in 1534, quelled with a severity which, although unprecedented in Ireland at that time, was a taste of things to come.

The Pale was tamed: from then on there would be English viceroys and soldiers in Dublin continously for nearly four centuries. When Elizabeth I sought to install military governors in Connacht and Munster, Munster rebelled and was duly crushed in 1583. Connacht acquiesced, and England had a presence and partial control over three-quarters of Ireland. Only Ulster, the most Gaelic, inaccessible and recalcitrant province, remained defiant.

Throughout the 1580s, England feared the threat of a Spanish invasion; this was only partially dispelled in 1588 when Drake defeated their Armada. England was reminded of Irish unreliability when Spanish troops aided the rebels in the wars of the 1580s. Elizabeth was forced to turn her attention to Ulster.

O'Neill and O'Donnell, the chieftains of Ulster, had both sworn fealty to the English Crown, taking the titles of the Earls of Tyrone and Tyrconnell respectively, but they increasingly understood the implications for Gaelic Ireland of the growth of English law and administration. In 1598, they defeated the English garrisons at the Battle of Yellow Ford and sparked off a rising in the rest of Ireland. The ensuing war, during which the Spaniards intervened yet again on the Irish side, lasted five years. O'Neill faced overwhelming odds. His final surrender to Elizabeth's deputy, Mountjoy, came six days after the English monarch had died in March 1603. The Tudor conquest of Ireland was complete.

Normally, in such a situation, England could then expect to command the loyalty of the Ulster nobility. It was usual for the defeated nobility to surrender to the Crown and then, in return, to be regranted their lands as servants of the Crown. But O'Neill and O'Donnell were proud men who found English rule humiliating. Neither they nor any other Ulster notables wished to witness and preside over the demise of the Gaelic way of life. In 1607, the Earls and their entourages went into voluntary exile, leaving Ulster leaderless, and their lands forfeited to the British Crown.

James I, King of England and Scotland, had now to find an alternative way to control this restless province. Since land was the source of wealth and the basis of power, one solution was that of 'planting' loyal settlers throughout the countryside on land taken from the natives. Machiavelli advocated the use of 'plantation', as this policy became known, in his advice to Princes:

But when states are acquired in a province differing in language, in customs and in institutions, then difficulties arise: and to hold them one must be very fortunate and very assiduous. One of the best, most effective expedients would be for the conqueror to go to live there in person . . . The other and better expedient is to establish settlements in one or two places which, as it were, fetter the state to you. Settlements do not cost much, and the prince can found them and maintain them at little or no personal expense. He injures only those from who he takes land and houses to give to the new inhabitants, and these victims form a tiny minority, and can never do any harm since they remain poor and scattered.

Plantation had already been used in Ireland in the 1570s and '80s in a small way (see map on page 199). But now, in 1609, a vast and carefully organised Plantation of Ulster was prepared. Plantation offered a way of attaining power over the rebellious regions of Ireland without the expense

Early in November 1641, news began to trickle through to London about a terrible and bloody rising in Ireland. In the absence of any clear and accurate account of what was going on over the Irish Sea, rumour flourished. It was soon being said that the Irish Catholics were torturing and massacring God-fearing Protestants by the thousand.

The illustrations opposite show various ghoulish tortures that were supposedly being practised against the Protestants in Ireland. They are taken from one of the many political pamphlets that were published in London at this time, on the eve of the Civil War, appealing to an electorate of growing size and political sophistication. This particular pamphlet was written early in 1642 by a Presbyterian, James Cranford. It was supposedly based on the evidence of Protestants who had fled from Ireland. The titlepage gives some idea of the hysterical atmosphere generated by the rising:

The teares of Ireland
Wherein is lively presented . . . a list of the
unheard of Cruelties
and perfidious Treacheries of bloud-thirsty Jesuits
and the
Popish faction.
As a warning piece to her Sister Nations to prevent
the
like miseries, as are now acted upon the Stage of
this
fresh bleeding nation.
Reported by Gentlemen of good credit living there,
but
forced to flie for their lives, as Job's Messengers,
to tell us what they have heard and seene with
their eyes, illustrated by Pictures.

Hatred of the Roman Catholic faith and of followers of Catholicism had a long pedigree in sixteenth- and seventeenth-century England. John Foxe's *Book of Martyrs* immortalised the sufferings of the Protestants burnt during Mary's reign and helped to keep alive fear of Catholics. On St Bartholomew's Day, 1572, in France, three thousand Protestant noblemen were murdered in their beds by Catholics, and this generated further fears amongst English Protestants, fears that were revived by the rebellion of the Catholic Irish in 1641. When Pope Pius V excommunicated Elizabeth I in 1570 and told the English Catholics that they no longer need be loyal to their sovereign, it seemed proof that Catholicism was equated with treason. England's arch-enemy, Philip II of Spain (1556-98), regarded the reconquest of

Protestant territory for the Catholic faith as his life's crusade. In 1588, he sent his Spanish Armada against England, and the defeat of this fleet was seen as not only a military but also a moral victory, a sign that divine pleasure courted Protestant England in her struggle with the Catholic superpowers. In 1605, a Catholic attempt to blow up the King and the Houses of Parliament was foiled, and the failure of this Gunpowder Plot is still celebrated annually on 5 November. 'Gunpowder, Treason and Plot' parties used to be essentially sectarian, with the burning of an effigy of the Pope at the centre of the ritual. But now the celebrations have become entirely secular and no more than an entertainment for children, whilst the effigy of the Pope has become the mock-up 'Guy' of today's bonfire parties. Outbreaks of anti-Catholic fervour recurred periodically throughout the seventeenth century. The 'Popish Plot' of 1678 (Titus Oates's revelations of the existence of a carefully prepared Catholic conspiracy to take over England and to plant the Catholic James II on the throne) is only the best known of many.

John Milton (1608-74) is an interesting illustration of this anti-Catholic hysteria that was deeply embedded in English attitudes at the time. Milton was one of the most enlightened men of his day. He was a keen supporter of civil liberties and argued for the complete freedom of the Press ('Give me the liberty to know, to utter and to argue freely according to conscience, above all liberties.'), as well as for a wide range of domestic liberties, such as free divorce and equal education of both men and women. These ideas mark him out as one of the truly radical thinkers of the seventeenth century. Yet, when it came to Catholicism, Milton shared the same forebodings as all his contemporaries. He believed that Catholicism was the only heretical form of Christianity and whilst the State should tolerate every variant of Protestant worship, Catholicism was 'not to be tolerated either in public or private.' He believed that Catholicism was 'idolatry', and he called it 'The worst of superstitions and the heaviest of all God's judgments.'

Clearly, there were deep psychological and political forces at work behind this recurring fear and hatred of Catholics in seventeenth-century England. The hysteria generated by suggestions of 'popish plots' had a positive function to play in the process of nation-building in the young English Protestant state. By rallying to defend their faith and their government, Englishmen were uniting themselves together in strength, behind an assertion of their Protestantism and their Englishness. Just as other societies have at times used anti-semitism or fear of blacks, so

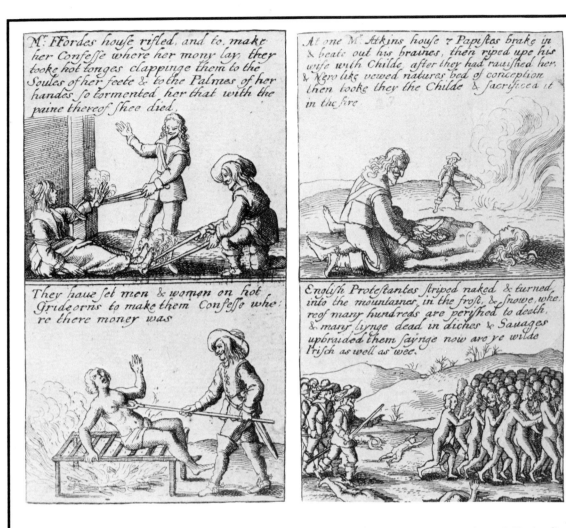

Mr Ffordes house rifled, and to. make her Confesse where her mony lay, they tooke hot tonges clappinge them to the Soules of her feete & to the Palmes of her handes so tormented her that with the paine thereof shee died.

At one Mr Atkins house 7 Papistes brake in & beate out his braines, then riped upe his wife with Childe, after they had ravished her, & Nero like vewed natures bed of conception then tooke they the Childe & sacrificed it in the fire

They haue set men & women on hot Grideorns to make them Confesse whe:re there money was

English Protestantes striped naked & turned into the mountaines, in the frost, & snowe, whe:reof many hundreds are perished to death, & many lyinge dead in diches & Sauages upbraided them sayinge now are ye wilde Irisch as well as wee.

anti-Catholicism in early modern England played a sort of bonding role in bringing the community together, against a commonly recognisable enemy. It was, of course, desperately unfortunate for Ireland that this hatred of Catholicism should have become a hatred of the majority of the Irish population, who were Catholic, and that the country should have become caught up in the assertion of England's Protestant mission just at the time in English history when she was about to launch herself as a world power. On the eve of England becoming the greatest economic and political force in the world, all that Englishmen hated and despised came together, represented by the Catholic Irish.

The ILLUSTRATION *on the left reads from top to bottom:*

1 *Mr Ffordes house rifled and to make her confess where her money lay, they took hot tongs clapping them to the soles of her feet and to the palms of her hand (and) so tormented her that with the pain thereof she died.*

2 *They have set men and women on hot gridirons to make them confess where the money was.*

The ILLUSTRATION *on the right reads from top to bottom:*

3 *At one Mr Atkins house, 7 papists broke in and beat out his brains, then ripped up his wife with child after they had ravished her, and, Nero-like, viewed nature's bed of conception then took the child and sacrificed it in the fire.*

4 *English Protestants stripped naked and turned into the mountains in the frost and snow, whereof many hundreds perished to death, and many lying dead in ditches and savages upbraided them saying: 'Now are ye wild Irish as well as we.'*

OLIVARIVS CROMWELL EXERCITVVM ANGLIÆ
TENENS ET GVBERNATOR HIBERNIÆ OXO

Cernimus hic omni Caput admirabile Mundo?
Quod Reges, Populi, Barbaries? stupent.
Regibus Hic Frater, Populis Pater, Hostis, undum
Barbariem, verá Relligione, domat.

REIPVBLICÆ DVX GENERALIS LOCAM-
NIENSIS ACADEMIÆ CANCELLARIVS

Nullius Ille timet quàm Summi Numinis arma
Nec timet, si Pacem Caldeat esse parat
Qui Bellum parere, Pacem et quærere Proelia Versis

CROMWELL

Oliver Cromwell completed the process of the English conquest of Ireland, begun centuries before, in 1169, by Henry II and his nobles.

By the end of the sixteenth century, Irish resentment was manifesting itself in full-scale rebellion, and in periodic attacks upon planter settlements by bands of woodkerne – groups who had been dispossessed of their lands and were forced into exile in the woods and bogs of Ireland. This general hostility to planter society, combined with opposition to the repressive regime of Strafford's Lord Deputyship in Ireland, produced the bloody rising of 1641. Because of the English Civil Wars, no army was sent out to put down the rising until after the wars had ended and Charles I tried and executed. It was at this moment, in the course of 1649, that the Council of State decided it could at last turn its attention to Ireland, and an expeditionary force was raised for this purpose.

The obvious man to lead this force was Oliver Cromwell, one of the founders of the New Model Army, and the brilliant military commander who had led it to victory against the King, and who now led the Council of State of the Commonwealth of England. Accordingly, he left with an army of fifteen thousand men on 12 August 1649, determined to subdue Ireland as quickly and as cheaply as possible. He began his whirlwind campaign by committing one of the grossest atrocities in the entire troubled history of Ireland; the sack and massacre of Drogheda. Cromwell warned the town, according to the customs of war, of the consequences of prolonged resistance, but the savagery of the slaughter that followed its capture was totally unlike anything that had happened in the English civil wars. All the defenders of the garrison and many of the civilian population of the town were put to the sword. The few survivors were transported to the West Indies. Cromwell ordered this massacre almost with a sense of divine mission at the opportunity to avenge the Protestants for the Catholic attacks upon them since 1641. On 16 September, Cromwell wrote to England with news of the massacre:

It hath pleased God to bless our endeavors at Drogheda . . . . The enemy were about 3,000 strong in the town . . . . I do not think 30 of the whole number escaped with their lives. Those that did are safe in custody for the Barbados. . . . I wish that all honest hearts may give the glory of this to God alone, to whom indeed the praise of this mercy belongs . . . this is a righteous judgement of God upon those barbarous wretches who have imbrued their hands in so much innocent blood.

Cromwell followed this up with an attack upon the port town of Wexford which was accompanied by an equally merciless slaughter of the population. Between fifteen hundred and two thousand soldiers and civilians were slain.

Meanwhile, Cromwell was setting in motion the process of land confiscation for which his name has also become famous in Ireland. Nearly all the land that had belonged to Catholic landowners was seized, to be given to soldiers for arrears of pay, and to adventurers who had loaned money to the Government and not been repaid. Cromwell had no qualms about the severity of his policy. He declared:

We come by the assistance of God to hold forth and maintain the lustre and glory of English liberty in a nation where we have an undoubted right to do it.

On 18 May 1650, Cromwell hurried home to England, his prestige enormously enhanced by his triumph over the Irish rebels.

Cromwell spent only nine months in Ireland, but the cruelty of his stay there is remembered to this day. To the Irish, he has become a folk-villain. Tales are told of a compact he is supposed to have made with the Devil. Generations of Irish boys and girls have been brought up knowing Cromwell as a bogey man; 'Cromwell will catch you,' they were told, if they were naughty. In rural areas it is still possible to hear occasionally the worst abuse possible from an Irishman, in the phrase, 'The curse of Cromwell on you.' This curse will be remembered long after everything else Cromwell did has been forgotten.

The ILLUSTRATION opposite, dated c. 1651, shows Cromwell as Governor General or Lord Protector of the English Republic, superimposed on a contemporary drawing of London.

13

to the government of maintaining a large garrison. State-sponsored colonisation in America was also being planned at the same time, through the Virginia Company. But, unlike in the 'New World' where most of the plantations were vast private franchises organised by single companies, in Ulster the plantation was carefully regulated by the Government. To take land from the dissident Catholic natives and to give it to loyal Protestant settlers would destroy the Irish political community and strengthen British control over the country.

The counties of Antrim and Down, in the north-east of Ireland, had enjoyed close links with Scotland for many centuries, and both had substantial Scottish colonies. At one point, Scotland and Ireland are separated by only 13 miles of sea, and the two counties were in some senses an extension of the Scottish lowlands. But the six counties of Armagh, Fermanagh, Coleraine, Cavan, Tyrone and Donegal were all systematically planted. The principal figures in the organised plantations were called Undertakers – landlords who were given between one and five thousand acres – on condition that they 'undertook' to bring in Scottish and English colonists, settle them in fortified villages, house them, and arm them. Land was also granted to Servitors, English military officials who had 'served' the Crown in Ireland and who were given land as a reward for their part in the 1590s wars. Co. Coleraine was an exception to this system. Here, the Undertakers were a consortium of businessmen representing the twelve great London companies, including the Merchant Adventurers, Clothmakers, Haberdashers, Skinners, Drapers and Saltersmen. They agreed to settle in Derry and rebuild the city's defences. Thus, Derry became Londonderry and Co. Coleraine became Co. Londonderry, a change resented by Catholics to this day.

All these planted settlements became Protestant sentinels, standing out as bastions of Anglo-Scottish rule in Ulster. They were garrisoned by those who would fight not only to defend their land, but also to defend English authority in the country. As the planters held their land entirely through grants from the Crown, their privilege was inexorably tied to the fate of British rule in Ireland, and their loyalty to England was guaranteed. By 1641, there were somewhere between fifty and a hundred thousand English and Scottish settlers 'planted' in Ulster.

The intention of those who drew up plans for the Plantation was to confiscate all the land from the native Gaelic Irish and to expel them completely from Ulster. However, this proved impossible in practice. There were too many of them, and there was no army powerful enough to aid the undertakers in wholesale evictions. The native Irish were allowed to stay on in Ulster, but usually only in the quarter of an estate that was made up of the worst and least cultivatable land; they were forced into subsistence on the poorest marginal land. Many of the Irish who were dispossessed of their lands fled to the forests and mountains to nurse their grievances. They became bands of outlaws known as 'woodkerne' and periodically attacked planter settlements.

The long tradition of Gaelic Ireland was overlaid, but not destroyed, by the Anglo-Scottish. The culture, language, the laws, the customs of the newcomers were strange. Even their farming techniques were different. As arable farmers, they levelled the forests and rejected the pastoral ways of the Gaels. Their houses were timber-framed or stone, thatched or slated, neat and tidy. They built markets, churches and schools, creating a way of life entirely foreign to that of the Irish. In retrospect, the most significant difference was that the settlers were Protestant and the natives Catholic. So, to the natural antagonism of the dispossessed and the apprehension of the planted was added a religious difference which at the time divided man from man with profound intensity. Language made communication awkward, culture and custom made understanding difficult and, of course, the very process of plantation militated against accommodation. Religion became a badge for these political divisions, and could be used to justify any injustice or outrage. The English solution to their Ulster problem left the native resentful and the settler beleaguered. It was unjust to the native and unfair to the settler; both were victims of a wider colonial design.

However, events in Britain presented the Irish Catholics with an opportunity to challenge British authority in Ireland. For the first time, but not for the last, England's difficulty was to be Ireland's opportunity. In 1640, Charles I, who had been trying to rule without calling Parliament, was forced back into the traditional constitutional practice of summoning a Parliament at Westminster. It immediately demanded reforms that would strengthen its own power and weaken that of the king. Civil War in England looked imminent and a victory by the overwhelmingly Protestant Parliament would threaten Ireland with further religious discrimination and plantation. So, as England moved towards the crisis of civil war, it became a propitious moment for the Irish to rebel. On 23 October 1641, a rising began at Dungannon, Charlemont and Newry (see page 10).

As Protestant refugees began to straggle into the walled towns from their isolated farms and plantation castles, they brought with them stories of atrocities. Settlers had been slaughtered in their beds, prisoners executed *en masse*, and thousands had been driven from their homes as the rebels drove a wedge between the settlements of Antrim and Down, besieged Drogheda, and invaded the Pale. Among historians, the extent of the massacre is contentious. The historical evidence, on which all assessments must be based, largely consists of some 30 volumes of Depositions, taken later by Protestant Parliamentary Commissioners and of dubious accuracy. Some historians even argue that no massacre took place at all. However, if there were excesses they sprang not from the policy of the rebellion's leaders but from the unbridled fury of Catholic Irish grievance feeding on sectarian passion. The fear and panic which the rising generated left Ulster Protestants with a lasting belief that the Catholics were potentially a murderous mob. Psychologically, 1641 proved to be a seminal event in Irish history, for it further consolidated the Protestant sense of siege. Time and time again, the spectre of 1641 has been raised to demonstrate Catholic treachery, and to argue that political assurances of Protestant security are not enough.

News of the rising in Ireland arrived in London at a particularly delicate

WILLIAM III
AND THE BATTLE OF THE BOYNE

William of Orange had been invited to England to preserve the Protestant religion from Catholic attack. He accepted the invitation because he saw England as a useful ally in his life-long struggle with Louis XIV's France. When James II landed in Ireland in April 1689 with French support, hoping to use this as the stepping-stone to England in an attempt to regain his throne, it was natural that English Protestants would want William to act to defeat James. Thus, Ireland became a part of a much wider strategic conflict with

France, and in May, William declared war on Louis XIV, to the delight of most Englishmen. Parliament voted him a huge sum to lead an army to Ireland. However, Ireland was a minor and irritating sideshow for William. He spent much of 1689 in diplomatic activity against France and turned his attention to Ireland only reluctantly in 1690.

On 14 June, William landed at Carrickfergus, near Belfast, with a large army. After the relief of James's 15-week siege of Londonderry in August 1689, Ulster

became the base of William's military operations. James retired to Dublin for the winter, having failed to starve out the citizens of Londonderry, and his army was reinforced by seven thousand French troops. On hearing of William's landing, James marched north, and deployed his army along the River Boyne, about three miles west of Drogheda. The two armies met here on 1 July 1690. William's commander, Shomberg, was killed in the battle, but William nevertheless won a decisive victory. Within days James had fled Ireland and William marched south to occupy Dublin. There, he realised that the war would drag on for some time, and so left his commanders to mop up the Franco-Irish army. Final victory did not come for another year, at the Battle of Aughrim in July 1691, and with the capture of Limerick in October of that year.

William had spent only a matter of weeks in Ireland but this Dutch prince was to become a folk-hero to the Irish Protestants. The Battle of the Boyne marked the final victory of the Protestants over the Catholics of Ireland. It ushered in the Protestant ascendancy, and the Protestant Dublin Parliament legitimised this ascendancy through a series of Penal Laws over the next few years (see page 23). To the Irish Protestants, their privilege dates from William's victory at the Boyne, and this Dutchman, who had little real interest in Ireland, became immortalised in the Protestant memory. July 12 (the correct date of the Battle under the new calendar) has become 'Orange Day' in Northern Ireland, and every year tens of thousands of Orangemen parade to honour the 'glorious and immortal memory' of William III (see page 56). King Billy, heroically astride a white mare, riding across the

Boyne, has become the symbol of the Irish Protestants. He appears on countless Orange banners, and his image is daubed in street murals in Belfast. 'Remember 1690' is scrawled over the walls throughout Northern Ireland. To the Ulster Protestants today, the memory of King Billy represents the triumphant assertion of the superiority of the Protestants over the defeated and subject Catholics. As long as this superiority is maintained, King Billy will be remembered as the legendary hero who saved the Protestants from popish superstition.

An early-nineteenth-century Orange Toast to King Billy went:

To the glorious, pious and Immortal Memory of King William III, who saved us from Rogues and Roguery, Slaves and Slavery, Knaves and Knavery, Popes and Popery, from brass money and wooden shoes; and whoever denies this toast may he be slammed, crammed and jammed into the muzzle of the great gun of Athlone, and the gun fired into the Pope's belly, and the Pope into the Devil's belly, and the Devil into Hell, and the door locked and the key in an Orangeman's pocket.

The ILLUSTRATION is an engraving of the Battle of the Boyne, made by the Dutch engraver who came over with William, Theodor Maas (1659–1717).

The PHOTOGRAPH shows a street decoration in Londonderry being prepared for the Apprentice Boys Parade in August 1971.

and crucial moment in the struggle between Crown and Parliament. It posed a fundamental political question: who would be put in command of the army raised to put down the rising, the King or Parliament? The Parliamentary leaders refused to trust the King with the command of an army that could always be directed against them once it had done its work in Ireland. In the panic provoked by the rebellion and fear of Charles's perfidy, gangs roamed the London streets shouting 'No popery! No bishops! No popish Lords', and a vast catalogue of grievances against the King, called the 'Grand Remonstrance', was passed in the Commons. In January 1642, Charles left the capital and spent a few months drumming up support throughout the country. Finally, in August, he raised his standard for war at Nottingham. The English Civil War had begun, and Irish affairs had become inextricably entangled with them.

The years from 1641 to 1649 were a period of confusion and strife in Ireland, and of civil war in England. After the defeat and the trial and execution of Charles I, Parliament turned to Ireland, and with the accounts of 1641 still ringing in Protestant ears, Cromwell was despatched to Dublin not only to re-conquer Ireland, but also to exact revenge (see page 13).

Cromwell carried out his orders coldly and expeditiously. Drogheda, where English Royalists were stationed, and Wexford, a rebel stronghold, were sacked. The garrisons in both were systematically massacred along with the Catholic clergy and most of the townspeople. If Cromwell's massacres were intended as a lesson to impress the Irish, they succeeded. Cromwell is remembered and hated in Ireland to this day.

Cromwell, like a large number of his contemporaries, held the Irish in genuine contempt. They believed that the Irish were culturally so inferior that their subordination was natural and necessary. As Christopher Hill, a leading English historian of the seventeenth century, has written: 'A great number of civilized Englishmen of the propertied class in the seventeenth century spoke of Irishmen in tones not far removed from those which Nazis used about Slavs, or white South Africans use about the original inhabitants of their country. In each case, the contempt rationalised a desire to exploit.' Related to this, no doubt, was the belief, later to become common amongst the English, in the unique benefits of English civilisation for the native, whether they were liked or not.

Essentially, however, Cromwell had the same preoccupation as the Tudors – strategy. In the European context, Ireland must not be allowed to threaten, or to help others to threaten, England or her Protestantism. Further transfer of land from Irish Catholics to English Protestants would secure English interests and subdue Ireland, and have the added attraction of paying for the war.

Landlords who had taken part in the Rebellion had their estates and properties confiscated. Those who could show that they had taken no part in the rising also lost their lands, but were compensated with holdings on barren soil in the west. The land in the rest of the country was taken over by the Government and given out to those who had lent money for the war and those who had fought in it. The peasantry was left largely undisturbed, and continued to work the land, but Protestants now owned much of Ireland. Cromwell had completed the conquest of Ireland and his settlement had created a Protestant English upper class in a country of Catholics. Ireland, now, was an English colony.

When James II, a Catholic, acceded to the English throne in 1685, he was determined to restore the Roman faith to England. He appointed the first Catholic viceroy in Ireland for a hundred years, Richard Talbot, Earl of Tyrconnell. As Catholic judges and privy councillors took office, it even seemed possible that they might repeal the Cromwellian land settlement and dismantle the Protestant ascendancy. Catholic hopes and Protestant fears grew. But the English Parliament, now resolutely Protestant, refused to accept James's Catholicism and, in a bloodless revolution, replaced him with the Protestant William of Orange from the Netherlands, James's son-in-law.

It was natural for the deposed King James to turn to Ireland for support, and in April 1689 he landed at Kinsale to begin the fight to regain his crown. Amid Catholic clamour, there was Protestant consternation as the spectre of 1641 rose again. Thirty-five thousand people crowded behind the fortified city walls of Londonderry before James's army laid siege to the city. The Apprentice Boys prevented the commander of the garrison, Lundy, from surrendering the city, and for 15 weeks, as thousands died of disease and starvation, the besieged citizens refused to consider terms. Finally a ship forced its way up the Foyle and relieved the famished city. Their determination to resist the popish hordes is now a part of Ulster folk memory, an example to the present, celebrated annually in the streets of the city by the Apprentice Boys' Parade. What is less well remembered is that the Pope, who was hostile to Louis XIV's ambitions for France, paradoxically was in alliance with William's cause in Ireland.

If Londonderry represents fortitude and the spirit of 'No Surrender', then the Battle of the Boyne in July 1690, the crucial engagement when William defeated James, represents Protestant triumph. That too is remembered when tens of thousands of Protestants swagger and strut to the sound of their Orange bands through the towns and villages of Northern Ireland, and it is no empty charade. William's victory set the final seal on the Protestant ascendancy, and the English dominance of Irish affairs that lasted two hundred years. The Irish had been defeated three times in a century. This time it was decisive (see page 16).

The Dublin Parliament, of course without Catholic representation, set about buttressing the Protestant ascendancy in a series of anti-Catholic Acts known as the Penal Laws, which sought to deny the Catholics any economic or political power (see page 23). Catholics were denied access to any form of political power, the priesthood was expelled, and Catholic education was outlawed. But the most important long-term effect of the laws was on land. The principle of primogeniture (the inheritance of a man's estate by his eldest son) is crucial to the survival of the gentry and land-owning classes.

In Ireland, under the Penal Laws, it did not apply to Catholics, whose land was divided on death equally among all sons. The ability of Catholics to hold their estates together was further weakened by regulations which said that if one son became a Protestant, then he automatically inherited the entire estate; that if a Protestant woman married a Catholic, her land passed to her Protestant next of kin; if a Catholic wife turned Protestant, she acquired control over part of her husband's estate. These regulations ensured Catholic land holdings would decline, and the laws prohibiting them from buying land prevented them from doing anything to remedy it. In 1641, Catholics owned 59% of Irish land; it had fallen to 22% by 1688, 14% in 1703 and only 7% by the mid eighteenth century.

The effectiveness of these laws has long been in dispute, and there is no doubt that over the years their application fell into abeyance. Catholic clergy and bishops were allowed to move about the country, although with difficulty; many Catholics sent their sons abroad for their education, and some Catholic families retained their estates intact throughout the period (usually only with the help of friendly Protestants).

Nevertheless, the impact of the Penal Laws in Irish society was immense. When states have one law for one group and another law for others, there is injustice. This sense of injustice, that Catholics were an inferior class in their own country, created an abiding, universal consciousness of grievance that was to lie at the heart of the Irish rejection of British rule. Nor was there much respect for the institutions of state that administered such laws as this, and this mistrust lent credence to those proposing to fight the cause not in parliaments or courts, but on the streets and in the countryside. For Catholics, the Church was the one institution that retained credibility, and the priest the one figure commanding respect. By driving Catholic worship underground, they gave both the Church and the priest an authority greater than in other countries, and the Church's hold on the Irish people effectively dates from the Penal Laws.

Throughout the eighteenth century, all European countries treated colonies as investments to be exploited, and Britain was no exception. Three-quarters of Ireland was owned by English or Anglo–Irish families, most of whom lived in England. Consequently, rents worth some three-quarters of a million pounds a year were leaving Ireland for England. Ireland paid a further £100,000 annually to Englishmen who held Irish sinecures and pensions used by the British Government as rewards and bribes for political purposes. This meant that Ireland was a very valuable asset to England. The value of the Irish revenues to the English economy in the early eighteenth century was roughly equivalent to the value of North Sea oil and gas to the United Kingdom economy in 1980. The profit that England was able to draw from Ireland provided some of the capital that fuelled the growth in the economy at the time of the Industrial Revolution. Furthermore, at a time when the entire revenue of Ireland was a little more than a million pounds, this transfer of capital to England represented an enormous drain on resources that might otherwise have been invested in Irish agriculture and industry.

However, the Irish economy was constricted not only by a shortage of capital, but also by discriminatory trade policies designed to protect English commercial interests. Irish ships could not trade with the colonies. The

AN ACT

For the Better Securing the Government by Difarming

PAPISTS.

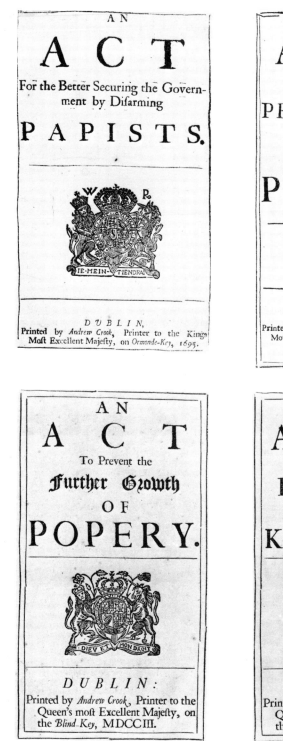

DUBLIN,
Printed by *Andrew Crook*, Printer to the Kings
Moft Excellent Majefty, on *Ormonde-Key*, 1695.

AN ACT

To Prevent

PROTESTANTS
Inter-Marrying
WITH
PAPISTS.

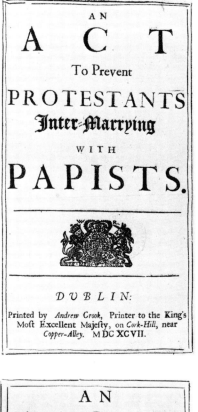

DUBLIN:

Printed by *Andrew Crook*, Printer to the King's
Moft Excellent Majefty, on *Cork-Hill*, near
Copper-Alley. MDCXCVII.

AN ACT

To Prevent the

Further Growth
OF
POPERY.

DUBLIN:

Printed by *Andrew Crook*, Printer to the
Queen's moft Excellent Majefty, on
the *Blind-Key*, MDCCIII.

AN ACT

To Prevent

Popifh Priefts

From coming into this

KINGDOM.

DUBLIN:

Printed by *Andrew Crook*, Printer to the
Queen's moft Excellent Majefty, on
the *Blind-Key*, MDCCIII.

THE PENAL LAWS

The page opposite shows the frontispiece of four of the many Acts passed by the Dublin Parliament between about 1695 and 1705, known generically as the 'Penal Laws' or the 'Penal Code', in that they set out to 'punish' all members of the Catholic religion.

William of Orange had marched into London after James's flight just before Christmas 1688, whilst the capital was enjoying a bout of its regular anti-Catholic fever, with the hunting of papists and the burning of Catholics' homes. It is hardly surprising that William should exploit this popular mood of anti-Catholicism, after he had decisively defeated James and the Irish Catholics at the Battle of the Boyne in July 1690 (although the Catholic Irish forces did not finally surrender until October 1691).

The Penal Laws attempted to destroy the Irish Catholic community. Catholics were barred from every form of public office; they could not join the army or the navy, they could not vote, nor be elected to Parliament; nor could they be members of the legal profession. The Catholic priesthood was expelled from the country and was liable to be hanged, drawn and quartered if they returned. A reward of £5 was put on the head of a priest and the profession of 'Priest-hunter' became popular and profitable for Protestants. All forms of Catholic education were made illegal, and Catholics were barred from sending their children abroad to study. But the most important effect of the Penal Laws was on the system of land ownership in Ireland, the root of all political power. The Laws prohibited Catholics from buying land, taking morgages on it, or leasing land for more than thirty-one years. They fundamentally altered the principles of land inheritance.

The severity of these laws extended right down to the smallest detail. Catholic gentlemen were subject to the penalty of whipping for keeping a gun, and if they were caught owning a horse worth more than £5 it could be confiscated. One Act actually proposed castrating all Catholic priests. The price on the head of a wolf, thought to be a danger to sheep and pastoral farming, was the same as that on the head of a Catholic priest; and one magistrate in Roscommon wrote, during Queen Anne's reign, 'We shall never be safe and quiet till a wolf's head and a priest's head be at the same rate.'

Similar laws were passed by Louis XIV's government in France at about the same time and some of the same Penal Laws were on the statute book in England, for instance those with regard to the holding of public office and some of the conditions regarding land ownership. But the position in Ireland was unique, for there it was the majority who were being legislated against by the minority. In Ireland,

the Catholic community was driven underground. Irish Catholics inherited a fundamental mistrust of laws and of the state, and by driving worship underground gave the priest an authority in the community greater than in most Catholic countries.

All these different aspects of the Penal Laws came together in the tradition in Ireland of illicit worship around the local Mass Rock. The scale of this illicit worship in wild out-of-the-way spots has recently been questioned by historians. What is not in doubt is that a folk-memory that thrives on a sense of injustice and of past wrongs has picked up the Mass Rock as a symbol of the underground, secretive practice of Catholicism.

In every rural area of Ireland today, it is possible for the old people to point out the local Mass Rock, usually a stone or rock, about table height, hidden in some dell or incline, and supposedly the site where Mass was said by the 'priest on the run' in Penal Times. The spot where the 'scouts' or 'look-outs' watched for the British soldiers, the 'Redcoats', or the Protestant yeomanry, is also remembered. A host of stories of miracles conducted at the Rock, of chases, escapes and arrests, surround the local folklore of the Mass Rock. All these stories encapsulate a sense of grievance and a sense of resistance to alien, Protestant, British rule.

The following extracts are taken from 'An Act to Prevent the further Growth of Popery':

. . . be it further enacted . . . that from and after the twenty-fourth day of March 1703 . . . in case the eldest son and heir of such popish parent shall be a protestant, . . . such popish parent shall become, and shall be, only tenant for life of all the real estate . . .

. . . that no person of the popish religion shall, or may be guardian unto, or have the tuition or custody of, any orphan child or children, under the age of twenty-one years . . .

. . . that every papist, or person professing the popish religion, shall . . . be disabled, and is hereby made incapable, to buy and purchase either in his or in their own name, . . . any manors, lands, tenements or hereditaments, or any rents or profits out of the same . . .

Provided always, that if the eldest son or heir-at-law of such papist shall be a protestant at the time of the decease of such papist . . . the lands . . . shall descend to such eldest son or heir-at-law . . . and if the eldest son or heir-at-law of any such papist, . . . shall become a protestant and conform himself to the Church of Ireland, . . . he shall be entitled to, and shall have, and enjoy from thenceforth the whole real estate of such papist . . .

1798 RISING

The French Revolution produced a wave of enthusiasm for reform in Ireland, especially amongst the Presbyterians in Ulster, who suffered exclusion from the political life of the nation because of the Penal Laws, just like the Catholics. The Society of the United Irishmen was formed in Belfast in 1791 by Wolfe Tone. Its aims were to unite Protestants and Catholics behind a revolutionary programme to radicalise the Irish Parliament in Dublin, and to remove British Rule from Ireland. From 1793, England was at war with France. It was natural for the United Irishmen to look to England's enemy for support. Wolfe Tone, Napper Tandy and others went to France to try to get French support for an insurrection in Ireland. The result of this was the fiasco of 1796. A French fleet with an army of fourteen thousand sailed for Ireland, but was broken up by storms in the Channel. The remnants of the fleet waited off Bantry Bay for ten days, but were then blown out to sea by gales and scattered. Hardly a single French soldier set foot on Irish soil.

The United Irishmen were meanwhile facing constant government suppression. They became more extreme, and although by now an illegal, clandestine organisation totally infiltrated by informers and spies, they decided to launch a rising in Ireland. It finally took place in May 1798. The rising was a disaster in political terms. Communications between bands of rebels were hopeless, and the situation was made no easier when the romantic leader of the rising, Lord Edward Fitzgerald, was arrested the day before the rebellion was due to begin. Leaderless and unco-ordinated, the rebellion was effective only in parts of Co. Antrim, Co. Down, and Co. Wexford. Here the rebels enjoyed their only real successes, holding out for some weeks through June 1798, until the government built up an overwhelming force to crush the rebels, who were finally defeated at the Battle of Vinegar Hill on 21 June. Another French fleet arrived in Ireland in August, unaware that the rising had already been put down. It was too little, too late. The French-Irish Army failed to provoke the broad popular uprising it expected, and finally surrendered to the government's army under Lord Cornwallis, at Ballinamuch on 8 September. Had the rising been better organised, had the plans been efficiently communicated to all the rebel groups, had the French landed earlier and marched to aid the rebels in Wexford, then the future course of Irish history could well have been very different. As it was, the rebellion was put down by government forces and by a militia (who frequently employed Orange societies) with an unprecedented cruelty.

Hangings, burnings and floggings were all quite common.

Some idea of the severity of the suppression of the rising can be judged by this poster displayed in one of the counties which had played almost no part in the rising, Tipperary:

NOTICE

TO THE INHABITANTS OF THE TOWN AND
NEIGHBOURHOOD OF TIPPERARY
IT IS ORDERED
That should a Shot at any Time be fired on the Military from
any House or Cottage whether in the Town or Country,
EVERY SOUL WITHOUT DISCRIMINATION found within will be
PUT TO THE SWORD AND THE HOUSE DESTROYED
That should the Daringness of the disaffected lead them
to Outrage or Cruelty on the Properties or Families of the
peaceable and well-disposed the WHOLE
NEIGHBOURHOOD
WILL BE LAID WASTE

T.H. FOSTER
Colonel, Louth Regiment

The scar of the repression of the 1798 Rising is set deep in Irish folk memory. Tales of floggings and tortures still abound in parts of Ireland today. Songs of the Rising are still sung. County Wexford is still sometimes called the 'rebel' county. Wolfe Tone, Napper Tandy, and Lord Edward Fitzgerald all became folk martyrs whose memory is regularly celebrated.

The *Irish Magazine* was a satirical publication that lasted from 1807 to 1815. Its cartoonist W. Cox visualised some of the stories of the suppression of the Rising, at the time when they must have been in common parlance.

The ILLUSTRATIONS from the *Irish Magazine* on the opposite page show:

1 'Plan of a Travelling Gallows used in the year 1798.'
2 'Dispatching the Superabundant Population.'
3 'Justice Knifeboard hanging a piper for playing Seditious tunes.'

Each drawing plays upon widely held beliefs in Ireland about the repression of the Rising and the severity of the methods used to punish the rebels.

English wool industry was protected by legislation which demanded that all Irish wool had to be exported to England for manufacture into cloth. Laws promoted by English brewers and glass-blowers forbade the export of hops to Ireland after 1710, and the export of glass from Ireland after 1746. Only the Irish linen industry, centred round Belfast, was left unscathed – but then Britain had no sizeable linen manufacturers. On the other hand, duties on British goods were low and the goods found a ready market in Ireland. By 1800, 85% of Irish exports and 79% of her imports went to and came from Britain, revealing an economic dependence on Britain made even more dramatic when it is considered that the reciprocal British figures were only 11% and 10%.

As the restriction of trade and commerce made the country almost completely dependent on agriculture, the landlord became a crucial figure in Ireland. History had assured that landlords would feel no paternal responsibility towards their tenants. Even if they were living in Ireland, they were, in the main, Protestant conquerors or their successors with little understanding or sympathy for the rebellious Catholic native. Absentee landlords sought a secure and steady income by renting their estates wholesale on long leases to middle-men, in effect land retailers who then sub-let. There were often several lets between the landlord and the man who actually worked the land, and at each stage the rent rose and the lease shortened. When it expired, no account was taken of improvements the tenant might have made; it was simply re-let to the highest bidder. It left tenants insecure and without incentive to improve their holdings. Some even ran down their farms towards the end of the lease so as to hold the price down to a level they could afford.

For a century and more, the Irish peasantry were caught up in impoverished serfdom. Regular famines in Ireland throughout the seventeenth and eighteenth centuries added to the miseries of those already exploited and neglected by their landlords. Contemporary reports are shocking. In 1750, the philosopher Berkeley asked 'whether there be upon the earth any Christian or civilised people so beggarly wretched and destitute as the common Irish?' 'I hoped to be excused for representing to His Majesty the miserable situation of the lower ranks of his subjects in this kingdom, that from the rapaciousness of their unfeeling landlords and the restrictions on their trade, they are amongst the most wretched people on earth,' reported the English Viceroy, no less, in 1770. Arthur Young, an English agricultural reformer, wrote in 1776:

Landlords of consequence have assured me that many of their cottiers would think themselves honoured by having their wives or daughters sent for to the bed of their masters, a mark of slavery that proves the oppression under which such people live . . . The cottages of the Irish which are called cabins, are the most miserable-looking hovels that can well be conceived . . . The furniture of the cabins is as bad as the architecture: in very many consisting only of a pot for boiling their potatoes, a bit of a table, and one or two broken stools; beds are not found universally, the family lying on straw.

In the middle of the eighteenth century, the potato was introduced into

Ireland. It was to have a lasting and dramatic effect. The potato is highly nutritional and provides a good basis for an adequate diet. It is also a very prolific crop. One acre of land was sufficient to provide enough potatoes to feed a family of six for a year and to supply seed potatoes for the next year's sowing. These qualities had two important effects. Firstly, the available land in Ireland could support more people, and consequently the population grew from about 3¼ million in 1760 to about 6½ million in 1815. Secondly, because the peasant did not need as much land to feed his family on potatoes as on grain, more of his land became available to grow crops which he could sell. Therefore, he could afford more rent. As a result of these two phenomena, landlords were able to charge more rent, because the peasant could afford to pay it, and with rising population, competition for land grew intense. One authority estimated that from 1760 to 1815, rents quadrupled. All this meant that, under these pressures, the average size of holdings grew smaller. Effectively, in land-hungry Ireland, rents equalled what could be grown on a plot of land after it had fed those who worked it. Any benefit that might have been bestowed on the peasantry with the advent of the potato was absorbed by the increase in population and higher rents. The peasant was left no better off but precariously dependent on one crop. Maria Edgesworth, the daughter of a Co. Longford landowner, wrote of the period before 1782:

Farms, originally sufficient for the comfortable maintenance of a man, his wife and family had, in many cases, been sub-divided from generation to generation: the father giving a bit of land to each son to settle him . . . the maintenance was hardly sufficient to keep them one step above beggary: and insufficient even for this, when the number of their children increased.

It is hardly surprising that such conditions should produce agrarian unrest. It showed itself in the form of secret societies, groups of peasants who bonded together to dispense rough justice on behalf of the poor. With names like the Whiteboys, Oakboys, Moonlighters, Peep O'Day Boys and Steelboys, these societies were secret and oath-bound with their own unwritten code. When land was enclosed, they tore down the fences. They dispersed the cattle, burnt hayricks, levelled houses, committed arson, and even murder, in their war against the landlords and their agents. Their activities increasingly worried the authorities, who were unable to get witnesses or convictions in the courts, although whether this was due to intimidation, or to the inherent sympathy of the local population, is unkown. The various groups were known generically as 'The Boys' — as the IRA are known locally today. By the end of the eighteenth century, Ireland had two laws: one underground and crude, the other official and aloof. So effective was the former that many a country house was constantly sentried and shuttered.

The American War of Independence in the 1770s had important ramifications in Ireland. America had a very similar constitutional arrangement with Britain (a local assembly under the ultimate authority of King and Parliament), and if the American colonists could successfully defy Britain, why not Ireland? The army was so stretched that troops had to be

THE FAMINE

In the autumn of 1845 a potato disease reached south-east Ireland from America and led to the partial blighting of the crop. The distress caused amongst a population which had nearly doubled in forty years, and about half of whom were entirely reliant upon the potato, was considerable but uneven. However, the situation worsened when the blight spread during the wet spring and summer of 1846, causing an almost total failure of that year's crop. In 1847 the disease was less acute, but many people had eaten their seed potatoes and the overall crop was again disastrously low. 1848 saw another failure of the potato. In 1849 and 1850 the blight was less severe. Only by 1851 did the period of hunger seem largely to be over.

During the years of the Famine, 1845–51, it is estimated that about one million people died of starvation and (more commonly) the diseases like typhus and cholera that followed in its wake. About one and a half million emigrated, mostly to Canada, the United States and England.

The catastrophe was not spread evenly across the population. It was almost entirely the labourer and cottier classes and the small farmer, reliant upon the potato, who suffered the most. Furthermore, the north and the east of the country escaped many of the worst miseries of the Famine, whilst the counties of the west and the south-west bore the brunt of the tragedy.

The scale of suffering endured by the Irish during the nightmare years of the Famine is almost unimaginable. The following account of a visit to the village of Skibbereen in Co. Cork was written by Nicholas Cummins, a magistrate of Cork, and published in *The Times* on Christmas Eve 1846:

. . . I shall state simply what I there saw. . . . On reaching the spot I was surprised to find the wretched hamlet apparently deserted. I entered some of the hovels to ascertain the cause, and the scenes which presented themselves were such as no tongue or pen can convey the slightest idea of. In the first, six famished and ghastly skeletons, to all appearances dead, were huddled in a corner on some filthy straw, their sole covering which seemed a ragged horsecloth, their wretched legs hanging about, naked above the knees. I approached with horror, and found by a low moaning they were alive — they were in fever, four children, a woman and what had once been a man. It is impossible to go through the detail. Suffice it to say, that in a few minutes I was surrounded by at least 200 such phantoms, such frightful spectres as no words can describe, either from famine or from fever. Their demoniac yells are still ringing in my ears, and their horrible images are fixed upon my brain. My heart sickens at the recital, but I must go on. . . . The same morning the police opened a house on the adjoining lands, which was observed shut for many days, and two dead corpses were found, lying upon the mud floor, half devoured by rats.

A mother, herself in a fever, was seen the same day to drag the corpse of her child, a girl about twelve, perfectly naked, and leave it half covered with stones. In another house, within five hundred yards of the cavalry station at Skibbereen, the dispensary doctor found seven wretches lying unable to move, under the same cloak. One had been dead many hours, but the others were unable to move either themselves or the corpse.

During the years of the Famine, a decline in the population of Ireland set in, one which has continued almost to the present. The bare statistics tell their tale:

	Population in Ireland (millions)	Population in England and Wales (millions)
1811	5.9	10
1841	8.2	16
1851	6.5	18
1976	4.7	50

The *Illustrated London News* was founded in 1842, on the eve of the potato blight in Ireland. Using black and white lithographs and engravings, the *News* aimed to provide its readers who turned for a break from the heavy columns of *The Times* with an accurate representation of the world about them. In this, the *Illustrated London News*, along with other journals like the *Illustrated Times* or the *Penny Illustrated Paper* were the pioneers of a new tradition in pictorial journalsim that has come down through magazines like *Picture Post* to the colour supplements of today. The *News* sent out its own illustrators to the west of Ireland to sketch scenes of misery and suffering in just the same way as newspapers would now send out photographers to cover an event. The DRAWINGS that the *Illustrated London News* carried through the years of the Famine have an impact that could only have come from direct personal observation of the tragedy. In their own day, these illustrations might well have had the same effect as film of Kampuchean refugees was to have in a later age. Some of the *Illustrated London News* illustrations are featured on the opposite page.

EMIGRATION

Nearly every Irish family knows of relatives living abroad, either those who have emigrated directly or the descendants of those who have emigrated. Emigration has had a profound effect upon Irish society, de-populating whole areas at home and planting ultra-Irish communities abroad.

In the ten years from 1845 to '55, it is estimated that some 2 million Irishfolk emigrated, mostly to the United States, Canada and Britain, some small number to Australia and New Zealand. Out of an 1845 population of about 8.5 million, this represents a huge exodus. Traditional hostility to emigration crumbled in the face of the tragedy and it was seen as the only way to escape the interminable poverty of life at home. Many landlords actually paid the fare for their tenants to emigrate, as it seemed the only alternative to eviction, and a lot cheaper than maintaining a man and his family on poor relief from the rates. It was estimated that the cost of emigrating a pauper was about half the cost of maintaining him in a workhouse for a year, and the solution was a final one in that it was very unlikely that the destitute would ever return. Conditions on the trans-Atlantic emigrant ships were appalling. There was overcrowding between decks, primitive or even non-existent sanitary conditions, a limited supply of fresh water, and poor food. It is hardly surprising that disease was rampant and that deaths were not uncommon during these voyages. In 1847, for instance, the *Larch* sailed from Sligo for Canada with 440 passengers, of whom 108 died at sea and 150 caught 'ship fever' on the voyage. The *Virginus* sailed from Liverpool to Quebec with 476 Irish emigrants. In the course of the nine-week crossing, 158 passengers died and 106 contracted fever, including the captain and most of the crew.

Stephen de Vere took a steerage passage on a vessel bound for Quebec in 1847 and wrote an account of the sufferings incurred by the emigrants on board:

Before the emigrant has been a week at sea, he is an altered man. . . . How can it be otherwise? Hundreds of poor people, men, women and children, of all ages, from the drivelling idiot of ninety to the babe just born, huddled together, without light, without air, wallowing in filth and breathing a foetid atmosphere, sick in body, dispirited in heart. . . . The fevered patients lying between the sound in sleeping places so narrow as almost to deny them a change of position . . . by their agonised ravings disturbing those around them . . . living without food or medicine except as

administered by the hand of casual charity, dying without spiritual consolation and buried in the deep without the rites of the Church.

On 1 June 1847, Robert Whyte set sail on an emigrant ship from Dublin, bound for Quebec, containing a party of tenants who were being sent abroad by their landlord. Whyte kept a diary of the voyage. Within two weeks of setting sail 'ship fever' broke out; Whyte noted on 15 June:

110 passengers are shut up in the unventilated hold of a small brig, without a doctor, medicines or even water.

The wind dropped and progress became very slow. As the ship held supplies for only fifty days, the captain was forced to reduce the ration of water. Fresh cases of fever occurred daily. On the night of 27 June, Whyte wrote that he was kept awake by 'moaning and raving from the hold' and cries for 'water, for God's sake, water.' By 9 July, over half of the emigrants and some of the crew had fever, and deaths were not unusual. Finally, on 25 July, the ship anchored off Grosse Isle, the immigration sickness centre in the St Lawrence River at Quebec. The supply of water for the passengers had by now entirely run out, and several of the sick died before they were unloaded for the Grosse Isle Hospital on 1 August. Whyte went to the funeral of one of the emigrants who had died, the wife of a tenant whose passage had been paid by his landlord. He recorded:

After the grave was filled up, the husband placed two shovels in the forms of a cross and said 'By that cross, Mary, I swear to avenge your death. As soon as I earn the price of my passage home I'll go back and shoot the man that murdered you — and that's the landlord.'

The Irish communities that were established in the United States and Canada burned with a sense of resentment at their suffering, and were filled with hatred against the landlords and the English Government who were blamed for the catastrophe of the Famine. A sense of fierce Irish nationalism was planted in these communities, and it is hardly surprising that much Fenian activity in the 1860s originated in the States. At the time of the Land War, hundreds of thousands of dollars were collected by the Land League in America to alleviate the miseries of the peasantry in Ireland. From 1919 to 1921, funds were raised in America to finance the construction of the new state, and finance the Irish Republican Army in its struggle with Britain.

Today in the United States, the Irish electorate constitutes an important lobby in American politics,

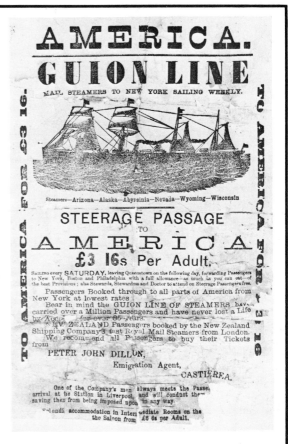

and the Irish National Caucus, with its various fund-raising organisations, preserves a potent sense of Irish nationalism tinged with the characteristic Irish–American hostility towards Britain's involvement in Irish affairs.

The ILLUSTRATION opposite is taken from the *Illustrated London News* of May 1851. It shows emigrants on the quayside at Cork harbour, waiting to depart for the New World.

The ILLUSTRATION above shows a poster for weekly sailings of Mail Steamers from Ireland to New York by an American Company, the Guion Line. Crossing the Atlantic in a United States ship to a US port was much more expensive than in a British ship to Canada. The US Passenger Acts were stricter and allowed fewer persons to be carried in proportion to the size of the ship. Hence, the relatively expensive fare of £3/16/- (£3.80) per adult promises 'a full allowance – as much as you can eat – of the best Provisions.'

withdrawn from Ireland for service in the American wars. Suddenly, Britain seemed vulnerable. To compound Britain's difficulties, France and Spain entered the War on the side of the Americans, and threatened an invasion of Britain through undefended Ireland. Once again, the strategic fears, that Ireland was England's back door, were revived. Irish Protestants rallied to the British side, and formed the Irish Volunteers to defend Protestant interests in Ireland against the Catholic states of Western Europe.

As the Volunteers drilled, they also began to talk. The men of industry spoke of the economic exploitation of Ireland by England; those of commerce complained of the damaging effect of the tariffs imposed on Ireland to protect British trade; Presbyterians knew that they had suffered nearly as much under the Penal Laws as the Catholics had done. With these shared grievances came a realisation of their power in Ireland, as they were the only army in the country. They began to demand political and economic reform. In Dublin, in 1778, they paraded a cannon bearing the placard 'Free Trade or This'. The British, unable to suppress these demands, were forced to concede to the Volunteers. But by now, in the Irish Parliament, further demands were being voiced for an independent legislature directly under the Crown. Henry Grattan, the leader of the Protestant Irish, was the most eloquent of these spokesmen. Defeated in America, the British gave ground, and in 1783 the Irish Parliament was granted considerable autonomy.

However, this independence was more apparent than real. The Dublin Parliament was still widely corrupt, and contained several members who were reliant upon Government support. Behind the scenes, the Lord Lieutenant was able to control Parliament effectively by the judicious use of patronage and through the direct influence he had over many MPs. In the 1780s, Ireland now had a Parliament of real power, but the problem remained of how to reform it in such a way that it might use its power in the Irish interest. Whilst many members were determined to hang on to their privileges, reform of Parliament could be easily frustrated.

Political discussion in Ireland was given new impetus when, in 1789, revolution broke out in France, a country with which Irish intellectuals had close links. The ideals of the French Revolution gave great sustenance to radicals everywhere; in the Irish context, 'liberty' implied that the Irish should have their own government, while 'fraternity' and 'equality' would mean the end of Catholic and Presbyterian disabilities. Wolfe Tone, one of the exponents of these ideas, felt that British rule was the principal grievance of Ireland. He advocated that the ideals of the French Revolution could be achieved only by an alliance of the two underprivileged groups in Ireland, Catholics and Presbyterian radicals, behind a programme of Catholic emancipation and parliamentary reform. Wolfe Tone was instrumental in founding the Society of United Irishmen to achieve these objectives.

The Relief Act of 1793, which gave some Catholics the vote in Ireland, failed to pacify the radicals, and there was talk of armed resistance among the United Irishmen. Their organisation began to take on a distinctly military style, and delegates were sent to France to raise support for a rising against the British. In the event, when the rising finally came in 1798, it was bungled (see page 25). Nevertheless, in the long view of history, it marked the re-birth of resistance in arms to British rule, and it proved to be the inspiration of the Republican Movement through the next two centuries. The rising was etched on the Irish mind by the awful vigour with which it was put down. In the months after the rising, it has been estimated, the security forces killed between twenty-five and fifty thousand people. It would never be forgotten, and when remembered, it would be to honour those who had risen in arms and established the tradition of insurrection in the Irish national movement. Irish Republicanism now had a history, an ideology, and martyrs.

The rising had frightened the British not only because it was inspired by revolutionary French Republicanism, which seemed to the English ruling class to threaten the very basis of civilisation, but also because it showed once again how unreliable and treacherous the Irish could be. At a time when Britain was fully extended in a European war, Irishmen had colluded with her enemies, risen in armed rebellion, and seriously threatened British security. Never again: the back door to England must be shut and firmly locked. The solution of the English Prime Minister, William Pitt, was the Act of Union: Direct rule.

Under the Act of Union of 1800, Ireland became part of Britain. It was to have no national government of its own, but would send MPs to Westminster which would be responsible for the affairs of both Britain and Ireland, or the 'United Kingdom', as it was to be known. In return, there would be Catholic emancipation. In British strategic and economic interest, Ireland was now not merely conquered, but ingested. Colonies normally retain some semblance of a separate identity in their relationship with imperial powers but, here, as in the case of French Algeria, its separateness was denied altogether. Until 1800 the Irish could see themselves as subjects, but as a people none the less. Now the British seemed to be demanding that the Irish should become British and extinguish their own Irishness. As the historian Oliver MacDonagh has written: 'The experience of being assimilated by, and resisting assimilation into a powerful and alien Empire — perhaps the master culture of the nineteenth century — was truly traumatic'. The Union meant that the destiny of Ireland was now in English hands, and to alter that arrangement would need the agreement of the British House of Commons (where there were to be 100 Irish members) and the House of Lords. This was such a daunting prospect that many doubted whether it could be achieved by constitutional means.

Pitt's promise of Catholic emancipation remained unfulfilled. George III refused to give it the Royal Assent, and Pitt resigned. However, with four Irishmen out of five Catholic, the first important political movement in nineteenth century Ireland was the Catholic Association, led by Daniel O'Connell, campaigning for Catholic emancipation. In the six years between 1823 and 1829, O'Connell and the Association organised the Irish peasantry into a formidable political weapon, largely by marshalling the authority and organisation of the Catholic Church, whose priests were not only spiritual advisers but also political activists. Solidarity was demonstrated in a series of huge meetings, and with rural unrest throughout Ireland and agitation in

EVICTIONS

The late 1870s saw agrarian distress and a huge rise in the number of evictions by landlords of tenants who could no longer afford to pay the rent. This in turn produced a revival in traditional agrarian outrages and attacks upon landlords and their agents. In 1879, Michael Davitt formed the Irish Land League to protect the tenantry against rack-renting and eviction, with the long-term objective of making tenants the owners of their own farms. In this atmosphere of agricultural distress, the Land League flourished, and Davitt and John Dillon tried to mobilise the tenants against the landlord class. In 1880, they successfully conducted a campaign ostracising a Captain Boycott, who had bought up land from an evicted tenant; a new word was introduced into the English language. Vast sums of money were accumulated by the Land League, much of it raised in America, as relief for evicted tenants and their families. As Ireland had virtually no industrial sector to soak up an excess population outside the north-east of Ulster, eviction from a homestead usually meant total destitution for a tenant and his family. The only prospects were starvation or emigration.

In August 1888, a celebrated eviction campaign took place on the Vandeleur estate near Kilrush in Co. Clare.

The evictions themselves were carried out by bands of henchmen employed by Vandeleur, the landlord, supported by the Police and the Dragoons and all the machinery of law designed to punish those who resisted eviction and the certainty of destitution. They lasted several days, and turned almost into pitched battles between the tenants and the army of men produced by the landlord. Robert French, landscape photographer of the William Lawrence Studios in Dublin (see page 40) witnessed some of the evictions and made a photographic record of them.

The following extract, from the newspaper *United Ireland* of 4 August 1888, is an account of one day in these evictions:

On Thursday the evictions were resumed. The eviction proceedings were carried out with the usual brutality by the sheriff, and opposed with determination and pluck by the tenants. The house of Matthais McGrath was defended with determination, the place was barricaded. The battering ram was drawn up in front, shouts of defiance came from the tenant inside. Thud, thud, went the lever against the masonry. After a while the wall yielded, but an immense barricade of

On the road to eviction.

Battering ram. 'Back with them, away with them.'

Eviction scene.

Eviction scene.

stonework was inside it. *Breach enough was effected to afford a view of the tenant's son bravely standing inside and determined, calling them to come on. Inspecto. Dunning called on him now to come out, but young McGrath answered sternly 'I am here within, and in with you'. The battering ram was again used, and the wall came down, a violent rush was made through the breach. District-Inspector Hill led on but his charge was abruptly stopped by his coming into contact with the battering ram and he was pitched helplessly into the kitchen, and pounced on by McGrath, who pommelled him soundly, but was himself attacked by Dunning and a constable named Atkinson from Kilrush, who assaulted him together, and were soon aided by a party of bludgeonmen, batoned and treated in a most savage and brutal manner. He was felled; numbers overpowered him. They struck and kicked with savage violence . . .*

The poor fellow had a severe wound on the crown of his head, and was kicked twice in the chest. The wrecking of the house was then proceeded with and complete . . . Colonel Turner stopped the work of the battering ram, smiling pleasantly, and had the emergency ruffians to stand at ease for the accom-modation of an amateur photographer to take a sketch of the ruined cottage. Continuing operations, the house was left a complete ruin before the villains ceased their work. A Coercion Court was improvised formally to try Pat McGrath with Removable Roche taking the justice seat on a stone wall. The formality being gone through he was removed in custody.

The PHOTOGRAPHS are four of Robert French's, recording an eviction. The captions below each are contemporary. The first shows, judging from the crowd of onlookers, that an eviction was something of a public event; the second is of a battering ram forcing an entry; the third shows the resignation of the family with its meagre possessions after the eviction. The fourth photograph shows the substantial nature of the forces of law and order present to ensure that the eviction was carried out.

It is not clear whether the 'amateur' photographer referred to in *United Ireland* is French, as he was, of course, a professional. If it was French, it suggests he was working on a commission for the landlord to photograph the eviction process.

England, the time was right. In 1829, Catholic emancipation was passed at Westminster.

O'Connell's political organisation now turned its attention to repeal of the Union itself, orchestrating this demand with a series of 'monster meetings' (as *The Times* called them) at places redolent of early Irish history, like Tara, the ancient seat of the Irish kings. A contemporary account gives a feel of one of these meetings:

The whole district was covered with men. The population within a day's march began to arrive on foot shortly after daybreak and continued to arrive, on all sides and by every available approach, till noon. It was impossible from any one point to see the entire meeting . . . . The number is supposed to have reached between 500,000 and 700,000 persons.

However, for the British Government to give way on Catholic emancipation was one thing; repeal of the Union was another. Sir Robert Peel, the Prime Minister, was unyielding. The dissolution of the Act of Union, he said, 'would not merely mean the repeal of an Act of Parliament, but dismemberment of a great empire . . . Deprecating as I do all war but above all, civil war, yet there is no alternative which I do not think preferable to the dismemberment of Empire.'

The repeal movement had thrown up a group of intellectuals called 'Young Ireland', more militant and radical than O'Connell, whom they regarded with a mixture of affection and impatience. When the Government decided to suppress the demand for repeal and banned a meeting in October 1843 at Clontarf, O'Connell acquiesced, making it clear that he would not go beyond legal means to attain his objectives. The intellectuals of Young Ireland were disappointed, believing that Britain should be challenged more directly, even at the risk of violence. As in the 1790s, a physical force party was emerging out of the failure of constitutionalism.

The movement centred around the journal *The Nation*, founded in 1842. It drew together several different strands of the Irish grievance. Thomas Davis, the leading figure of 'Young Ireland', warned of the decay of Irish culture, language and custom under British influence, and called for an assertive sense of pride in all things Irish. In so doing, he was to be the inspiration of the Gaelic revival at the turn of the century. Others, like John Mitchel, revitalised and sustained the central tenet of Republicanism as handed down from Tone and on to Padraig Pearse – an unabiding hatred of England as the source of all Ireland's ills. Mitchel wrote:

England! all England, operating through her government: through all her organised and effectual public opinion, press, platform, parliament has done, is doing, and means to do grievous wrongs to Ireland. She must be punished; that punishment will, as I believe, come upon her by and through Ireland; and so Ireland will be avenged.

Fintan Lalor argued that the core of the Anglo-Irish conflict was the land question, and that its solution lay in the marshalling of the peasantry and the removal of the injustices of British rule where they were most obvious, in the countryside. This is precisely what the Land League was to do forty years later. Perhaps Lalor summed it up for them all when he wrote:

The entire ownership of Ireland is vested of right in the people of Ireland: that they, and none but they are the land owners and law makers of this island: that all ties to land are invalid if not conferred or confirmed by them: and that this full right of ownership may and ought to be asserted and enforced by any and all means which God has put into the power of men.

In the heady clamour of 1848, when revolution was in the air and when monarchies were collapsing in the capital cities of Europe, 'Young Ireland' demanded repeal on threat of insurrection. But their bluff was called, and they ended up by mounting a rebellion that was, as one of them said, more like an escapade than an insurrection. It petered out after only a week, in a cabbage patch in Co. Tipperary. The British deported and imprisoned the leaders, but they could not deport their ideas. O'Connell had organised and radicalised the masses and created the basis for a parliamentary Nationalist Party, but it was 'Young Ireland' that would have a profound influence on succeeding generations of Republicans. For the moment, however, Ireland lay in the darkest shadow of her history — the Famine.

By 1844, radical shifts had affected Irish agriculture, largely in response to the needs of the British market. Throughout the latter part of the eighteenth century, British demand had both grown and changed. As Britain was prepared to pay high prices for grain, particularly during the Napoleonic wars, more and more pasture (Ireland's natural agriculture) was put to the plough. Irish agriculture boomed and the population continued to increase, from 6½ million in 1815 to well over 8 million in 1841. Changes in agriculture were of most benefit to the landlords. The balanced husbandry of cereals required a crop rotation that included potatoes which, in turn, could sustain the increased population required to raise the crops. With a rapidly rising population, the land-hungry peasant had no choice. Provided the agrarian population would live on potatoes, all the profits from increased prices and greater production would accrue to the landlords.

When peace came in 1815, with the end of the Napoleonic wars, the Irish agricultural boom collapsed. The price of wheat in Dublin fell from 17/6 to 11/6 per hundredweight (34%) in little more than six years. At the same time, the demand for cattle rose, and their export more than doubled between 1821 and 1835. The obvious course for the landlords to take was to revert to pasture, but to do this would be to deprive the labourer of either his land or his job, or both. Pasture simply could not support as many people as tillage, and with the population still rising, this double pressure forced the peasant onto more and more marginal land. The ridges where potatoes were grown (known to the Irish as 'lazy beds') can still be seen in Ireland today, high on mountain slopes. With this pressure on the peasantry, agrarian distress and disorder grew. There was a revival of the secret societies and their traditional methods of resistance to evictions, which grew as more land returned to pasture. Resentment first flared up in a strike in Leinster, a strike against the tythes paid to the Protestant Church of Ireland. Which was not only alien, but, as far as the Catholic peasantry was concerned, heretical. The strike spread so rapidly that the Government was forced to intervene in 1832. In that same year there were 242 murders, and hundreds of assaults on property and persons. Faced, yet again, by a silent and unhelpful population, the courts were powerless, and the British introduced a Coercion Act in 1833. This empowered the Government to 'proclaim', for a limited period, certain districts where disturbances were occurring, and to put them under martial law.

An increasing proportion of the population lived on the very edge of destitution. In each generation the land was divided between the sons, a practice which enlightened landlords viewed with increasing concern but were unable to stamp out. Gustav de Beaumont, a French visitor, wrote of rural conditions in Ireland in 1839:

Imagine four walls of dried mud (which the rain, as it falls, easily restores to its primitive condition), having for its roof a little straw of some sods, for its chimney a hole cut in the roof, or very frequently the door through which alone the smoke finds an issue. One single appartment contains father, mother, children and sometimes a grandfather or grandmother; there is no furniture in this wretched hovel: a single bed of straw serves the entire family. Five or six half-naked children may be seen crouched near a miserable fire, the ashes of which cover a few potatoes, the sole nourishment of the whole family.

On the eve of the famine, 45% of the tenancies in Ireland were for land of between one and five acres. In some areas in the west of Ireland, the figure was as high as 70%. The total cultivated acreage was 14½ million acres: 8 million to grass, nearly 4 million to cereals, and 2½ million to potatoes. Of a population of 8¼ million people, two-thirds lived off the land, and one-third was wholly dependent on the potato. Irish agriculture as it was constituted was incapable of maintaining the agrarian population of Ireland to a decent standard of life. Without the potato, it was incapable of sustaining it at all. The obvious economic solution was to consolidate the small holdings into large ones, with consequent clearance of the surplus population. As Malthus would have said, the size of the population had outgrown the supply of resources and so needed to be reduced. This was not a solution open to man. It was open to nature.

In 1845, a disease of the potato plant appeared in Ireland, first blighting the leaves, then reducing its tubers to a black suppurating slime. It held rural Ireland in its deadly grip for over four years (see page 29). About one million died, and one million emigrated. That totalled one in three of the rural population. It was the greatest disaster in Ireland's troubled history and left the rural economy and the Irish psyche indelibly changed.

Although the British administration attempted to alleviate the situation, the catastrophe was of such proportions that it was beyond the resources of the Victorian state, and the imagination of its politicians, to do anything effective. Government schemes to relieve the distress were hampered not only by administrative confusion and inefficiency — no government had ever tried to alleviate the effects of a disaster of this magnitude before — but also

ROBERT FRENCH'S IRISH SCENES

William Mervin Lawrence opened a photographic studio in Dublin at 7 Upper Sackville Street (now O'Connell Street), right opposite the General Post Office, in March 1865. Photography was one of the great growth industries of the Victorian era, and from the early beginnings of metal 'daguerrotype' plates and paper 'calotype' prints, photographic technology soon advanced, making the rapid production of photographic prints an easy and highly profitable business. Every major city in Europe and America had its photographic studios, catering mostly for portraiture and the seemingly insatiable demand of the Victorians for photographs of themselves. Dublin was no exception, and in 1865 the city's Trade Directory listed thirty-four photographers at work. William Lawrence combined all the skills and the acumen of the classic Victorian business entrepeneur, with a clear sense of where a new market could be exploited, and soon developed his business into the most successful photographic studio in Ireland. Initially, he specialised in portraits, because the wet-collodion photographic process made it cumbersome and difficult for the landscape photographer to travel. As the glass plate negatives had to be sensitised and processed within minutes of exposure, it was necessary for the photographer to travel with all the paraphernalia: jars of chemicals, a portable darkroom and boxes of glass plates. However, with the advances of Dr Maddox and the advent of dry-plate photography in the early 1870s, all this changed. Now, the only equipment needed by the travelling photographer was his camera, tripod and a supply of dry-plate negatives. William Lawrence was quick to exploit this new technology, and made his views of Irish scenery the most popular in all of Ireland. Before long, it was possible for visitors to cross Ireland with guide-books illustrated by Lawrence pictures, in trains displaying Lawrence scenes, and staying at hotels which sold Lawrence photographs of all the local sites.

Robert French was the principal photographer who worked for Lawrence. French had joined the Lawrence studios in the late 1860s, starting at the bottom of the profession as a printer, working himself up to the position of Photographer by the mid-70s, just as the dry plate revolution was taking place. French then spent the next forty years travelling through every province of Ireland, recording scenic views of all the well-known and little-known beauty spots. Over this period, he took tens of thousands of negatives, often visiting the same location over and over again through the years, recording the changes and the continuities in the Irish countryside. Unfortunately, as it might seem to us today, his brief was not to photograph people or to observe social conditions, but to photograph scenes, although obviously his townscape photographs in Dublin and Cork show something of the bustle of these cities in late Victorian times.

CORN MARKET. CORK. 2158 W L.

French's eye for a scene and meticulous attention to detail mark him out far and above the level of most commercial scenic photographers, as the photographs on these pages clearly show. He retired in 1914 at the age of seventy-three, but lived to see the destruction of the Lawrence studios and many of the negatives accumulated over the years, in the 1916 Rising, which left much of Sackville Street in ruins. However, 40,000 of the glass-plate negatives of Irish scenes taken by French survived, and were finally bought by the National Library of Ireland in 1943 at a price of £300.

ENGLISH CARTOONS

In the affairs of nations, as well as individuals, the perception each side has of the other, its assessment of their potential and their limitations, their probity and character, is crucial. Behind much of the way Britain has handled its Irish problem has been a popularly held image of the Irishman which verges on a caricature. As far back as the twelfth century, Geraldus Cambrensis, the chronicler of Henry II's invasion of Ireland, held the Irish in contempt. But, of course, conquerors are unlikely to have a high opinion of the conquered. In fact, it is probably no exaggeration to say that much in the Anglo-Irish relationship has been conditioned by popular preconceptions, assumptions and representations constructed by the English of the Irish and then, in return, constructed by the Irish about themselves and about the English.

In the nineteenth century, the most clear expression of this English attitude can be found in the political cartoons of the magazine *Punch*. In an age before the advent of radio and television, the Victorian political cartoon is a clear indication of popular prejudices about all manner of people and issues. Historians have only recently come to acknowledge this rich source as an index of popular culture and attitudes. Out of the many comic weekly magazines, *Punch* was the most popular, and has been the most enduring. Founded in 1841, its success was due partly to skilful financial management, but also to the long line of talented cartoonists and illustrators who elevated the major weekly *Punch* cartoon almost to the level of importance of a *Times* leader.

From the 1860s onwards, the representation of the Irishman in *Punch* took on quite distinct, regular features. He was given a huge projecting mouth, a jutting jaw, a sloping forehead, and he was usually covered in hair.

In short, he was made to look like an ape. Quite unlike the other ethnic and political caricatures popular in Victorian Britain, the Irishman assumed his own inimitable identity as a barbaric, stupid, less-than-human ape-man. Interestingly, this was happening just at the time that the Darwinian theories of evolution were becoming widely debated, and the Irishman was being represented quite clearly and distinctly as belonging to an early, primitive stage in the evolution of man. It was no accident that this cartoon-image became popular at the time of the Fenian troubles from 1865 onwards, and was especially common during the time of the Land War and the agitation in Parliament for Home Rule in the late 1870s and 1880s. Also, the cartoons must be seen in

the context of the equally popular and standard representation of John Bull or Britannia, the self-image of the English. John Bull was seen to have exactly the opposite characteristics to Paddy. He was calm, patient, enlightened, civilised, humane and protective. Whereas Paddy was patently unfit to govern himself, John Bull had all the attributes of a civilised and fair master. These cartoons reflected, but also helped endorse, a moral justification for England's domination over Ireland.

The CARTOONS on these pages from *Punch* illustrate the image of the ape-like Irishman, common to all the comic weeklies at the time.

1 *Punch*, 4 November 1843. An interesting early example of the Irish stereotype drawn by J. Kenny Meadows (1790–1874) the first of the great *Punch* cartoonists. Daniel O'Connell and the Repeal Movement is given the grotesque features of an 'Irish Frankenstein', which are some way along the line in the development of a full apish Paddy.

2 *Punch*, 28 December 1867. This drawing of 'The Fenian Guy Fawkes' followed the Fenian rising in Ireland and bomb-blasts in Manchester and at

1

THE FENIAN GUY FAWKES.

TWO FORCES.

2

Clerkenwell Prison. It was drawn by John Tenniel (1820–1914) who was the senior cartoonist on *Punch* for over forty years from the 1860s, and is perhaps the best known of all Victorian cartoonists, being knighted in 1893. The cartoon clearly plays upon anti-Catholic prejudices from the 5 November Gunpowder Plot rituals. The Irishman is menacing, destructive and aggressive, but also stupid — he sits with a lighted torch on a keg of gunpowder imperiling the lives of himself and the innocent children around him.

3 *Punch*, 29 October 1881. 'Two Forces', again drawn by John Tenniel. A classic confrontation between the forces of good and evil. Interestingly, this cartoon also includes the good side of the Irish

3

spirit, personified by 'Hibernia' protected by a staunch Britannia with the sword of 'law'. This female symbol epitomised what the English thought the Irish should be — soft, delicate, submissive, dependent upon England's consolation and protection. All these female characteristics made it 'natural' for Ireland to be subject to England, just as it was 'natural' in Victorian society for women, as an 'inferior' class, to be dependent upon their men. Images like these further help to justify England's civilising mission in Ireland.

These crude stereotypes have become a part of English culture and the rough, stupid, thick-set Irish Paddy has been the butt of countless jokes down to the present day. 'Have you heard the one about the Irishman who . . . ?'

by the overriding ideology of the day, which believed that free market forces would themselves adjust economic difficulties. This attitude scorned the sort of governmental intervention and regulation necessary to tackle a problem like this.

Throughout the years of the Famine, during which England too suffered from a shortage of foods, Ireland continued to export wheat, barley, cattle, sheep and pigs to Britain. 'Famine' is therefore in one sense a misnomer for the tragedy of those years, since food was plentiful in Ireland. Her economy however, was so tied to the needs of Britain that it was impossible for the food and starving masses to be brought together.

During the course of the disaster, people with nothing left but the prospect of starvation and death headed for the ports. Many found their way to Liverpool, then a town of 250,000. In one week alone, in January 1847, the Poor Law Guardians had to dispense relief to 130,000 people. By June, it was estimated that 330,000 Irish had passed through Liverpool docks. But the greatest exodus was to the New World. In 1846, 116,000 somehow raised the passage for the wretched voyages to America and Australia (see page 30). The following year, 250,000 followed them. In the decade beginning in 1845, two million Irishmen, a *quarter* of the population, left Ireland for ever, and by 1925 a further three million had departed for the New World. Psychological resistance to the idea of emigration was swept aside by the famine, and it became an acceptable if wrenching alternative to the impoverished life on the Irish soil. Emigration was a part of a mood of depression and resignation that the Famine left in its wake in many country districts – what one historian, Gearoid O'Tuathaigh, has called 'a state of almost chronic melancholia'. With the dreadful memory lingering on in the collective mind, holdings were no longer split up to facilitate early marriage, and the land now passed from father to son, though not necessarily the eldest son.

Emigration steadily brought down the population until it levelled out at 4½ million in 1911. Today, it is still under 5 million. Instinctively, it seems, social forms and traditions arose to ensure against the over-population that had existed before the famine. By 1951, after a century of these constraints, 97% of men and 81% of women between the ages of 20 and 24, were unmarried; while one farmer in four between the ages of 64 and 75 was a bachelor, and the rural population declined from 7 million to 3 million since the Famine.

It was those who were suffering most from Ireland's distorted agricultural economy that were swept away by the Famine. Only a quarter of the old holdings, of one to five acres, remained. The shift from pasture to tillage continued, and the number of larger farms of over thirty acres trebled. Entire communities disappeared. Whole villages were deserted and left to crumble. Many landlords went bankrupt under the crippling burden of the Poor Law rates and rent default, and after the Famine, one quarter of the land of Ireland changed hands. The fall in land prices attracted speculators, who proved to be no worse nor better than the old owners.

In terms of Anglo–Irish relations, the importance of the Famine was that, to Irish Nationalists, it finally and incontravertably demonstrated that Britain was unfit to govern Ireland. Although the Republican accusations of attempted genocide by Britain were totally unfair, there remains a nagging suspicion that had a catastrophe of this dimension descended on the Home Counties, then the reactions of the British Government would have been quite different in kind. Certainly, in the minds of the Irish on both sides of the Atlantic, the Famine was a crime for which Britain bore heavy responsibility, and it brought a new bitterness to the hatred of British rule, and a lasting determination to overthrow it.

From Britain, the Irish problem looked very different. It was put down to Irish backwardness and obduracy, to defects in the Irish character. Despite the Union, the British did not regard the Irish as equals, and this is evidenced by English popular culture through the nineteenth century, which clearly portrays the Irish as a primitive and inferior species (see page 42). Even Queen Victoria claimed in 1867 that 'the Irish people are a really shocking abominable people – not like any other nation.' One MP claimed in 1886 that England had a duty to govern Ireland which 'if left to herself, would afford such a spectacle of misery as mankind has ever witnessed.' If the Irish bemused the British, then so would the Irish question. Disraeli expressed this bafflement when he said: 'I want to see a public man come forward and say what the Irish problem is. One says it is a physical question, another a spiritual. Now it is the absence of the aristocracy, then the absence of railroads. It is the Pope one day; potatoes the next .' Ireland, a poor Catholic rural society, was welded to a wealthy, imperial, Protestant industrial power, Britain. Their cultures were profoundly different, and their relations became confused in a mirage of misleading prejudices and bewildering misconceptions. In fact, as J.S. Mill put it when Britain was in the throes of industrial revolution and on the verge of her great Imperial adventure:

Ireland is not an exceptional country but England is. Irish circumstances and Irish ideas as to social and agricultural economy are the general ideas of the human race: it is English circumstances and English ideas that are peculiar. Ireland is in the main stream of human existence and human feeling and experience: it is England that is in one of the lateral channels.

Although resentment at British rule continued to ferment in Ireland, and now in the ghettos of England and America, it was not until the 1860s that a new Republicanism emerged. In 1858, veterans of 1848 set up the Irish Republican Brotherhood, the predecessor of the IRA, whose oath gave allegiance to 'the Irish Republic now virtually established', by which they meant that British rule in Ireland was illegal and Irishmen had a moral right to oppose it. They committed themselves to do their 'very utmost, at every risk, while life lasts to defend its independence and integrity', thus making clear their commitment to overthrow British rule by insurrection. Its sister organisation in America, the Fenian Brotherhood, failed to provide the funds the IRB hoped for, but it grew rapidly in the early 1860s as a result of agricultural depression and a number of well-publicised trials. By 1865, the separatists (or 'the Fenians' as they became generally known in England and

IRISH CARTOONS

In response to this constant denigration of the Irish character in English popular culture, the Irish constructed a counter-image for themselves and of the English. While the English represented Ireland as a barbarous, uncultured country, inhabited by sub-human, violent ape-men, so the Irish created a romantic and noble representation of their country as a dignified, upright and Christian nation. To the English, Paddy was aggressive, stupid, primitive, and unfit to govern his own affairs. To the Irish, Pat was gentle, loving, honest and heroic, and worthy of his equal place amongst the commonwealth of nations, which only England had denied him.

Inherent in these contradictory images is a particular attitude towards history. To the English, Irish history was a continuous saga of turbulence and violence, a long line of brutal and treasonable uprisings against benevolent English government. To the Irish, their history was pure, sacred and heroic, rooted in an age when Ireland was inhabited by saints and scholars and kept Christianity alive in Europe through centuries of Dark Ages. If the English looked to a recent past of troubles and tragedies, the Irish looked to an idealised vision of a distant past, when a pure Gaelic culture dominated Ireland. The

Gaelic Revival in the last decades of the nineteenth century gave an enormous boost to these attitudes. This politicisation of Irish culture at the time must be seen in the context of a dominant English culture which tended to deny the very existence of Irish civilisation.

These ideas in Ireland found visual expression in political cartoons just as the dominant English attitudes had done in the pages of *Punch*. Dublin produced a wave of political comic weeklies towards the end of the nineteenth century like *Pat* and *The Jarvey*, and in addition several Dublin newspapers began to publish cartoons as weekly supplements. From the 1880s, the development of the printing process of chromolithography meant that many of these cartoons were in colour. The two central images of these cartoons were produced in conscious contrast to the English images. Pat was a proud, upright yeoman, honest and fair. With a smile on his lips and a twinkle in his eyes, he was an attractive epitome of Irish masculinity. But the more haunting image was Erin, an epitome of Irish femininity. Erin was drawn in flowing robes, usually white, with long, falling hair. Her face was strikingly beautiful, but she was also melancholic and wise. She represented all

THE IRISH JUGGERNAUT.

that was courageous, chaste and pure, and became the complete antithesis of *Punch's* Hibernia, suppliant and submissive. Erin represented moral strength and resistance. On the other hand, England was usually personified by the agents of English rule that would have been familiar to most Irishfolk. England became an evil force represented by the judiciary, the landlords or the army. Now, it was the English who were the bullies and the brutes, out to rape and pillage Ireland.

The significance of the cartoons on the previous few pages is that they represent not the work of a few obscure, demented illustrators who sketched out their own private obsessions. They were published in magazines and newspapers that enjoyed enormous popularity in England and in Ireland. They represent a genuinely popular expression of the attitudes and prejudices of the mass of the population for whom they were intended. As commercial organisations, these magazines and papers would soon have died if they did not express what their readers wanted; indeed many of them *did* fold when they became obtuse or remote. In addition to simply reflecting popular feelings, they helped to sustain and to concentrate such ideas. If at first Paddy was just a joke, then the characteristics he possessed were soon attributed to the real live thing. Irishmen were actually thought to be inherently violent in character and somehow less human than other beings. If the rape of Erin by England was initially a metaphor, then it soon became a deeply rooted belief amongst thousands of Irishmen that all their problems would be solved if only the British presence in Ireland could be ended. These powerful mental representations actually created a framework in which it became increasingly difficult for both sides to see reality.

They made it difficult for an informed and concerned public to emerge. It was much easier to go along with *Punch* and believe that Irish problems defied solution becase of defects in the Irish character, than to analyse the real cause of the problem.

It became a tragic feature in Anglo–Irish affairs that two nations, so naturally and geographically close as England and Ireland, should have been driven so firmly and so incurably apart by the widespread popular misconceptions each held about the other. Furthermore, if the English view of the Irish favoured an ideology of domination, then the

Irish view of themselves and of England's role in their past went to sustain a powerful ideology of rebellion. The culmination of this ideology came in the events of 1916.

The four CARTOONS illustrate these features quite clearly. They show the four common Irish representations of the English. The first '*The Law's Delay*' depicts the judge who sleeps while injustice is done (from the *Weekly Freeman*, 12 July 1884); the second cartoon '*The Irish Juggernaut*' shows the landlord who crushes the peasantry (from *United Ireland*, 22 September 1888); the third '*Heroines of Irish History: the Torture of Anne Devlin*' illustrates the military force which assaults the courageous epitome of Ireland (from the *Irish Fireside*, 5 August 1885); and the fourth cartoon '*Ha! Ha! Revenged!!!*' depicts the jailer who keeps Erin imprisoned (from the *Weekly Freeman* 23 May 1885).

Ireland as well) claimed to have 80,000 members including several thousand Irish soldiers in the British Army. Despite bitter opposition from the hierarchy of the Catholic Church, it was the first movement in Ireland that drew its strength both in its leadership and membership from working men — artisans, labourers, small farmers and shop-keepers. Particularly important for the future was its success, under the leadership of O'Donovan Rossa, in radicalising the rural poor in the western counties of Clare, Galway and Mayo. Organised in cells as a secret society, it was in fact riddled with informers, and when in 1867 the Fenians held an insurrection, it proved no more effective and no less fanciful than its predecessors. But it affirmed the faith again. Its proclamation was to have a familiar ring:

Our rights and liberties have been trampled on by an alien aristocracy, who, treating us as foes, usurped our lands and drew away from our unfortunate country all material riches . . . The soil of Ireland at present in the possession of an oligarchy belongs to us, the Irish people, and to us it must be restored.

The call to arms and the offer of sacrifice had been made in yet another generation: it was a further phase of the struggle that would see fruition some fifty years later. However, there was a more immediate impact. The executions of three Fenians who attempted to free their leader as he was being transported to prison in Manchester were followed by an explosion, killing twelve at Clerkenwell Prison in London. This attracted more concern in Britain than events in Ireland ever could. Some people called for more stringent policies, but for others it strengthened the impression that something was sadly amiss in Irish society, and prepared both politicians and public for a reappraisal of Irish affairs. Among them was Gladstone. He was deeply affected by the acts of violence and told the House of Commons that the sense of shock and horror at such 'an inhuman outrage' would come home 'to the popular mind' and make people realise 'the vast importance of the Irish controversy'. Clearly, outrages perpetrated on the mainland were a great deal more effective than those committed in Galway.

When Gladstone took office in 1868, he began to try and pacify Irish nationalism. His 1870 Land Act was directed at the heart of the Irish grievance — landlordism. It stipulated that evicted tenants should get compensation for any improvements for which they had been responsible and that tenants evicted for reasons other than failing to pay their rent should receive 'compensation for disturbance'. Since few tenants were evicted for 'other reasons', the Act made little impact, but it did mark the beginning of the end of *laissez faire* policies. The Government had now accepted the need to intervene in the most fundamental aspect of Ireland's economic life, the relationship between landlord and tenant.

In the later 1870s, competition from America, depression in England, and in 1877 and 1879 partial potato crop failures, threatened famine again in the west of Ireland. With prices depressed, tenants could not find the rent and evictions began: over a thousand families in 1878, two thousand in 1880. The formation of the Land League in 1879 was to ensure, for the first time in Irish history, that the discontent in rural Ireland would be forged into a serious political movement. Its immediate aims were to organise the tenantry to protect itself against rack-renting and eviction; its long-term ambition was to make the tenants the owners of the land. Evicted families were sheltered and fed; embargoes were placed on evicted farms; the families of those imprisoned were looked after; evictions were made the occasion of great demonstrations; those who broke the Land League's code were ostracised (see page 34). It became so effective in some areas that it virtually superseded English rule. In 1880 the Irish correspondent of *The Times* reported:

Its code is clear, its executive resolute its machinery complete and its action uniform. There is a government de facto *and a government* de jure — *the former wielding power which is felt and feared, the latter exhibiting the paraphernalia and pomp but little of the reality of power.*

The Land League was peaceable, but agrarian outrages kept pace with the evictions — 236 in 1877, 863 the following year, and 2,590 in 1880, and they were becoming more precisely directed. Between 1847 and 1878, only 1% of 'offences against the person' were directed at landlords and their agents, but in 1880 it was 20%. Gladstone's Coercion Act did nothing to stem the flow. Despite the arrest of nearly a thousand local leaders in 1881, acts of agrarian violence nearly doubled.

The Land War convinced British politicians that the landlord system in Ireland was no longer tenable. Gladstone's second Land Act of 1881, which effectively undercut the Land League, introduced protection against unfair eviction. It regulated rents through land courts and granted fair compensation for the improvement to lettings made by tenants. Although it was complicated and by no means comprehensive, it was a direct challenge, and began to undermine the power of the landlords. The land courts, in their first three years, reduced rents by an average of 20%, and the landlords began to sell out to their tenants. Conservative administrations then followed this up with the Ashbourne Land Act of 1885 which began to make large sums of money available to enable tenants to borrow funds to purchase land, and with the Wyndham Land Act of 1903, which established a state system of mortgages for tenants and compensation for landlords to complete the process. Slowly, the structure of land-ownership in Ireland was transformed. Of the 22 million acres that make up the country, 9 million changed hands between 1903 and 1920, and a further 2 million were in the process of being sold. Ireland had become a nation of small farmers, and the land seized by the English in the sixteenth and seventeenth centuries had largely reverted to the Irish.

However, the Land War had implications beyond the economy, since as a movement of national self-assertion, it contributed to the development of Irish nationalism and self-confidence. For a country to become a nation it needs its own cultural identity, and towards the end of the century, the Irish began to assert their 'Irishness' in what is known as the Gaelic Revival. Douglas Hyde put it simply in his pamphlet *The Necessity of de-Anglicising Ireland* in 1892:

On the morning of Monday 24 April 1916, Easter Monday, Padraig Pearse marched with a tiny contingent of supporters to the General Post Office in what is now O'Connell Street. There, in the smart green uniform of an Irish Volunteer, he read out to a small, uncomprehending audience of passers-by, a document that fundamentally shifted the parameters of Irish history. Pearse and his colleagues, barely a hundred and fifty men, proclaimed the existence of an independent Irish Republic, and it is the fundamental existence of this state to which Irish Republicans declare their allegiance to this day. Pearse's declaration ran:

POBLACHT NA EIREANN
THE PROVISIONAL GOVERNMENT OF THE IRISH REPUBLIC
TO THE PEOPLE OF IRELAND
IRISHMEN AND IRISHWOMEN:

In the name of God and of the dead generations from which she receives her old tradition of nationhood, Ireland, through us, summons her children to her flag and strikes for her freedom . . .

We declare the right of the people of Ireland to the ownership of Ireland, and to the unfettered control of Irish destinies, to be sovereign and indefeasible. The long usurpation of that right by a foreign people and government has not extinguished the right, nor can it ever be extinguished except by the destruction of the Irish people. In every generation the Irish people have asserted their right to national freedom and sovereignty; six times during the past three hundred years they have asserted it in arms. Standing on that fundamental right and again asserting it in arms in the face of the world, we hereby proclaim the Irish Republic as a Sovereign Independent State, and we pledge our lives and the lives of our comrades-in-arms to the cause of its freedom, of its welfare and of its exaltation among the nations.

The Irish Republic is entitled to, and hereby claims, the allegiance of every Irishman and Irishwoman. The Republic guarantees religious and civil liberty, equal rights and equal opportunities to all its citizens, and declares its resolve to pursue the happiness and prosperity of the whole nation and of all its parts, cherishing all the children of the nation equally, and oblivious of the differences carefully fostered by an

alien government, which have divided a minority from the majority in the past . . .

In this supreme hour the Irish nation must, by its valour and discipline and by the readiness of its children to sacrifice themselves for the common good, prove itself worthy of the august destiny to which it is called.

The Rising itself was as confused and clumsy as all the others had been. Eoin MacNeill, the Commander-in-Chief of the Volunteers, had not been told of plans for a Rising, as he was known to oppose them. On finding out, he cancelled the orders to mobilise which had been set for Easter Sunday. The Rising continued, a day late, although thousands of Volunteers all over Ireland failed to turn up because of the confusion. Only in Dublin did the rebels amount to more than a tiny number.

The British authorities finally got the upper hand over the rebels by pouring troops into the city, and from the Wednesday morning the gunboat *Helga* began shelling each centre of the rebel operations

from Dublin Bay. The damage done by the *Helga's* high explosive and incendiary shells was immense. On the Thursday, Major-General Sir John Maxwell arrived in Dublin to take full control of the civil and military authorities, and set out to destroy Irish revolutionary nationalism. On the Friday evening, Pearse and a wounded Connolly, carried on a stretcher, evacuated the General Post Office and agreed to sign a cease-fire order on the basis of unconditional surrender.

When Pearse, Connolly and their little band of revolutionaries walked out into the streets of Dublin on Easter Monday, they knew they had no chance of military success. Their aim was to arouse the conscience of the Irish people in a gesture that at the time seemed futile, but with the hindsight of history, can be seen to have been decisive.

The PHOTOGRAPH on the left shows British troops on guard near some of the worst destruction in Dublin. The photograph above shows the shell of the General Post Office and the ruins of Sackville Street (now O'Connell Street) which had been one of the finest in Europe.

When we speak of the necessity for de-Anglicising the Irish nation we mean it, not as a protest against imitating what is best in the English people, for that would be absurd, but rather to show the folly of neglecting what is Irish and hastening to adopt pell-mell and indiscriminately everything that is English simply because it is English.

The Gaelic League was formed in 1893 to promote the use of Irish and to encourage the publication of Gaelic literature old and new, and it helped to generate a new cultural nationalism. It was so successful that by 1906, it had a membership of 100,000 and 900 branches throughout Ireland. With it came a revival of Irish sports, like Gaelic football and hurling, which was important because it brought a sense of pride in Irish culture to a wide constituency, while a renewed interest in Ireland's past preoccupied many intellectuals like A.E. Russell and W.B. Yeats. What emerged, in the popular mind at least, was a highly romantic vision of Ireland before the English conquest, based on rediscovered folk tales and historic legends. The Nationalist Moran thought that 'the prospect of such a new Ireland rising up and out of the old, with love and not hate as its inspiration, has already sent a great thrill through the land.' It brought to Ireland a heady romantic nationalism. Yeats later remarked: 'All the past has been turned into a melodrama with Ireland for a blameless hero; and poet, novelist and historian had but one object: that we should hiss the villain.'

The political tradition of Fenianism was carried forth by Sinn Fein, an organisation formed by Arthur Griffith in 1905. Sinn Fein is a difficult phrase to translate, literally meaning 'ourselves' with connotations of 'self-reliance'. It represented the core of the Republican tradition, gaining support from those who grew sceptical of a parliamentary solution to Irish affairs. Sinn Fein aimed to re-establish the independence of Ireland by a withdrawal from Westminster and the establishment of an independent Irish Parliament in Dublin, defending it by force if necessary.

To this was added a younger tradition, the labour movement. In Dublin at the turn of the century, 30% of the population lived in slums and 2,000 families lived in single rooms. Unemployment may have been as high as 20% and many of those in work received wages that were sufficient only for a bare existence. James Larkin and James Connolly, leading Trade Unionists, organised labour in Dublin, resulting in a major confrontation with the city's industrialists in 1913. They believed that the struggle for Irish freedom was not only national, implying a struggle against Britain, but social and economic too, involving resistance to capitalism. Connolly, the movement's mentor, wrote:

. . . the national and economic freedom of the Irish people must be sought in . . . the establishment of an Irish Socialist Republic and the consequent conversion of the means of production, distribution and exchange into the common property of society, to be held and controlled by a democratic state in the interests of the entire community.'

This was the language of revolutionary socialism.

Meanwhile, Padraig Pearse was using a different language to justify an armed uprising. By invoking the Irish martyrs of the past and by calling upon the Christian tradition of sacrifice, Pearse said that a nation could attain the right to statehood only through struggle. In 1915, Pearse read the oration at the funeral of the Fenian hero O'Donovan Rossa. He declared: 'Life springs from death and from the graves of patriot men and women spring living nations. The Defenders of the Realm . . . think they have pacified Ireland . . . but the fools, the fools, the fools, they have left us our Fenian dead and while Ireland holds these graves, Ireland unfree shall never be at peace.' Pearse and his band of supporters decided to take up the succession from Tone and the United Irishmen of 1798, the Young Ireland rebels of 1848 and the Fenians of 1867, and to redeem Ireland as Christ had redeemed mankind, by affirming the Irish nation through a blood sacrifice. Pearse wrote mystically: 'Ireland will not find Christ's peace until she has taken Christ's sword . . . Christ's peace is lovely in its coming, beautiful are its feet on the mountains. But it is heralded by terrific messengers; seraphim and cherubim blow trumpets of war before it.'

All these separate ingredients came together in the Easter Rising of 1916 when 1,600 members of the IRB and Connolly's Citizen Army challenged British rule in Ireland (see page 51). When Padraig Pearse read the Declaration of Independence from the steps of the Post Office in Sackville Street, Dublin, he called upon the Fenian tradition by proclaiming the existence of an independent Irish Republic as a moral, legal and indisputable right: 'We declare the right of the people of Ireland to the ownership of Ireland and to the unfettered control of Irish destinies, to be sovereign and indefeasible.' The demand was made in the name of history and Ireland's martyrs: 'In every generation the Irish people have asserted their right to national freedom and sovereignty: six times in the past three hundred years they have asserted it in arms.' It proclaimed also the socialism of Connolly: 'The Republic guarantees religious and civil liberty, equal rights and equal opportunities to all its citizens and declares its resolve to pursue the happiness and prosperity of the whole nation . . .'. They re-affirmed the need for sacrifice: 'In this supreme hour the Irish nation must, by its valour and discipline, and by the readiness of its children to sacrifice themselves to the common good, prove itself worthy of the august destiny to which it is called.'

The 1916 Easter Rising was the climactic act in the Irish Republican tradition. Connolly's call for a workers' Republic, Pearse's call for a blood sacrifice, and the echo of the Fenian martyrs were to reverberate through Ireland. Although the rising was put down by the British within a week with their superior firepower, this dramatic gesture of defiance proved to be the beginning of the end of British rule in twenty-six of Ireland's thirty-two counties.

2: PARTITION

The Act of Union in 1800, by which Britain absorbed Ireland, marks a watershed in Anglo–Irish history. Throughout the nineteenth century, Irish affairs would be determined at Westminster in London. Both Catholic Nationalists, for whom the Union was an outrageous denial of the Irish identity, and Protestant Loyalists, for whom it was the guarantee of privilege, knew that the battle for Irish independence would be directed against the Union in the setting of the British Parliament.

In giving up the Dublin Parliament, over which they had complete authority, the Protestants were losing control of their own destiny. It was for this reason that they accepted the Union, at the beginning, with reluctance. When they saw that their privilege and position could be guaranteed only by Westminster, they naturally gave crown and country a loyalty that might seem exaggerated by English standards. The Act itself assured them that Britain and Ireland would 'for ever, be united into one Kingdom' and that the Protestant Church would 'remain in full force for ever'. So, it is not surprising that for Irish Protestants it took on the quality of a timeless trust with a special authority beyond ordinary law. Thus, they would see any attempt to reconcile Irish Nationalism as an abrogation of that trust. For Nationalists, the Union meant they must press their cause in a foreign legislature where they had less than 100 votes in a chamber of 650. It had been part of the intent of the Act to muffle Irish protest. Pitt, the architect of the Act, had been advised: 'By giving the Irish 100 members in an assembly of 650, they will be rendered impotent.' However, it was to prove that a well-organised Irish party could be devastatingly effective in parliaments when governments had slender majorities.

Ulster, the historic nine counties in the north-east of Ireland, has always had a distinct character. The traffic of people and goods across the channel to Scotland meant that in Antrim and Down there had long been a Scottish influence. At the same time, Ulster was somewhat cut off from the rest of Ireland by the natural terrain of forest, bog and mountain. The result is, as a modern geographer, Professor E. Estyn Evans, has put it, that while Ulster is a part of 'the essential unity of Ireland', it has a 'strong regional variant in habitat, heritage and history'. Northern Ireland he describes as 'a land and a people of strong personality in some ways more British than the British, yet in other ways more Irish than the Irish.'

Unlike the rest of Ireland, where the Protestant minority is tiny, the population in Ulster's nine counties is evenly balanced between the two religions. In the north, rural disturbances of the eighteenth century took on a sectarian character. A general increase in the population led to land hunger, and in Armagh landlords who had traditionally rented to Protestants began to let to Catholics who, more desperate, were prepared to pay higher rents.

This led to growing hostility and suspicion between rival gangs, the Protestant Peep O'Day Boys and the Catholic 'Defenders'. Skirmishes between the two groups became more frequent, and in 1795 there was a 'battle' at the Diamond in Armagh. In its wake, the Protestants organised a society to protect their advantaged position in society. It was called the Orange Order (see page 56).

Custom, culture and religion had always divided Catholic from Protestant, and in the nineteenth century economics began to divide Ireland, north from south. From 1800, the population of Belfast doubled every decade. As it was caught up in the English Industrial Revolution, it became a part of the industrial conurbation that included Glasgow and Liverpool (see page 63). Ship-building boomed. So did the linen industry. The trade policies that suppressed the economy of southern Ireland encouraged the growth of Belfast. Belfast became a classic, northern, English industrial city, which had more in common with Bolton than Dublin by 1900. The people who migrated to Belfast to work in the new industries brought with them the religious antagonisms of the countryside and the violent tradition of the agrarian secret societies. Protestants and Catholics flocked into the city, but gravitated to their own separate areas. Amongst the unskilled labourers, the Protestants went to the north and east of the city, in a conurbation spreading north from Sandy Row and the Shankill Road, whilst the Catholics went to the area called the Pound, overflowing west along the Falls Road. As the Protestant farmers of Armagh in the eighteenth century had feared the Catholic migration would put up rents, so Protestant workers in Belfast feared that Catholics would force down wages. Tension and antagonism were never far below the surface in the ghettos, and there was serious disorder in Belfast in nearly every decade of the nineteenth century.

Sectarian rhetoric was a feature of nineteenth-century Ireland. In 1857, the Grand Chaplain of the Orange Lodge, a Reverend Drew, declaimed: 'The Word of God makes all plain, puts to eternal shame the practices of persecutors, and stigmatises with enduring reprobation the arrogant pretences of Popes and the outrageous dogmata of their blood-stained religion.' Meanwhile, Archbishop Cullen of Dublin denounced 'the bigoted fanatical proselytising Orange faction'.

The disturbances of 1857 began when Revd 'Roaring' Hugh Hanna held an illegal open-air meeting in the centre of Belfast. A Royal Commission reporting on the troubles, which continued for two months, took the view that the July Orange March represented the celebration of the triumph of one class over another. It found the overwhelmingly Protestant police to have been partisan, and recommended 'a total change should be made in the mode of appointment and the management of the local police'. In 1864, a riot in Belfast, occasioned by the unveiling of the O'Connell monument in Dublin, lasted 18 days, left 12 dead and needed 2,000 British troops to subdue it. Riots in 1872, sparked off by a Catholic march on Lady Day left several dead, and resulted in 837 families abandoning their homes and 247 houses being completely destroyed.

As Protestant fought Catholic in the north of Ireland, there was growing

THE ORANGE ORDER AND 12 JULY

The Orange Order came into being in September 1795, after the so-called 'Battle of the Diamond', which was in fact little more than a bloody clash between groups of Protestant 'Peep O'Day Boys' and Catholic 'Defenders' on a field near the town of Armagh. The Order was basically a more formal reorganisation of the 'Peep O'Day Boys', and the various Orangeboys or Orange Societies, to defend Protestant privilege. The popular symbol of the Protestant hero King William was used as their emblem, and his colour as their identification.

The celebration of 'The Glorious Twelfth', commemorating King Billy's victory over the Catholics at the Battle of the Boyne in 1690, was adopted by the Orange Order from its very earliest days as a means of bringing Protestant Loyalists together by parading behind banners and flags. A letter written by Lord Gosford, the Governor of Armagh, dated 13 July 1796, gives an account of the first 'Glorious Twelfth' parade held in Co. Armagh by the newly formed Orange Order:

They accordingly came here about five o'clock in the evening, marching in regular files by two and two with orange cockades, unarmed, and by companies which were distinguished by numbers upon their flags. The party had one drum, and each company had a fife and two or three men in front with painted wands in their hands who acted as commanders. The devices on the flags were chiefly portraits of King William, with mottos alluding to his establishment of the Protestant religion, and on the reverse side of some of them I perceived a portrait of his present Majesty with the crown placed before him, motto God save the King.

They were perfectly quiet and sober . . . I recommended to the heads of their companies to keep their people sober and to go to their respective homes quietly which they assured me would be the case, for they had entered into resolutions that no more liquor should be drunk than what their commanders might deem a necessary refreshment upon their march . . . . The number who paraded through my place amounted, I should imagine, to about fifteen hundred. I have had no particular account as yet from the other side of the County except that similar bodies paraded there and all ended quietly.

This description shows how little the ritual of Orange marches has changed over the years. The beating of drums, marching behind banners and the defiant slogans and songs have often created a near hysterical atmosphere, so the history of Orange Parades has been a troubled one. The Orange Order was formally dissolved in 1836, but revived again a decade later, and the 12 July marches in 1849 resulted in sectarian violence and the death of several Catholics. This incident became known as the 'Battle of Dollis Bray', and troops had to be sent in to quell the rioting. There was also serious rioting in Belfast after the 1857 Orange Day.

The continuous tradition of annual Orange Day parades dates from 1872 when the ban on public marches was formally lifted. In the mid 1880s, the Orange Order became the nucleus of the organisation of Protestant resistance to Home Rule in Ulster. This in itself greatly enriched the Order; the early primitive flags became ornate silken banners, and Orange Halls were built in all the Protestant towns and villages of Ulster. The parading of Orangemen past the Catholic ghettos infuriated the Catholic population, and troops were called to quell rioting in Belfast after Orange Parades in 1886 and 1935.

It was a similar march held by the Apprentice Boys of Londonderry, (another annual commemoration, this time of the lifting of the siege of Londonderry in 1689) on 12 August 1969 that led to the cycle of events known as the 'Battle of the Bogside' and the sending in of the British Army to the streets of Northern Ireland on 14 August, to keep the peace.

The flag OPPOSITE, the oldest surviving banner of the Orange Order, date about 1800, belongs to Lodge No. 1020 from Newtown Mt Kennedy. It is now in the Ulster Folk and Transport Museum.

The PHOTOGRAPH shows the 1979 Orange Parade passing down the Lisburn Road, Belfast, and the illustration below is a crude drawing of King Billy, inscribed 'The Immortal Memory of 1690', taken from a purse belonging to an Orangeman, c. 1800.

GLADSTONE

Gladstone's long political career had been unusual in that he had started it as a staunch conservative, opposing reform of the parliamentary franchise in 1832, and had ended it as a devotee of nineteenth-century liberalism and a supporter of Home Rule for Ireland. Throughout his life, the drive and energy with which he threw himself into a cause was remarkable. One of his private secretaries once remarked that if one hundred could represent the energy of an ordinary man and two hundred that of an exceptional man, Gladstone's energy would represent a figure of at least one thousand. Although he visited Ireland only once he showed a persistent concern for the plight of the Irish. He regarded the Irish question as one of the great unresolved troubles of British politics, and he believed it was the duty of politicians to grapple with the unpopular subject of Ireland to try and bring justice to that unhappy land. Early in his career, on 12 October 1845, he wrote prophetically to his wife saying:

Ireland! Ireland! That cloud in the West! That coming storm! That minister of God's retribution upon cruel, inveterate and but half-atoned injustice! Ireland forces upon us these great social and great religious questions. God grant us that we may have the courage to look them in the face!

Gladstone's real involvement with Ireland began some twenty years later, as Liberal Prime Minister, 1868–73. On hearing of his victory in the election of 1868, whilst chopping down a tree on his estate, he is reputed to have uttered the momentous phrase, 'My mission is to pacify Ireland'.

But, by 1885, his policy of reform of the Church, education and the land had failed to solve the Irish problem, and Gladstone decided that the only solution was some form of devolved government. Accordingly, he faced the complete destruction of the Liberal Party, and introduced a Home Rule Bill in 1886, which was eventually defeated in the House of Commons. In his final speech on the Bill, Gladstone, now aged 76, spoke of the abominable way in which Ireland had been treated by England which was a 'broad and black blot' upon the British record. He ended his speech by saying:

Ireland stands at your bar, expectant, hopeful, almost suppliant. . . . Think, I beseech you, think well, think wisely, think, not for the moment but for the years that are to come . . . .

The defeat of Gladstone's second Home Rule Bill by the House of Lords in September 1893 drained the stamina of the 'Grand Old Man' of English politics, and he retired a few months later, recognising the failure of his mission 'to pacify Ireland'.

Whether Gladstone's commitment to the Irish question was motivated more by his crusading moral mission than by the need to ensure the support of the Irish MPs for his various Liberal administrations, is very difficult to assess. In any case, Gladstone is one of the few English politicians who has staked his career and the future of his party on a just settlement of the Irish question, and was prepared to court great unpopularity to see this through.

The ILLUSTRATION above shows Gladstone introducing the second Home Rule Bill in the House of Commons in 1893, aged 83.

PARNELL

Charles Stewart Parnell was by birth a Protestant, a landlord and a member of the Anglo–Irish ascendancy. He was educated at Cambridge, and seemed devoted to the life of a country gentleman. This was hardly the ideal background for the man who entered Westminster in 1875 and in five years assumed the leadership of the nationalist MPs who, by their policy of obstruction, threatened to bring Parliamentary business to a standstill. Yet his passionate patriotism convinced Parnell that repeal of the Union was the key to Irish nationalism. In 1885 he said at Cork:

We cannot ask for less than the restitution of Grattan's Parliament, with its important privileges, and wide, far-reaching Constitution. We cannot under the British Constitution ask for more than the restitution of Grattan's Parliament. But no man has a right to fix the boundary of the march of a nation.

Despite his background as a landlord, Parnell was President of Davitt's Land League through the bitterest phase of the Land War between the peasantry and the landlords. It was Parnell's tactics that produced the resounding success of the Boycott campaign. But Parnell decided that the best future for his own career was to remain inside Westminster and to continue the struggle in a constitutional arena.

The years of 1885 and 1886 mark the pinnacle of Parnell's influence. He held the balance of power in the Commons between the Liberals and the Conservatives, and Gladstone's 'conversion' to Home Rule at this critical moment brought one of the English parties over to the Irish Nationalist cause. The break up of the Liberal Party, and Gladstone's failure to deliver Home Rule, showed the limits of Parnell's power, and perhaps suggests that the constitutional struggle for Irish independence was always likely to be frustrated.

Parnell's career ended with the revelations of a long-standing affair with Mrs Katherine O'Shea, the wife of one of his supporters, which became public through the divorce courts in 1890. It was revealed that Parnell and Mrs O'Shea had been living together more or less continuously since 1886, and that they had two children. Nothing rocked and outraged Victorian society more profoundly than a good scandal; Parnell had committed the grave sin of being found out. Parnell's Irish supporters stood firmly behind him, but in England the clamour for his retirement from politics intensified, until Gladstone asked him to step down, saying that the Liberal–Irish alliance would be in jeopardy if he stayed on. When the Irish Catholic bishops came out against him, and his party divided over whether to continue to support him, it was the end. Parnell finally withdrew in 1891, and died later in the year, aged only 45, in the arms of Katherine, whom he was finally able to marry.

The DRAWING below shows the suspension of Parnell from the House of Commons during the period of his policy of obstruction.

Republican resistance to British rule in the south. Mass meetings in the 1840s, and Fenian risings in 1848 and 1867, had begun to convince British politicians that there must be reform in Ireland. Among them was Gladstone, the most formidable politician of his age. Irish violence, he became convinced, was the product of Irish grievance. Despite general English indifference to the Irish question, he was the first major British politician to have a policy on Ireland that went beyond simple expediency (see page 58). To remedy injustice and placate Nationalist Ireland, he dis-established the Protestant Church of Ireland and introduced legislation designed to protect tenants against the more rapacious landlords. To Protestants, it was ominous. The Protestant Church lost its privileged position in Irish society, assured in the Act of Union and regarded by many as an immutable part of the Union. In attacking the power of the landlords and the privilege of the Church, Gladstone was striking at the twin pillars of the Protestant ascendancy. The Protestant establishment grew anxious as it faced the possibility that Westminster, under Nationalist pressure, might slowly and systematically dismantle its privilege, or even the Union itself. However, Gladstone had failed to accommodate the Nationalists either. The Land Act was largely ineffective, and Gladstone's failure to establish Catholic universities led to further disillusionment. Only repeal of the Union would really satisfy them. To achieve this end, during Gladstone's Ministry of 1880–85, Irish Nationalist MPs at Westminster brought Parliamentary business to a standstill. They delayed, obstructed and hampered in every conceivable way the business of the House. This 'filibustering', a clever use of the House's procedures to stop the process of legislation, threatened to bring the government of Britain to a halt. They developed into a political party in the modern sense, under the astute leadership of Charles Parnell, disciplined, organised and, above all, completely committed to support the party (See page 59).

At the end of January 1881, the Irish Parliamentary Party, opposing Gladstone's Irish Coercion Bill, kept the House sitting continuously for 41 hours. The Bill was passed at the end of this marathon session only when the Speaker, on his own initiative, ended the debate by putting the question from the chair. It was an entirely new procedural device, yet without it, there was no constitutional way of bringing the debate to an end. The Government then introduced into the House's rules of procedure a resolution to enable debates to be foreclosed — now known as the guillotine. This measure was itself passed only after nearly every Nationalist MP had been suspended.

While in opposition during the summer and autumn of 1885, Gladstone reflected on Ireland. The Irish question was threatening the government of both Britain and Ireland, and the policies of coercion and reform, both separately and together, had been ineffective.

In the November election of 1885, the first with adult male suffrage, two Irelands were clearly revealed. The Loyalist minority in the north-east half of Ulster returned Unionists, while every other seat returned Home Rule candidates, except Trinity College, Dublin, which was a Protestant enclave. In the House of Commons there was a 'hung' Parliament, 335 Liberals, 249

Tories and 86 Irish Nationalists. No party could take power without making an alliance with another. In one of the momentous changes in British politics in the nineteenth century, Gladstone's son announced his father's 'conversion' to Home Rule. Historians have argued over Gladstone's motivation ever since. It is tempting to see this as a cynical bid for power. However, the 'conversion' is in line with Gladstone's moral fervour and he must have known that he was threatening to split and destroy a Liberal party of whom some hundred or so MPs were deeply and ideologically opposed to Home Rule. Indeed this was to prove fatal to Gladstone's brief ministry of 1886. However, Gladstone took office with Parnell's support and a commitment to Home Rule — limited independence for Ireland.

In Ulster there was consternation. The Orange Order underwent a great revival, drawing into its orbit middle- and upper-class supporters as well as extending its traditional working-class base, and joined with the newly formed anti-Repeal Union to resist and organise against Gladstone's proposals. Even in 1886, there was no doubt that Ulster Protestants would resist Home Rule – Rome and Dublin rule, as they saw it – by force if necessary. They would not be persuaded to take any steps down a road that might lead them into a Roman Catholic independent Ireland, where they would be a minority. And in this they were to find staunch allies amongst British Conservatives who saw the demand for Irish independence as a threat to Empire, for if the Irish were seen to repudiate Britain's imperial role, might not others seek to follow suit? A leading Conservative, Lord Randolph Churchill, described Gladstone's Home Rule Bill as plunging the knife into the heart of the British Empire and when, at the invitation of the Anti-Repeal Union he addressed the Belfast crowds in February 1886, he told them that if Ulster chose to fight, then 'there will not be wanting to you those of position and influence in England who are willing to cast in their lot with you — whatever it may be — and who will share in your fortune.'

As Home Rule was debated in London throughout the spring of 1886, provocative oratory and journalism fed the feverish atmosphere and in Belfast, inevitably, trouble between Catholic and Protestant broke out on 3 June in the shipyards, where only 7½% of the workforce was Catholic. After several days of rioting, British troops had to be called in to subdue a Protestant mob. Finally, at one o'clock in the morning of 8 June, the long and bitter debate (16 days were spent on the second reading alone) in Parliament ended. The House of Commons divided, and the Bill was defeated by 343 votes to 313. 93 Liberals had defected. Gladstone went to the country on the issue and lost resoundingly. In Belfast, where the election coincided with the round of Orange marches in July, it produced the most serious sectarian violence of the century, with 32 dead, 442 arrests and hundreds injured. This pattern was repeated in 1893, when Gladstone, again briefly in power, introduced his second Home Rule Bill, which got through the Commons only to be defeated by the assuredly and reliably Unionist House of Lords. Nevertheless, the Gladstonian conversion was a watershed. The Union had been questioned and debated in *Britain*: it was no longer sacrosanct, and was now a live issue in British politics.

1

2

BELFAST

During the nineteenth century, Belfast became one of the great growth cities of the Industrial Revolution, enjoying close links with the industrial centres of the north of England. Its population of about 20,000 in 1800 rose to about 100,000 in 1851, and reached a total of 350,000 by 1900.

The basis of Belfast's industrial progress was the linen industry which, from the 1830s onwards, became increasingly concentrated in large centres of production, the huge linen mills that can still be seen throughout the city. The linen industry was transformed from a hand-craft cottage industry to a centralised and highly industrialised factory production system. The mills required machinery, and this gave a lead to the engineering industry which was needed to construct and maintain the machines. From the 1850s on, the engineering industry was itself revolutionised, by the opening up of Queen's Island as a centre of ship-building. The entrepreneurial genius of Edward Harland combined with the maritime expertise of G.W. Wolff produced one of the most successful business partnerships in Ireland. From 1869, the massive Harland and Wolff shipyards worked in close collaboration with the White Star line, whose demand for large passenger ships led to the construction of some of the world's largest ocean liners. The tonnage of ships built in Belfast rose from just over 1,000 tons in 1842 to over 250,000 in 1914.

The PHOTOGRAPHS on these two pages were taken by Robert John Welch (1859–1936). Welch was a keen naturalist, and took thousands of geological, botanical and zoological photographs in Ireland. He was also the official photographer for Harland and Wolff for many years at the turn of the century. He took photographs of the construction and the launchings of all the major ships built in Harland and Wolff's yards. In April 1912, he sailed on the trial run of the *Titanic* before its fateful maiden voyage later that year.

Photograph 1 gives some idea of slum conditions in Belfast. It was taken in February 1894 in the Pepper Hill district at the City end of the Shankill Road. This photograph shows that conditions in the Protestant working-class districts of Belfast were poor, little better than in the Catholic ghettos.

Photograph 2 is a fine industrial landscape showing workers leaving the Harland and Wolff factories in 1911. In the rearground can be seen the giant gantries on which the *Titanic* is being constructed. By 1914, Harland and Wolff were employing over 12,000 men, and their shipbuilding rivals, Workman and Clark, another 10,000. But, in a city whose population was about one-quarter Catholic, the prosperous ship-yards were almost exclusively a Protestant preserve. The 1911 Census recorded that only about 7.6% of shipyard workers were Catholics.

Photograph 3 is one of Welch's official photographs taken for Harland and Wolff, showing the dining room of one of the great White Star liners. The photograph gives some idea of the size and the splendour of this ship, constructed in the heyday of the popularity of the ocean-going liners.

3

It was the Conservatives who were to dominate British politics for two decades and with them the Union was secure. To Ireland, they brought a policy of reform, attempting to 'kill Home Rule with kindness'. Local government was re-organised, and a series of land reforms effectively transferred the ownership of the land from landlord to tenant (see page 49). By 1920, two-thirds of the population owned their land.

To an extent, these reforms placated Ireland, and Nationalism in Ireland went through a period of gestation. Parnell's successors in the Nationalist Party lacked his political adroitness; they had no hung Parliament to exploit, and in any case the Liberals, the only English party committed to Home Rule, were in the political wilderness.

In 1905, a Liberal Government was returned. It had a large majority, and without the need of Irish parliamentary support had little reason to pursue Home Rule. A brilliant and radical Government, it was beset with rising unemployment and falling living standards which were accentuating the misery and inequalities of Edwardian England. It set about reform with zeal 'to wage implacable warfare against poverty and squalidness', as Lloyd George, Chancellor of the Exchequer, put it. In two years, it reversed the Conservative Party's anti-trade-union legislation, suppressed 'sweated' labour, introduced free meals and medical services into schools, passed a rudimentary state pension scheme, and set up labour exchanges. In 1909, to pay for this welfare legislation and increased defence spending, Lloyd George's 'People's Budget' raised income tax to 1/2d (6p) in the pound, increased death and other duties, and introduced a new land value duty.

These radical reforms were too much for the Conservative Party, led by the right-wing Arthur Balfour; the land duty, in particular, was seen as a wilful attack on the landed classes from whom the Conservatives drew support. So it was decided to use the huge Conservative majority in the House of Lords to defeat the budget in the same way as it had been used to kill Gladstone's second Home Rule Bill in 1893. But this broke the convention of 250 years that financial matters were the Commons' preserve.

A major constitutional crisis arose which lasted nearly two years. After two elections and the King's agreement that, if necessary, he would create enough Liberal peers to outvote the Conservatives, the House of Lords backed down and accepted a curbing of its powers on major legislation to those of delay. The Irish Nationalist Party, now led by John Redmond, emerged from this crisis in a very powerful position. Not only had the constitutional barrier to Home Rule, the House of Lords veto, been removed, but the second election left the Liberals and Conservatives tying with 273 seats each; the Irish Nationalists holding the balance. If the Liberals wanted to stay in power and redeem their pledges for Irish support during the constitutional crisis, they would now have to put a Home Rule proposal before Parliament.

Ulster Protestants were already marshalling for the fight ahead, and had found a leader of charisma. In February 1910, Sir Edward Carson, a southern Unionist, a powerful orator and able politician (remembered also as the lawyer who prosecuted Oscar Wilde), had accepted the leadership. The

Union was, he said, the guiding star of his political life, and he was utterly convinced Ireland could never prosper outside the United Kingdom. On 23 September 1911, Carson addressed a crowd of 50,000 Orangemen and Unionists at Craigavon House near Belfast. There was no doubting his determination: 'with the help of God, you and I joined together . . . will yet defeat the most nefarious conspiracy that has ever been hatched against a free people.' There was no equivocation: 'We must be prepared . . . the morning Home Rule passes, ourselves to become responsible for the government of the Protestant province of Ulster'. Two days later, the Ulster Unionist Council, which was organising the campaign against Home Rule under the direction of Sir James Craig, appointed a commission 'to frame and submit a constitution for a provisional Government of Ireland'. For the moment, Liberals deluded themselves that it was all bluff. Winston Churchill told a Dundee meeting in October: 'I dare say when the worst comes to the worst we shall find that civil war evaporates in uncivil words.' Churchill misjudged the Unionist temper. To the Ulsterman, the Home Rule proposals represented nothing less than betrayal. Essentially, they believed that the relationship between loyal Protestants and Britain was a compact, a bargain, whereby in exchange for fidelity to the British crown, they could expect their privileges in Ireland to be maintained. Any concession to the Nationalists that undermined Protestant ascendancy was a repudiation of the compact, and released them from their obligation of loyalty. Their loyalty was, in short, conditional and need not inhibit their resistance to British proposals. At this time, many politicians under-estimated the resolution with which they would resist being pushed into a United Catholic Ireland where, they feared, their Protestant heritage would be eroded and their way of life impaired. 'Ulster will fight and Ulster will be right' is no mere catch phrase; it expresses their righteousness and resolution (see page 68).

Politicians in England were searching for a solution to the Irish question in a situation of great unrest. On the industrial front, there was near anarchy. The army was used against striking Welsh miners in 1910. In the following year it was used again, this time in Liverpool during a railway strike while London was paralysed by a dock strike. 1911 saw nearly one million workers involved in industrial disputes that cost more than ten million working days; that figure was *quadrupled* in 1912.

The Suffragettes' demands for women's votes were becoming increasingly militant, and many were shocked by stories of the rigours of forcible feeding endured by women in prison who had resorted to hunger strike to make their case. In an atmosphere of fierce class-hatred, it seemed that the clouds of rising discontent in England and the threatening rebellion in Ireland might be massing for a revolutionary storm. It even affected parliamentary politics, which the constitutional struggle had left sour.

Andrew Bonar Law, the new Conservative leader, bitterly opposed to Asquith's reforming ministry, was in no mood for accommodation: 'I am afraid I shall have to show myself very vicious, Mr Asquith, this session', he said as they walked back in procession from the King's speech in February 1912. In taking up the Unionist cause, he was to denounce government policy

UNIONIST AND NATIONALIST

As the division amongst Irishmen themselves, between Nationalists and Unionists, became more apparent towards the end of the nineteenth century, then the political cartoons of the period again provide an insight into how each side saw the other.

To the Nationalists, the Unionist rhetoric of 'No Surrender' and 'Remember 1690 and King Billy' was just a lot of ballyhoo. The Nationalists either ignored the Unionists, or regarded their utterances about fighting to defend their religion and Empire as bluff. Even the 1886 and 1893 campaigns to mobilise the Protestants of Ulster failed to make the Nationalists take them seriously. It seemed incredible that these Protestants would put their loyalty to Britain above their Irishness. Most Irishmen did not realise that there was an Ulster problem. Their leaders refused to consider it, and newspapers failed to report it effectively. Those who knew of the Ulster Protestants assumed that their motivation came from an excess of religious bigotry. The Dublin newspapers, in their weekly cartoon supplements, mocked the pomp of Orange rituals: the drums, the flags and banners, the bombast. As long as the Unionists were reduced to the level of laughing stock, then their resistance to becoming a part of a United Ireland could be ignored.

It was only during the course of 1913 and the early months of 1914, with the appearance of the Ulster Volunteer Force as a well-armed, well-disciplined force, pledged to fight to defend the Union, that the Nationalists realised that a United Ireland, free from Britain, would never come about without an accommodation with the Protestants of Ulster. That remains true to this day.

Meanwhile, the Protestants of Ulster, for their part, refused to consider becoming a part of a United Ireland governed from a Dublin 'papist' parliament. From the moment of Gladstone's conversion to Home Rule, it had become a distinct possibility that the Protestants of Ulster would be a minority in a Catholic Ireland. The common catch-phrase in Ulster at this time was 'Home Rule means Rome Rule'. Traditional fears of the Catholics were revived. It was thought that Catholic government would be absolutist by nature, and that the Protestant minority would be ignored. It was feared that Catholic government would be bad for business and unsympathetic to the Protestant virtues of enterprise and hard work. The spectre of the massacres of Irish Protestants in 1641 and 1798 were revived. Protestant families would not be safe in their beds. Protestant landownership would not be secure. Education would be in the hands of nuns and priests who would

bring up a new generation to believe in the ways of Rome. So the rumours went on, and the fears built up. Cartoons in newspapers like the Belfast-based *The Union*, and the host of Unionist posters and postcards reflected these fears. Again, the possibility of political compromise and reconciliation was

lessened by the construction of popular stereotypes that were far removed from the realities of politics.

This nightmare image of life as a minority in a Catholic Ireland helped to feed an ideology of resistance in the North. Ulster would fight, and Ulster would be right.

The first CARTOON opposite depicts Lord Randolph Churchill during his visit to Belfast, leading on 'The Demon of religious strife to do the work of Hell in the North of Ireland' (from the *Weekly News*, 27 February 1886). The second, 'The Orange Nay! (?Neigh?)', mocks Orange ritual in their 'decisive and characteristic answer to the Home Rule question'. The other ILLUSTRATIONS are from Unionist postcards showing Belfast under Home rule. Decaying and ovegrown, cattle are grazing in the central square as statues to 'King Redmond' are erected, and Protestants queue at the Emigration Office.

ULSTER UNIONISM

In the mid 1880s the Unionists in Ireland began to organise to resist the threat of Home Rule and to mobilise themselves behind the Union with Britain. In May 1885, the southern Unionists had formed the Irish Loyal and Patriotic Union. In January 1886, the Ulster Unionists, led by the redoubtable Unionist MP Colonel E.J. Saunderson, formed the Ulster Loyalist Anti-Repeal Union. In February, they received a great boost by the visit to Belfast of one of the leading young lights of Tory politics, Sir Randolph Churchill. Churchill, ambitious for power and influence, had allied himself during the autumn of 1885 with the Irish Nationalists, and opposed a policy of coercion in Ireland. Now, out of office again, seeing Gladstone about to introduce a Home Rule Bill, he changed sides. He wrote to his friend James Fitzgibbon, Chief Justice for Ireland:

I decided some time ago that if Gladstone went for Home Rule, the Orange card was the one to play. Please God it may turn out to be the ace of trumps and not the two.

A phrase, attributed to Churchill, became a slogan in the North at this time: 'Ulster will fight and Ulster will be right.'

The defeat of Gladstone's first Home Rule Bill in the House of Commons in June saw a month of rioting in the streets of Belfast, and then a temporary respite until his second Home Rule Bill in 1893. Again, Ulster resistance was made manifest, and there was even talk of armed opposition to Home Rule. After the defeat of this second Bill in the House of Lords there followed a period of 'killing Home Rule with kindness' under the Conservative administrations of 1895–1905, a quiet period in Ulster Unionism.

The two elections of 1910 left another 'hung' Parliament, with the Liberal Government once again reliant upon the Irish Nationalist MPs. In return for their support, the Prime Minister, Herbert Asquith, agreed to introduce a Home Rule Bill, and after the Parliament Act of 1911 became law, the power of the Lords to veto such a bill was removed. Now, they were able to delay it only for a maximum of three

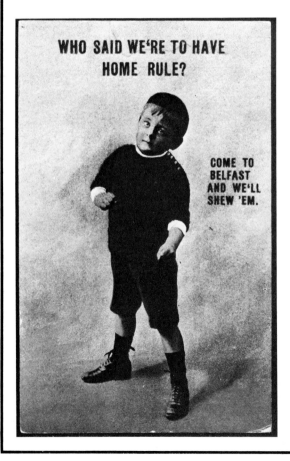

successive sessions. Thus, a Home Rule Bill introduced in 1912 would be bound to become law in three years' time, that is in 1914.

It was in this context that the Ulster Unionists began to organise their fiercest resistance to the Home Rule Bill. Sir Edward Carson, a successful Dublin lawyer, was appointed to lead them. Rarely has a more suitable man been found for a job. His brilliant and lucid oratory, his uncompromising forthright air, his theatrical sense and his drive and energy all mark him out as the most powerful champion Ulster Unionism has ever found. There followed a series of well-orchestrated mass meetings addressed by Carson, his deputy in Ulster, James Craig, and his allies from the conservative wing of English politics.

On 28 September 1912, having whipped up excitement to fever pitch, Carson led a vast multitude of Ulstermen in signing the Ulster Solemn League and Covenant. 218,000 men and 229,000 women signed this Covenant stating that:

Being convinced in our consciences that Home Rule would be disastrous to the material well-being of Ulster as well as of the whole of Ireland, subversive of our civil and religious freedom, destructive of our citizenship and perilous to the unity of the Empire, we . . . do hereby pledge ourselves in solemn Covenant throughout this our time of threatened calamity to stand by one another in defending for ourselves and our children our cherished position of equal citizenship in the United Kingdom and in using all means which may be found necessary to defeat the present conspiracy to set up a Home Rule Parliament in Ireland.

With Ulster Unionism clearly tangled up in English politics, it was obvious that a major confrontation was coming. The situation became even more menacing when, in January 1913, the Ulster Volunteer Force began drilling throughout the North.

The ILLUSTRATIONS on these pages show something of the colour and of the appeal of Ulster Unionism in these years leading up to 1914. Most of them were produced as postcards to spread the word as widely as possible. The PHOTOGRAPH shows Sir Edward Carson signing the Ulster Solemn League and Covenant on 28 September 1912.

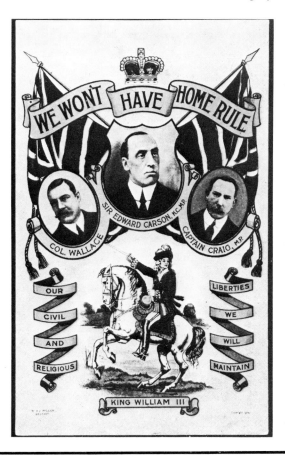

as a betrayal of Empire, and of the Ulsterman's birthright, prosperity and religion, and was even to question the constitutional legitimacy of the Liberal government.

In Ulster, Unionist demonstrations took on an increasingly military look. On 9 April 1912, 100,000 men marched past a saluting base on their way to hear Bonar Law, on the same platform as Carson, proclaim that the Conservatives 'would do all that men could do to defeat a conspiracy as treacherous as had ever been formed against the life of a great nation.' Above him, on a 90-foot flag pole flew the largest Union Jack ever made.

Two days later, Asquith's Home Rule Bill was introduced. There was to be a separate Irish Parliament with jurisdiction over internal affairs. Foreign policy, defence, and the effective control of revenue, were to be retained by Westminster, where there would be less Irish representation. It was a form of modest devolution. Unionist rhetoric reached a new peak. At a meeting at Blenheim Palace, Bonar Law, having denounced the Liberal Government as 'a revolutionary committee which has seized upon despotic power by fraud', went on: 'There are things stronger than parliamentary majorities . . . If an attempt were made to deprive these men [Ulster Protestants] of their birthright as part of a corrupt Parliamentary bargain [a reference to the Liberal alliance with the Irish Nationalists] they would be justified in resisting by all means in their power, including force . . . I can imagine no length of resistance to which Ulster can go in which I should not be prepared to support them.' This was the language of sedition. Bonar Law clearly believed that the state itself was under attack, and anything necessary to preserve the state was legitimate, even if it meant civil war. Unionists and Conservatives alike were convinced that this was an exceptional issue involving fundamental constitutional principles, principles which the Liberals were prepared to betray in order to hold on to the votes of disloyal Nationalists. Clearly, Home Rule had touched a sensitive nerve in the Conservative mind. It raised the whole issue of Empire and its legitimacy.

The rationale of Empire, as the British saw it, was a duty to civilise, a responsibility to the less fortunate to bring sound government and good order, and to bestow on all her subjects the benefits of British civilisation. To question Empire was to challenge the quality of British civilisation itself: to demand independence was to suggest that, for some at least, there might be better ways than the British way. Such demands must be resisted.

For many Conservatives, it would have been psychologically traumatic to question the idea of Empire seriously. If the British were not in India to benefit the Indians, they could only be there for self-interest. The same was true of Ireland. Without the veneer of Imperial pageantry, without the rhetoric of Kipling and without absolute conviction in the veracity of the British Imperial role, too many of the unsavoury aspects of Empire might emerge — that the British economy was exploiting the world; that British conquest had destroyed good government and stable societies; that other cultures too were civilised – some, indeed, more civilised than Britain. Such thoughts were unthinkable. The Empire was *the* British achievement, her jewel, and to question it was heresy. No Conservative, therefore, could contemplate Home Rule — it struck at the heart of the British Imperial adventure and the idea of what is was to be British.

There were, of course, more prosaic reasons to resist Home Rule. The strategic importance of Ireland, one of the reasons for England's original involvement, remained, and even increased as Britain's dependence on trade grew. Commercial interests in Ulster feared that Home Rule might hinder access to the British market. To the general mass of Ulster Protestants, Home Rule, they had been told, meant Rome Rule, an end to Protestant privilege and the destruction of the Protestant way of life. September 1912 saw an extraordinary demonstration of Ulster Protestant solidarity, when well over half the adult Protestant population signed the Solemn League and Covenant, pledging themselves to resist by all means attempts to set up a Home Rule government, and to refuse to accept the authority of any such body (see page 69). Under an obscure law, it had been discovered that Justices of the Peace could authorise drilling if it were 'for the purpose of maintaining the constitution of the United Kingdom as now established', and for some eighteen months, members of Orange Lodges had been training. In January 1913, the Ulster Unionist Council decided to bring these various groups together as the Ulster Volunteer Force, organised as a militia of about 100,000 men (see page 72). They were put under the direction of a retired Indian Army General, Sir George Richardson. For the moment, most drilled only with wooden rifles. It was time for London to make a new initiative.

The idea of Partition had come up during the Parliamentary debates on Home Rule in the summer of 1912, when a Liberal member proposed the exclusion of the four most Protestant counties; Antrim, Armagh, London-derry and Down. In January 1913, Carson proposed that the nine counties of Ulster be excluded. Towards the end of 1913, Redmond was under increasing pressure from Asquith to allow some form of temporary exclusion but Redmond was still under the illusion that the Ulster protest was no more than a bluff. Finally, in early 1914, Redmond agreed that individual counties might opt out of the Home Rule proposals for six years. The Nationalists seemed to have conceded considerable ground but Carson rejected the offer on 9 March with the brusque comment that Ulster would not accept 'a sentence of death with a stay of execution for six years'.

The curt rejection of the proposal angered members of the Cabinet, who were also alarmed by intelligence reports of arms and ammunition being hoarded in the north. So, in the spring of 1914, plans were drawn up to increase and re-organise the military presence in Ulster. This involved some risk, since many of the officer class were Anglo–Irish Protestants, and many more had Unionist sympathies. Armies, after all, tend to be conservative.

In anticipation of orders, and amid confusion about their nature, 52 officers at the Curragh Camp near Dublin proffered their resignations rather than face the prospect of having to subdue their kith and kin. The plans were hastily withdrawn. This was not a mutiny, the officers had not refused orders, but it was clear that the army was not reliable, and that the Liberals no longer had the option of coercion. Asquith confided to a friend 'there is no doubt if

ULSTER VOLUNTEER FORCE

In January 1913, the Ulster Unionist Council, led by Carson, decided to bring the various ad hoc groups who were drilling in northern Ireland into one unit, the Ulster Volunteer Force. This was to be organised on a military basis under the command of a retired professional army officer, Sir George Richardson. Volunteers started assembling and drilling openly throughout Ulster, although at first they carried only wooden replicas of rifles and it is probable that they were not taken seriously. Soon, however, their numbers amounted to some 100,000 men.

One of the most fanatical of Ulstermen, Major Fred Crawford (who had signed his name in blood on Ulster's Solemn League and Covenant), brought several thousand rifles, some machine guns and a large stockpile of ammunition into Ulster during the year to arm the UVF. The Government, alarmed by the growth of this private armoury, clamped down and in December prohibited the import of arms and ammunition into Ireland. With instructions from the Ulster Unionist Council and with funds raised in England and Ireland, Crawford disappeared to Germany to purchase whatever weaponry he could, planning to smuggle it back into Ulster by sea. On the night of 24 April 1914, 20,000 German rifles and 3,000,000 rounds of ammunition were landed at three Ulster ports and distributed throughout the UVF within twenty-four hours. The gun-running restored a position of military supremacy in Ireland to the Ulster Unionists, at a crucial time during the delicate negotiations over Home Rule. It helped to persuade Asquith and the Liberal Cabinet that the Ulster threats were no bluff.

By July 1914, the Ulster Volunteer Force was well armed and well trained. In the case of a complete breakdown in the Home Rule discussions, they threatened open war against anyone who tried to impose a Dublin Parliament on Ulster. UVF units were standing by, awaiting the telegraphed order from Carson to move into action. Detailed and intricate plans had been made to evacuate the women and children from Belfast in the event of an outbreak of fighting. The UVF medical corps was prepared to deal with thousands of casualties. Then, suddenly, the problems of Ulster were overwhelmed by a far greater conflagration.

The PHOTOGRAPH shows Sir Edward Carson, with his characteristic blackthorn stick, inspecting a UVF unit in 1914, after the Larne gun-running. Note the German rifles and the military regalia.

IRISH VOLUNTEERS

The formation of the Ulster Volunteer Force as a well-disciplined, well-trained military unit was a threat that the Irish Nationalists could not allow to pass unchallenged. In November 1913 the initiative came not from one of the Republican revolutionaries, but from a known moderate Eoin MacNeill, co-founder of the Gaelic League and Professor of Early Irish History at University College, Dublin. At a meeting in Dublin he declared that the policy of the Tory party and of the Ulster Unionists had made:

the display of military force and the menace of armed violence the determining factor in the future relations between this country and Great Britain.

He called for the formation of a body of Irish Volunteers whose objective would be:

to secure and to maintain the rights and liberties common to all the people of Ireland . . . Their duties will be defensive and protective and they will not contemplate either aggression or domination.

Some 3,000–4,000 volunteers enrolled immediately, by May numbers had swollen to at least 75,000 and by September they stood at about 180,000.

However, the Government embargo on the import of arms meant that despite the drilling, following the example of their UVF, the Irish Volunteers were in no sense a real army. After the drama of the Ulster gun-running episode, the Irish Volunteers again responded by following the lead set by their UVF rivals.

Sir Roger Casement, Bulmer Hobson and Erskine Childers arranged the purchase of some 1,500 Mauser rifles and 45,000 rounds of ammunition in Germany. Compared to the weaponry smuggled in by Major Crawford for the UVF this was paltry, but it represented a significant escalation of affairs as Ireland divided into two armed camps. Childers successfully landed most of the guns in broad daylight in Howth Harbour, on the north of Dublin Bay, on 26 July 1914, only two days after the Buckingham Palace Conference had failed to resolve the deadlock over the Home Rule Bill, and only two days before Austria–Hungary declared war on Serbia and began the sequence of events which were to engulf Europe in war.

The PHOTOGRAPH shows John Redmond, Irish Nationalist Party leader, inspecting Irish Volunteers, probably early in 1914. Note the wooden rifles that some of the Volunteers are drilling with.

MR. CARSON ARRIVES AT BELFAST.
While descriptions of affairs in Ulster may be distorted for political purposes, the "Gazette" cinematograph cameras cannot deceive.

PRINTED ON SAFETY-FILM   PATHÉ FRÈRES CINEMA L.

1

2

LARKIN'S OWN
The Dublin Strikers have now organised an "army" of their own.

PATHÉ FRÈRES CINEMA L.

3

4

5

6

PATHÉ NEWS

It took fifty years from the invention of still photography to solve the problem of the photographic reproduction of movement. Men had long been aware of the optical trick of 'persistence of vision', in which images viewed at speed create an impression of continuous movement. Several popular optical toys had employed this principle from the 1820s on. Advances in the development of flexible roll film called celluloid film, combined with the development of the projector, coming out of the Victorian magic lantern tradition, completed the evolution into cinematography. The Lumière brothers organised the first public cinema screening in Paris in December 1895. The invention proved a rapid success, and within a few years cinematographic operators were touring fairs, amusement arcades and vaudeville shows. Initially it seemed that the appeal of the new device would be for its tricks, but one of the earliest fascinations of the moving picture, like that of the photograph, was its ability to act as a window on the world, to show to an audience events and parts of the world which they could never hope to see themselves.

Moving film could easily be shot at ceremonies and parades, when events could be predicted in advance and the heavy cameras on their large tripods could be set up to record the action. An 1896 film of that year's Derby proved very popular. In 1897 Gladstone's funeral was recorded on film. From 1889 to 1902, short sequences of the Boer War proved very popular to audiences who thought that for the first time they were able to see the 'reality' of war on moving film. As the cinema became more established as an industry, with picture palaces opening up all over Europe and America, it was natural that these early news films, called 'Topicals', should become more organised into regular news film reviews of world events. The lead was taken by the French Pathé Frères company, who launched the first regular newsreel in France in 1909. They were rapidly followed by their rivals in the Gaumont company, and both organisations introduced a British edition of their newsreels in 1910. The newsreels had arrived, and became a regular feature of cinema life until their demise in the late 1960s.

The six PHOTOGRAPHS on the opposite page give some idea of how the early newsreels covered events in Ireland in the years leading up to the First World War.

1 and 2   Title and single frame from an early silent newsreel made by Pathé and released in July 1914. The claim that the 'cinematograph cameras cannot deceive' was clearly a boast of one-upmanship over the popular press. Whereas a reporter could exaggerate events or misconstrue what actually happened, it was felt that 'the camera could never lie'. Hence, moving pictures must have a 'reality' about them that could not be matched by other media. This ignores the fact that someone still has to decide what events will be filmed, how they will be filmed, and then how they will be edited and finally presented. As will be seen, it is very easy to manipulate newsreel film, and the apparent illusion of actuality of moving pictures can be very deceptive.

3 and 4   Two frames from a Pathé newsreel released in October 1913 at the time of the wave of strikes in Dublin. 'Larkins Own' refers to the Citizen Army organised by James Connolly, as a military wing of the Irish Socialist movement and separately organised from the Irish Volunteers.

5 and 6   Two frames from a later version of a newsreel supposedly showing Carson inspecting Ulster Volunteers near Belfast. The shot of the group of men drilling, apparently in front of Carson, is of the same men who had previously been called 'Larkins Own'. The Ulster Volunteer Force was a completely separate organisation from the Citizen Army. But the newsreel editors, short of film, were quite willing to use the groups interchangeably– presumably on the assumption that to most of the cinema audience, one group of marching Irishmen looked much like another, and no one would spot the difference.

were to order a march upon Ulster that about half the officers in the Army . . . would strike.'

A month later, on the night of 24–25 April, a brilliantly executed gun-running operation landed 20,000 rifles and 3,000,000 rounds of ammunition at the ports of Larne, Bangor and Donaghadee on the north-east coast of Ulster. The British could do nothing. Within twenty-four hours, the Ulster Volunteer Force no longer drilled with wooden rifles. To the South, at least, it had become clear what Bonar Law had meant when in supporting the Unionists, he said, 'there are things stronger than parliamentary majorities'. The Nationalists concluded that force could only be answered with force. In November 1913, they formed their own 'People's Army', the Irish Volunteers (see page 73). In July 1914, arms (1,500) Mauser rifles and 45,000 rounds of ammunition) were landed in daylight at Howth near Dublin. There were now three armies in Ireland — British, Unionist and Nationalist.

Later in the same month, Asquith, under pressure from the King, agreed to a meeting at Buckingham Palace of all the main protagonists: himself, Lloyd George, Redmond and his deputy John Dillon on the one side; Bonar Law, Lord Lansdowne, Carson and his deputy Sir James Craig on the other. For three days they argued over the areas of exclusion but could not agree. Asquith noted that they always returned 'to that most damnable creation of the perverted ingenuity of man, the county of Tyrone'. But for the moment greater events were to overtake the Ireland problem. Only a week after the breakdown of the Buckingham Palace Conference, armies were mobilising and ultimatums were being sent. By 4 August 1914, when Britain declared war on Germany, nearly all the European powers were at war.

The Irish controversy was shelved: the Home Rule Bill was put on the statute book with two provisos — it would not be implemented until the end of the war and before the Ulster question had been resolved.

The war put Carson in something of a dilemma. Politically, if the British Government ever decided to force Home Rule, the UVF was the trump card. Yet, after all the protestations of loyalty to King and Empire, he had little choice. He told the Unionist Council in Belfast on 3 September: 'England's difficulty is not Ulster's opportunity . . . We do not seek to purchase terms by selling our patriotism.' The services of the UVF were offered to and accepted by the British Army, and it became the 36th (Ulster) Division. They were among the first troops into action at the Battle of the Somme in 1916. Their gallantry and heroism affirmed their loyalty in the starkest way possible (see page 78). The Covenant had now been signed in blood.

Most of the Nationalist Volunteers of southern Ireland also fought alongside the British Army in the war. Constitutional Nationalists like Redmond calculated that this declaration of loyalty would assure Home Rule a sympathetic hearing after the war. Others disagreed: some saw no reason to fight in a war that was not Ireland's war, but for others, hard-line Republicans, the war offered the English difficulty that presented the Irish opportunity.

On Easter Monday 1916, about 1,600 men made open rebellion on the

Dublin streets and proclaimed an Irish Republic. Intending to be martyrs, they hoped not for victory, but to bear witness to Ireland's inalienable right to independence. Connolly put it succinctly: 'We are going out to be slaughtered.' On Saturday 1 May, after a week of fighting, Pearse surrendered unconditionally. As the week had progressed, public opinion about the rebels in Dublin had moved from bafflement to hostility. The Nationalist *Freeman's Journal*, with the largest readership in Ireland, summed up the prevalent feeling: 'The insurrection was no more against the connection with the Empire, than it was an armed assault against the will and decision of the Irish nation itself, constitutionally ascertained through its representatives.' Since Britain was fully extended in a European war, the authorities saw the insurrection as treason. General Sir John Maxwell declared a state of martial law, arrested 3,500 people, and interned more than half of them in Wales and decided to execute the leaders. At Kilmainham Jail on 3 May, they shot Pearse and two others. They were denied the presence of a priest. Next day, it was the turn of four more; another was shot on the following day. Now, each day, Dublin awaited news of new executions. On 8 May, another four were executed. Public opinion began to move dramatically. On 12 May, two more leaders were shot; one, the severely wounded Connolly, was strapped in a chair. These executions transformed Irish opinion. When Sinn Fein prisoners had been marched through the streets on their way to Wales in May, they had been reviled and spat at: when they returned to Dublin during 1917, they were rapturously received as heroes. 'We shall be remembered by posterity and blessed by unborn generations', wrote Pearse in his death cell. He was right. Here begins the momentous swing in Irish opinion from the Nationalist constitutionalists to the Republican revolutionaries.

After Asquith had visited Ireland in mid-May, he instructed Lloyd George to open up discussions again. Lloyd George conducted separate negotiations with the Unionists and Nationalists, assuring Carson in writing that the exclusion of the six counties was permanent, and Redmond, verbally, that it was temporary. When this duplicity came out into the open, Redmond was forced to withdraw from the negotiations and was effectively discredited as a Nationalist leader. The initiative further moved to the Republicans.

During 1917, Sinn Fein won four by-elections: North Roscommon in January; South Longford in May; East Clare in July, where De Valera openly canvassed the values for which the Easter martyrs had died; and Kilkenny in August. The executions, continued martial law, the failure of the Home Rule negotiations and, above all, the fear that conscription might be introduced in Ireland, had left Ireland in an ugly and militant mood. Then came the death of Thomas Ashe.

In Mountjoy Jail, 30 Sinn Fein prisoners, sentenced for drilling and making seditious speeches, were on hunger strike. Refusing to be treated as criminals, they demanded to be classed as prisoners of war. Then, on 25 September, after he had been forcibly fed, Ashe died. The Suffragettes had already made forcible feeding an emotive issue, and when the coroner's jury described it as 'inhuman and dangerous', the Republicans had scored a

THE BATTLE OF THE SOMME

With the outbreak of the War in August 1914, Lord Kitchener appealed for volunteers to come forward to join the army and to help defeat the 'dastardly Hun' and to 'protect small nations'. Soon, Kitchener's dour face was staring down from hoardings throughout the country with the simple but brilliantly effective finger-pointing appeal: 'Your country needs YOU'. The patriotic clamour to join the war effort and to fight for 'freedom and democracy' astonished everyone. Half a million men volunteered in the first month alone and thereafter the recruitment rate settled at about a hundred thousand a month for well over a year.

The Ulster Unionists had pledged their undying loyalty to King and Empire. Wary at first, Carson soon had no alternative, and in a series of meetings with Kitchener, he offered 35,000 UVF members to the war effort. Kitchener agreed to the inclusion of 'Ulster' in the names of all the units that might be formed. Craig arranged with Moss Bros. an order for all the uniforms needed, and as men streamed into recruiting offices in Belfast, they were issued with uniforms, boots and equipment all supplied from UVF funds. The 36th (Ulster) Division was quickly organised out of the UVF recruits, and training began around Belfast. The Division was kept training in Ulster, much to the annoyance of the men who were worried that the War would be over before they reached the Front. Then, on 8 May 1915, as bands played and crowds cheered, they marched ceremoniously out of Belfast, and crossed to France in October.

The opportunity for the Ulster Volunteers to seal their covenant in blood was not long in coming. General Haig, the new Commander-in-Chief of the British forces in France, had an offensive planned, to be launched from the point where the French and the British lines joined in the region of the River Somme. After five days of continuous bombardment, the troops of thirteen British divisions went over the top at 7.30 a.m. on 1 July 1916. The men who went forward were the volunteers who had joined up in the heady days of 1914, the 'flower' of British youth.

Amongst the units that advanced on that day was

the 36th (Ulster) Division, who held a section of the line from the north-east of Thiepval Wood astride the River Ancre. As the Ulstermen advanced towards the German lines on the day that was the original anniversary of the Battle of the Boyne, many of them wore Orange ribbons and some shouted 'No Surrender' and 'Remember 1690'. At first the Ulster Division attained its objectives, but elsewhere the British were repulsed by the steady fire of German machine guns. The troops had been quickly and crudely trained; all they knew was how to advance uniformly in line. As the first line was gunned down, a second appeared and as that was shot to bits there came a third and then a fourth and so on. All along the Front the German lines held out and the British army suffered the heaviest losses it had ever known in a single day: 20,000 men dead and another 40,000 wounded. The 36th (Ulster) Division, despite conspicuous bravery that was rewarded by four Victoria Crosses, lost 5,500 officers and men, killed and wounded, in the first two days of the attack. In one unit, the West Belfast Battalion, 'The Shankill Boys', only 70 men survived out of 700.

The initial news of the offensive spoke of magnificent successes, vast numbers of the enemy captured and ground won. It took a few days before the full casualty lists were published in the newspapers. Belfast and the rest of Ulster went into mourning. In house after house, the blinds were drawn down as a sign of bereavement. The casualty lists named the UVF units to which the men had belonged. All the Orange processions were cancelled on 12 July and on the 'Glorious Twelfth', all traffic and business stopped as a sign of respect. Just as the Republicans had made their 'blood sacrifice' in the streets of Dublin some two months before, now Ulster had made its own 'blood sacrifice' for King and Empire.

The PHOTOGRAPH on the opposite page shows men of the 36th (Ulster) Division resting in a communication trench on 1 July 1916. The central figure in this photograph was taken out of the group and used as the lone soldier staring out of the title sequence for the BBC's *Great War* series.

Every year in Belfast on 1 July, there is a commemorative ceremony for the Battle of the Somme and the losses suffered by Ulster families on that day. The photograph above shows veterans of the Ulster Volunteer Force and the 36th (Ulster) Division at the 1979 commemoration service, held in front of Belfast's City Hall.

considerable propaganda victory. At a military funeral more impressive than Parnell's, Michael Collins delivered the oration. It was short: 'Nothing additional remains to be said. That volley we have just heard is the only speech which it is proper to make above the grave of a dead Fenian.'

Irish Americans were following events in Ireland with increasing concern, and when America entered the European War in 1917, Britain was under diplomatic pressure from the American Government to launch some kind of political initiative. A convention was called in July 1917, and sat through the winter. But it was a charade. The Unionists, who had actually considered boycotting it, were unyielding and Sinn Fein, disdaining compromise and claiming Britain had no right to Ireland, stayed away. The Nationalists who did attend no longer had any credibility to speak for the South.

On 21 March, the Germans mounted a massive offensive on the Western Front. In four days, they advanced 40 miles. Britain and France, it seemed, might lose the war. American troops were on their way, but 150,000 new soldiers were needed urgently and in Britain, men up to the age of 50 had already been conscripted. The British War Cabinet turned to the men of Ireland and introduced the Military Service Bill on 18 April 1918, giving the government powers to conscript in Ireland. Nothing could have been designed to inflame Irish passions more. 'All Ireland will rise against you,' warned Dillon, who had replaced Redmond as the leader of the Irish Nationalists, as he led his party out of the House of Commons. Dillon's prediction proved accurate, and most of Ireland united behind Sinn Fein.

Irish politicians of all persuasions met at the Mansion House, Dublin, on 18 April and affirmed: 'Denying the right of the British Government to enforce compulsory service in this country, we pledge ourselves solemnly to one another to resist conscription by the most effective means at our disposal.' Ireland had declared rebellion.

The new Lord Lieutenant of Ireland, significantly, was an army general, Field Marshal Lord French. During the night of 7 May 1918, 73 leading members of Sinn Fein were arrested by the security forces, and on the following day French announced that Sinn Fein had been involved in treasonable negotiations with the Germans. There was only the flimsiest of circumstantial evidence for this and undoubtedly the 'German Plot', as it came to be called, provided the excuse to arrest the leaders of the anti-conscription movement. It is also likely that Sinn Fein were warned of the arrests, but acquiesced, knowing the impact they would have on public opinion. On 3 July, Sinn Fein, the Irish Volunteers, and the Gaelic League were all but proscribed. The British adopted a policy of firm repression, yet despite this and countless arrests, the Republican Movement became more potent as it went underground.

In retrospect, the British policy since 1916 had been astonishingly inept. The suppression of the rising was neither lenient nor tough enough; it was too lenient to destroy Sinn Fein, but tough enough to generate sympathy for the rebels. This sympathy grew as the British timed and spaced the executions so as to maximise their impact on Irish opinion. Hostility to the rebels turned to support when the British maintained martial law and maltreated Irish

FUND-RAISING FOR THE NEW STATE

The 69 Sinn Fein MPs elected in December 1918 refused to take up their seats at Westminster, and instead established their own assembly, called Dail Eireann. Here, they declared Ireland an independent nation and the Dail its sovereign authority. Despite the fact that many members were serving sentences in British prisons, this constituted the establishment of an alternative government to the British regime, based in Dublin Castle. There were no formal government offices. Each ministry tried to operate as effectively as it could, although it was frequently necessary to move whole departments from building to building to escape police raids. Despite these almost insuperable difficulties, Robert Barton in the Ministry of Agriculture succeeded in establishing a Land Bank and a Land Commission. Michael Collins in the Ministry of Finance succeeded in raising a loan for the government by selling Republican bonds. This helped the construction of an alternative state in Ireland.

The photographs above are single frames from a fund-raising film made for the Dail Eireann National Loan in the autumn of 1919. The short film is about ten minutes in length, and shows Michael Collins (seated at the table) selling bonds to several prominent members of the Republican Government. Each person comes up, one by one, and buys a bond from Collins who signs it and passes it across. The short film was shot by John MacDonagh, a director of the Film Company of Ireland, during the shooting of a feature film about the troubles in Ireland in the Penal Days. The location for the filming was, suitably

enough, St Enda's School, just outside Dublin, the school founded by Padraig Pearse in 1908 from where he had gone out to lead the Rising of 1916 and proclaim the Irish Republic.

The completed film was taken by Republican supporters from cinema to cinema in Ireland, and projectionists were instructed at gun point to screen it. As it was only ten minutes long, by the time the authorities got to hear about it and the police arrived at the cinema, the film had finished and the Republicans had vanished taking the film with them. It must have been an effective use of film as propaganda. The loan succeeded in raising a total of over £300,000.

Arthur Griffith, shown buying Republican bonds in the left-hand PHOTOGRAPH, was a total separatist who believed that the only way to realise Irish nationalism was to opt out of all conventional political activity. As editor of *United Irishmen* and co-founder of Sinn Fein, he was committed to attaining a self-reliant Irish nation, utterly separate from Britain. Griffith served as Minister for Home Affairs in the alternative government established by the Dail.

Eoin MacNeill, shown buying Republican bonds (right), was a scholar and leading member of the Gaelic League. At the end of 1913 he had formed the Irish Volunteers but although leader of the Volunteers he had been opposed to the 1916 Rising. He was Minister for Industries in the alternative government.

prisoners. Support became committment over the issue of conscription, for which, in retrospect, the British had no real need. The war was, after all, won, without the conscription of a single Irishman. It could almost be said that the British contributed as much to the rise of the Republican phoenix as the men of Easter themselves, for British policy was the perfect counterpoint to Sinn Fein's strategy.

In the election of December 1918 that followed the end of the war, Sinn Fein swept the country on a platform that they would boycott Westminster and set up an Irish Parliament. Before the poll, the Nationalists held 68 seats and Sinn Fein 7 – most of these won in recent by-elections. Afterwards, Sinn Fein held 73, the Nationalists 6. The Sinn Fein MPs, including Countess Markievicz, the first woman ever to be *elected* to the House of Commons, met in Dublin, declared themselves a Republic, and set themselves up as the Government of Ireland.

Of the 73 members of the Assembly, the Dail Eireann, as it was known, 34 were in prison. Nevertheless, they renewed the Declaration of Independence and reaffirmed the right of Ireland to be a nation as sanctified by the men of Easter. They agreed: '. . . we, the elected Representatives of the ancient Irish people in National Parliament assembled, do, in the name of the Irish nation, ratify the establishment of the Irish Republic and pledge ourselves and our people to make this declaration effective by every means at our command.' They further made an appeal 'to the free nations of the world', hoping that the Versailles Peace Conference at the end of the war would look favourably on her claim to nationhood and 'guarantee to Ireland its permanent support for the maintenance of her national independence.'

The Dail's avowed intention of superceding the British administration by setting up its own alternative government was severely hampered in September 1919 when the British declared it illegal. Although it met clandestinely six times in 1920 and 1921, it was not able to direct affairs effectively. Some ministries, which had been set up earlier, operated out of private houses, and although constantly harassed by the British, managed to begin the process of state-building. But this policy of supplanting British government by Irish was most successful at a local level. As a result of local elections held in January and June 1920, Sinn Fein found themselves in control of many local councils and Poor Law Boards. The Dail felt strong enough to direct the councils to break away from the British local government and by October, most of them had done this, despite the financial problems it created. The British administration was further embarrassed when the Republicans burnt down the local government offices in the Customs House and destroyed their records. By 1921, there was also an alternative system of justice in operation; some nine hundred Parish Courts, county courts and a 'supreme' court were functioning effectively outside British jurisdiction. The British administration was breaking down.

However, most attention now focused on the violence that was becoming more common throughout Ireland. The Anglo–Irish War (or Irish War of Independence, or the Black and Tan War, depending on one's perspective) developed from small beginnings. There was a tradition of hostility to the

Royal Irish Constabulary throughout much of the Irish countryside, where the police were often regarded as the enemies of the people. Unlike its British equivalent, the RIC was armed and was closely associated in the public mind with the enforcement of unpopular policies; the police were nearly always present to protect the landlord's interests during evictions, for instance. Significantly, police stations were known as 'barracks' in Ireland, and it was against these police barracks, often small isolated buildings, that the IRA directed its initial attacks. Between May and December, 18 RIC men were killed. Although these individual attacks upon the agents of law and order were very much in the tradition of local agrarian violence, behind them was a carefully worked out plan by Michael Collins, the IRA's Director of Intelligence. Funds were raised in America and arms were acquired in post-war Europe. Collins's intention was to demoralise the police and to undermine the British hold on Ireland. The army garrison in Ireland was increased and army patrols reinforced police activity. As Robert Kee has put it, 'the Volunteers were goading the Government into goading the people into rebellion.'

As the violence in the countryside escalated, Lloyd George's Cabinet responded with the Government of Ireland Act, which was passed through Westminster in 1920. It embodied the Home Rule idea, current in politics since 1885, whilst acknowledging the special position of Ulster. The Act proposed two Home Rule Parliaments, one for the 26 counties of the South to meet in Dublin, and another for the 6 counties of the North in Belfast. There was to be a Council of Ireland with representatives from North and South to provide the basis for the re-unification of Ireland. Proportional Representation was to be used in the elections of members of both Parliaments to ensure that the minorities (a large Catholic minority in the North, a small Protestant minority in the South) were properly represented. In the South, where Dail Eireann did not accept the authority of Westminster to legislate for Ireland, the Home Rule Parliament remained a dead-letter, although the electoral procedures of the Act were used in May 1921 to elect a new Dail. In the North, the Ulster Unionists accepted the Act grudgingly, as they would have preferred to remain fully integrated in the United Kingdom. Craig described it as the 'supreme sacrifice', but it was as much as the Unionists could reasonably have expected. There had been strong support in the Cabinet for a nine-county province as this would contain an equal number of Protestants and Catholics and would conform to the boundaries of the ancient province of Ulster. But under great pressure from the Unionists, the Cabinet finally agreed on a six-county province with a population ratio of two Protestants to each Catholic, ensuring that the Protestant Unionists would be able to maintain their domination over Northern Ireland (as the new province was to be called). The Unionists hoped that a six-county state would be large enough to be economically viable and small enough to be politically manageable by the Unionist majority.

The problems that would face Northern Ireland were demonstrated immediately. The divide between the Catholic and Protestant communities now left the Catholics feeling beleaguered by Partition that cut them off from

IRISH REPUBLICAN ARMY

As the 'alternative' government of the Republic of Ireland struggled to assert itself throughout the course of 1919, it was clear that one area that was going to be vital in the months ahead was the military wing. In order to orchestrate an effective campaign to oust the British from Ireland, the Dail was going to need an army. Through the course of the year, the Minister of Defence of this underground government, Cathal Brugha, slowly turned the various Irish Volunteer units into the standing army of the Republic, all swearing an oath of allegiance to the new state. This new creation was called the Irish Republican Army and had Richard Mulcahy as Chief of Staff and Michael Collins in the vital post of Adjutant-General and Director of Intelligence.

It seems that from its inception, Collins wanted the IRA to make Ireland ungovernable; to create an atmosphere of violence and disorder within which effective control of the situation by the British authorities would be impossible. Irish history had been full of individual risings; grand gestures but military fiascos. Now Collins wanted to develop a strategy that would wrench effective control of Irish affairs from Britain and force the British government to recognise Irish Independence. His tactics were to carry out attacks and assassinations upon selected targets: police barracks, policemen, and the agents of British rule in Ireland. They began on 21 January

1919, the day the Dail Eireann met to proclaim Irish Independence, when Dan Breen and Sean Tracey attacked a Royal Irish Constabulary patrol at Soloheadbeg in Co. Tipperary. They captured a cartload of explosives, and killed two policemen.

Throughout 1919, there were sporadic attacks on police barracks, which were often isolated buildings and hard to defend. Relying upon the traditional hostility to the police throughout the Irish countryside, the raiders would vanish into the community after an attack and make it impossible for the security forces to identify them. By the end of the year, fourteen policemen had been killed and twenty wounded.

As the situation escalated throughout 1920, the IRA was organising itself into an effective guerilla army. Late August and September 1920 saw the formation of small, well-trained, highly mobile units called 'flying columns'. These 'flying columns' usually consisted of twenty to thirty well-armed men, who were constantly on the move and often operated on their own initiative, striking at police patrols or military transports and melting away into the countryside to regroup later. These attacks provoked a new level of frustration amongst the security forces who replied with furious outbursts of reprisals. Ireland was caught in a cycle of violence and counter-violence. In 1920, the police suffered 176

deaths and 251 casualties; in the army, 54 soldiers were killed and 118 wounded.

The best known commander of these IRA guerilla units was Tom Barry, who had served in the British Army in Mesopotamia and Palestine during the First World War. Barry led the 3rd West Cork Brigade 'flying column', and became renowned for his ruthless and daring attacks on the security forces. On 28 November 1920, he led the most devastating attack of the war, when his men ambushed an Auxiliary patrol at Kilmichael in Co. Cork. This particular group had become lax in their routine, often sending out patrols along the same route.

Barry and his unit lay in wait for two lorryloads of Auxiliaries as they were returning to their barracks. The lorries were stopped by a trick and as the men climbed down they were fired on from all sides by Barry's men. Sixteen Auxiliaries were killed and only one man survived the ambush, having been left for dead. Barry's men lost two dead. These 'flying columns' developed a devastatingly effective philosophy for guerilla warfare during these months. They avoided major engagements of a classic military kind but only struck the enemy when it suited themselves, maximising their destructive capability but above all surviving to fight another day. In an interview for *The Troubles* series, the late Tom Barry said:

The purpose of guerilla warfare was to drive the British out. We had no other way of doing this other than by improvising attacks on them. The only way to do this at the time was by guerilla warfare. We had no precedent for this, even in South Africa [during the Boer War against the British] the situation was different. They [the Boers] had an established army and ammunition and they were backed by various countries . . . but this was the only way to stop the repression of the colonial power.

The two PHOTOGRAPHS show the damage caused by IRA raids on bridges in Co. Cork. British soldiers, probably from the Essex Regiment, look on. In the second photograph, local civilians, drafted in to repair the damage, can be seen at work. It is likely that these actions took place in the sector where the Essex Regiment confronted Tom Barry's 3rd West Cork Brigade 'flying column'.

their co-religionists in the South, and vulnerable as a minority in a majority Protestant state. Rioting broke out in Belfast and Derry and continued throughout the summer. As the Ulster Volunteer Force was revived, and Protestant vigilantes started to drill, the Government began to consider plans for the formation of a Special Constabulary in Ulster (see page 106). In Derry, the rioting left 18 dead, and 1,500 troops were needed to keep the peace in a town of 40,000 people; that is, one soldier for every 26 people. In Belfast, rioting took on the traditional sectarian form and led to attacks upon the Catholic minority in the city. One authority claimed that as many as 11,000 Catholics were expelled from their jobs (out of a Catholic population of 93,000 in the city) and hundreds of Catholic families were driven from their homes. The summer rioting of 1920 led to 62 deaths and over 200 serious injuries and set the pattern which was to dominate the new state.

Anglo–Irish affairs now entered their most confused phase. To many, it seemed that the root causes of Irish grievance had been removed. For centuries, the religious problem had plagued Irish affairs but now, outside Ulster, this was largely forgotten. The economic exploitation of Ireland by England had infuriated Irishmen for generations, but that had now been settled by the land reforms. The land of Ireland was once again owned by the tillers of the soil. For decades leading up to the Great War, the Irish had been demanding Home Rule, but now a Home Rule Act was on the statute book, awaiting ratification. So, what was the cause of the present conflict? A growing number of Irishmen, inspired by the ideals of the men of 1916, and maddened by British policy in Ireland since the Rising, were no longer satisfied with Home Rule. Most people wanted a completely independent Ireland, a separate Republic, in which Irishmen would have full control over their own destiny, just like any other nation. The British proposal, modest devolution, had been resoundingly defeated by the electorate in open elections. How could the British impose a moderate settlement that conformed to British ideals of Empire, on an unwilling nation who had democratically voted to reject it? The Government decided that the Irish campaign against them was being run by a few 'murder gangs' which were not in any way representative of the bulk of the population. They concluded that if the Republican men of violence could be crushed, there would be a return to constitutionalism and a negotiated settlement along the lines of the Home Rule Parliament in Dublin. So the Government turned back to its classic policy towards Ireland, of coercion.

With the growing number of attacks upon the police, the morale of the RIC was rapidly declining, and fewer and fewer recruits were coming forward to replace the large numbers that were resigning from the service. Consequently, it was decided to recruit men in Britain, to form auxiliary police units to augment the regular RIC. They began to arrive in Ireland early in 1920 (see page 88). The IRA was in the process of organising itself into a fast-moving guerilla army, one which could attack Crown forces with devastating speed and efficiency and then melt away into the countryside, relying upon the tacit support of the local population for aid (see page 84). The auxiliary policemen, who were nicknamed Black and Tans, found this kind of warfare increasingly frustrating and, unable to strike back at the IRA, began to take vengeance on the local population whom they thought to be harbouring the rebels. Although the army was furious at the indiscipline of these policemen, they could do little to prevent such outrages, since the Black and Tans and the Auxiliary Division of ex-army officers all came under the authority of the RIC, and not that of the British Army. The problem with a policy of coercion was that it drove many of the population into supporting the rebels, and instead of isolating the men of violence, actually generated sympathy for them. Furthermore, such a policy depended upon the defeat of the terrorists before any political dialogue could continue; the inevitable logic of this is that it was a policy of military repression.

During the latter months of 1920, the situation reached a new low. IRA attacks were mounting in its campaign to make Ireland ungovernable. Assassinations of individuals and ambushes of police and military convoys were almost daily occurrences. The security forces took to reprisals. Towns were looted, houses and villages were destroyed, and creameries wrecked, a serious blow to Ireland's dairy economy. On 21 November, the IRA assassinated 12 British officers suspected of being spies. That afternoon, the Black and Tans fired on a crowd at a football match in Dublin, killing 12 and wounding 60 more. The day became known as 'Bloody Sunday'. In December, after 17 Auxiliaries had been killed in an IRA ambush, a group of Black and Tans descended on Cork, first looting and then burning part of the centre of the city. They deliberately obstructed the local firefighters from coming to put out the blaze.

Public opinion in Britain was outraged by such wanton acts of destruction. Asquith, the ex-Liberal leader, said: 'Things are being done in Ireland which would disgrace the blackest annals of the lowest despotisms in Europe.' But the Government blundered on, convinced that the use of policemen, even though they were armed ex-soldiers, was preferable to overt military rule. The Cabinet was, however, deeply divided on its policy towards Ireland, and wavered between the 'hard military line' advocated by ministers like Winston Churchill, the Secretary of State for War, and the 'soft civil line' of other ministers like Austen Chamberlain, the Chancellor of the Exchequer. Few, however, would probably have fully agreed with Bonar Law who said that 'the Irish were an inferior race' and called for a short, sharp period of coercion to be followed by ten years of enforced calm. A request for an organised policy of reprisals against the homes of suspected IRA sympathisers was turned down by the Prime Minister, Lloyd George, in September, but a few months later a policy of 'official reprisals' was agreed.

In December 1920, General Macready, C-in-C of the British Army in Ireland, told the Cabinet that military governors in areas under martial law (most of the south and west of the country) had been authorised to inflict punishments after rebel attacks, on the following conditions:

A. *Punishments will only be carried out on the authority of the Infantry Brigadier, who before taking action will satisfy himself that the people concerned were, owing to their proximity to the outrage or their known political tendencies, implicated in the outrage . . .*

BLACK AND TANS

At the end of 1919 it was decided that the Royal Irish Constabulary, already about 12% under strength, must be reinforced to defend itself from the growing number of attacks it was facing from the IRA. The Cabinet had decided that the Irish situation was a police problem and not one for the military, and so the decision was made to form auxiliary police units to augment the regular RIC.

As recruitment in Ireland was so low, and by the middle of 1920 men were resigning from the RIC at the rate of 200 per month (mostly because of threats of intimidations against their families), it seemed obvious that recruits would never be found in Ireland and so must be raised in England. By the beginning of 1920 it was not difficult to find men in England willing to join up. The war had ended, over a million servicemen had been demobilised, and the soldiers of the Great War were returning to 'Homes fit for Heroes' as Lloyd George had promised them. But the initial post-war boom soon became a worsening slump, and thousands faced the prospect of unemployment. Moreover, after years in the trenches, many men found it impossible to re-adapt to civilian life. Recruitment to a semi-military organisation that offered the possibility of drama and excitement seemed appealing. The very high rates of pay that were offered made it even more attractive.

Some of the men who went to Ireland at this time were approached for interviews during the making of *The Troubles* series. Many were reluctant to talk at all, others insisted on giving anonymous interviews, knowing that the notoriety of their exploits are remembered with bitterness in Ireland to this day. The comments they made all show the same motivation to join up:

I came back from the First War and I thought that anything was better than standing in a queue. There were so many millions out of work. And then I saw this advertisement for the Royal Irish Constabulary and it said apply to Scotland Yard and I joined, and then I had to go down to Chelsea to pass a test which I did. The next night I caught the train from Euston and I was in Dublin the next morning.

I had a flare for a little adventure, and I was about to join the Foreign Legion. But on enquiring, I found that the pay was only ten centimes a day for a five-year period. On going back to my room—where I lived—I happened to pick up a current edition of the Daily Mail

and I saw in it this advert for recruits wanted for the RIC with good pay, danger money, prospects for promotion and a pension at the end. So I thought to myself; why should I risk my life and perhaps my limbs for ten centimes a day when I could join the RIC for good money? So I decided to join up there and then.

And, of course, there was good money [in the RIC]. It was £6 per week and I think I'd been getting 28 shillings [£1.40] a week when I'd finished up in the Army. . . . The average wage [in the RIC] was about two to three times what the men could have earned in England.

After a brief training in the civil law, the recruits were sent out to police barracks where, as ex-soldiers accustomed to a military discipline, they soon felt the laxity of police discipline. On 28 April a group went out on a spree in Limerick breaking windows and assaulting civilians. This earned them the immortal name of 'Black and Tans', partly after a local pack of hounds and partly because of the strange mixture of army khaki uniforms and dark green police belts and hats.

Recruitment to this new force really picked up after the appointment of Major-General Henry Tudor as 'Police Adviser' to the Government in Ireland in May of 1920. Despite the serious misgivings of General Sir Nevil Macready, the Commander-in-Chief of the British Army in Ireland, who strongly believed that armed men should be under military command and not that of the police, Tudor was allowed to step up recruitment to the Black and Tans. Over 300 arrived in Ireland in July, over 600 in both August and September, and 1,300 in October. Ex-officers of the British Army were formed into a separate unit, the Auxiliary Division, under Brigadier-General Frank Crozier, an ex-UVF member. Again, although formed on military lines, they were nominally under police control. Fighting a fast-moving, unseen enemy who was evolving tactics of a new-style guerilla warfare, these recruits found their experience on the Western Front almost useless. If the enemy could not be confronted in battle then the Black and Tans went out and raided the villages and towns that gave him support. The scale of these acts of reprisal soon grew dramatically. On 20 September a number of policemen went on the rampage in Balbriggan, Co. Dublin, looting and burning four public houses, damaging 49 other houses and bayoneting to death two 'suspects'. On the next day in Co. Clare, a wave of reprisals followed an IRA ambush, and four people, including a young boy, were killed. The Army was furious at these reprisals and influential opinion in London was outraged. *The*

Times firmly declared that a policy of reprisals would weaken 'to a dangerous degree any respect that survives in Ireland for the constitutional virtues of law and order.'

Despite these powerful attacks, Tudor defended his men forcibly. He had the ear of Winston Churchill, and the Cabinet alternated between moods of hostility and acquiescence to the Black and Tan outbursts.

This lack of control over the Black and Tans culminated in a series of outrages. On 21 November 1920, known as 'Bloody Sunday', twelve British officers were shot on Michael Collins's instructions for being secret service agents. Auxiliaries responded that afternoon by firing wildly into a crowd at Croke Park football stadium, killing twelve, seriously wounding another eleven, and injuring fifty more. Then on the night of 11 December, after an ambush near Cork, Auxiliaries and Black and Tans went into the city, looted and wrecked buildings and fired the town. The Chief Secretary for Ireland, Sir Hamar Greenwood, claimed in the House of Commons that Cork was set on fire by its own citizens, but a military enquiry into the event had to be hushed up for fear

that its findings would seriously discredit the Government.

The tension between the army and the police surfaced after a series of ugly scenes in Trim, Co. Meath, early in February 1921. Five Black and Tans were arrested and court-martialled by the army, but were released on the orders of Tudor, who insisted on protecting his men to maintain the morale of the police force.

The whole of the Black and Tan episode was a grim sign of the depths to which Anglo–Irish affairs had sunk. The irony was that all the efforts of the army and the police were apparently designed to impose on the Irish the 'moderate' settlement of a Home Rule Parliament in Dublin, as in the 1920 Government of Ireland Act. It was partly because of this deadly state of affairs and the feeling in London that such measures would have to be stepped up to bring any sort of political success, that the politicians started looking for a way out. By June it was beginning to seem to both sides that the situation must not deteriorate further. It was time for a political initiative.

The first two PHOTOGRAPHS show Patrick Street, Cork, smouldering after being burnt down by Black and Tans and Auxiliaries. An eye-witness remembered it in an interview for *The Troubles*:

You could see the whole of the centre of Cork, the main street which is Patrick Street, the Regent Street of Cork, burning. . . . . It was as bad as anything I've seen in the Blitz in London.

An Auxiliary officer described in an interview how the burning of Cork was used as a threat by the Black and Tans later in the war:

Talk about Western films, they weren't in it! The Black and Tans used to carry a holster on the thigh with a revolver . . . hanging from the ring of the revolver they had a half-burnt cork and they used to say 'If you ambush us, then you know what's going to happen; half of Cork has been burnt and be careful or we might burn down your place.'

The last PHOTOGRAPH shows a group of Auxiliary officers and Black and Tans at Union Quay, Cork, 1921. Note the protected truck it was necessary to travel in, and the motley collection of uniforms.

B. The punishment will be carried out as a Military Operation and the reason why it is being done will be publicly proclaimed.

The people to be punished were given an hour to remove 'any valuable foodstuffs, hay or corn but not furniture' from their homes which were then to be wrecked by explosives. For terrace houses, where fires might spread, the furniture was to be removed and burned separately in the street. The first of these 'official reprisals' took place in Midleton, near Cork, on 29 December 1920. After an IRA ambush, during which three policemen were killed, six houses were destroyed by the army. Over the next few months, hundreds of homes were destroyed in Ireland as part of official British policy.

By 1921, Ireland was fighting a very effective guerilla war. Despite constant denunciation by the Catholic clergy who abhorred the violence of the IRA, its campaign continued unabated. On 19 March, at Crossbarry in Co. Cork, a battle was fought between Tom Barry's encircled 3rd West Cork Brigade flying column and the 17th Brigade of the British Army. General Macready called this battle 'the nearest approach to actual warfare, as contrasted with ambushes, that has yet occurred.'

In April, Army searches led to extensive IRA arms finds, but the war reached a crescendo in the months of May and June with a record number of engagements (well over two thousand in each month). In the May elections, held under the Government of Ireland Act, the Sinn Fein Republicans took every seat in the 26 counties outside Trinity College, Dublin. The Sinn Fein representatives refused to attend the Home Rule Dublin Parliament.

In a memorandum to the Cabinet on 24 May 1921, General Macready suggested that a full military victory against the guerilla troops of the IRA was almost an impossibility. The measures, he said, that would be necessary to placate Ireland involved total martial law and the sort of draconian regulations that even the Cabinet baulked at (see page 92). In June, all telegraph offices were closed down in an attempt to destroy communications between the rebels, and large scale searches rounded up hundreds of suspects, though few of them were identified as IRA men. Although 16 battalions of army reinforcements arrived in Ireland in June, it seemed to many in the Cabinet that a military victory was slipping from their grasp.

The IRA, too, was in difficulty. Although internment and trials by military tribunals seem to have affected it little, and morale was high, the successive arms raids had seriously weakened its military capability. Faced with reinforced British garrisons, the prospects for the IRA were bleak. Collins is reported to have said later, 'You had us dead beat. We could not have lasted another three weeks.' Simultaneously, Lloyd George and De Valera, the President of the Dail, began to feel that total military victory was unattainable. The will to fight on in Ireland was fading. It was time for negotiations to begin.

On 22 June, George V travelled to Belfast and opened the Northern Ireland Parliament that had been formed after the May elections in the North, where 40 Unionists had been elected out of 52 seats (see page 92). George V's speech was intended as a gesture of conciliation, and three weeks later, on 11 July, a truce was signed in Dublin between the Army and the

GEORGE V OPENS THE BELFAST PARLIAMENT

On 22 June 1921, King George V travelled to Belfast on the royal yacht, the *Victoria and Albert*, to open the Home Rule Parliament for the six counties of Northern Ireland. It was ironic that under the 1920 Government of Ireland Act, the one part of Ireland that had been the fiercest in its opposition to Home Rule should be the first to open its own Parliament. But the six-county Parliament of Northern Ireland was little more than a devolved assembly within the United Kingdom, and the Ulster Unionists were prepared to accept control of a six-county province as a practical compromise from their original ambitions of remaining an integrated part of Great Britain.

George V had repeatedly shown concern about the situation in Ireland. In the middle of July, 1914, when stalemate seemed to have been reached in the Home Rule discussions, civil war looked likely, and the King had intervened by calling a Conference between all the parties at Buckingham Palace. At the opening of this Conference, he addressed those assembled:

For months we have watched with deep misgivings the course of events in Ireland. The trend has been surely and steadily towards an appeal to force and today the cry of civil war is on the lips of the most responsible and sober-minded of my people. We have, in the past, endeavoured to act as a civilised example to the world, and to me it is unthinkable, as it must be to you, that we should be brought to the brink of fratricidal strife upon issues apparently so capable of adjustment as these you are now asked to consider, if handled in a spirit of generous compromise.

But the time had not been right. The King's appeal was in vain. The Conference broke down and civil war looked even more likely when, suddenly, everything was caught up in the maelstrom of war.

When the Great War ended, George V's worst fears of 'fratricidal strife' seemed to be realised in Ireland. For over two years, the Irish had fought the security forces, but now both sides seemed exhausted and the King, despite fears of an assassination attempt, went to Northern Ireland to appeal for a peaceful settlement to the fighting. He wanted to make a speech that went further than the stock phrases. He consulted General Smuts, who suggested to Lloyd George that the King might make an appeal for peace. The Cabinet had just been told of the measures to which Britain would have to resort to achieve a full military victory in Ireland. They included total martial law, the suppression of all newspapers, the licensing of all public traffic on the roads, the issue of identity cards and the suppression of the Dail as a treasonable assembly. The Cabinet decided these measures were too extreme to be acceptable, and so favoured conciliation. Hence, Lloyd George approved of the King's appeal for peace and George V went to Belfast where he used these words:

I speak from a full heart when I pray that my coming to Ireland today may prove to be the first step towards an end of strife amongst her peoples, whatever their race or creed. In that hope, I appeal to all Irishmen to pause, to stretch out the hand of forebearance and conciliation, to forgive and forget and to join in making for the land which they love a new era of peace, contentment and goodwill.

This time, the appeal was exactly right. The British Cabinet was hoping that conciliation would be a way of avoiding the use of draconian measures to impose a 'moderate' settlement in Ireland. Meanwhile, in Dublin, De Valera also feared that prospects looked black. Sixteen new battalions had arrived in the country to reinforce the British garrisons there. The IRA was being weakened by arms raids and to a lesser extent by internment. Three weeks after the King's appeal, a truce was signed in Dublin, on 11 July.

The PHOTOGRAPH on the opposite page shows King George V at the opening of the Belfast Parliament reading out his appeal for 'a new era of peace, contentment and goodwill'.

IRA. On the next day, Eamon De Valera went to London with his negotiating team, which consisted of Arthur Griffith, Robert Barton, Austin Stack and Erskine Childers. Lloyd George offered Ireland limited independence, a form of dominion status under the Crown, and insisted upon a recognition of the Northern Ireland state and the partition of Ireland. De Valera and his team gloomily returned to Dublin and discussed Lloyd George's terms in the Dail during August and September. Many objections to the restrictions placed upon Irish sovereignty were aired there, naturally enough. Another team returned to London to continue the talks in mid-October, this time without De Valera. The negotiations dragged on for several weeks into November. The two issues, Ulster, and the position of Ireland inside the Empire, proved to be the major stumbling blocks which on more than one occasion nearly brought the collapse of the talks and the departure of Griffith's delegation for Ireland. The dispute over Ulster finally came down to a refusal by the Republicans to recognise the partition of Ireland and the existence of the six-county state in the North as *permanent*.

The suggestion of a Boundary Commission to review the border seemed to be a reasonable compromise. Lloyd George's proposal of the Boundary Commission was accepted with enthusiasm by Michael Collins who believed that it would whittle down the Northern Ireland state to a size so small that it would cease to be viable. No impartial commissioner could fail, he thought, to award substantial areas of Tyrone and Fermanagh, as well as some parts of Armagh, Derry, and Down, to the Free State, thus rendering the North politically and economically unworkable, and re-opening the issue of a United Ireland.

It was the status of the Irish State that mattered to the British Government. They could not accept Irish independence if it meant Ireland was to be independent in the same way that, say, France or Sweden were. Ireland must remain within the Empire and swear loyalty to the Crown. Lloyd George was still leader of a Coalition Government and had to satisfy the Conservatives in the Cabinet to whom the ideology of Empire was fundamental. The Irish, of course, wanted complete independence.

The position of Ireland inside the British Empire eventually focused on a semantic debate about the precise wording of the Oath of Allegiance to the Crown that Irish ministers would have to take. It now seems incredible that centuries of conflict between Britain and Ireland should finally come down to a dispute about the phrasing of a ritualistic oath. But by the end of November, the Irish were putting forward an oath that went:

I . . . do solemnly swear true faith and allegiance to the constitution of the Irish Free State, to the Treaty of the Association and to recognise the King of Great Britain as Head of the Associated States.

The British, however, insisted on a version:

I . . . do solemnly swear true faith and allegiance to the constitution of the Irish Free State as by law established and that I will be faithful to His Majesty King George V, his heirs and successors by law, in virtue of the common citizenship of Ireland with Great Britain and her adherence to and membership of the group of nations forming the British Commonwealth of Nations.

The negotiations staggered from one difficulty to another. At one point they broke down completely for a short while after Gavan Duffy had uttered the comment, 'Our difficulty is to come into the Empire, looking at all that has happened in the past.' Austen Chamberlain leapt to his feet and shouted: 'That ends it,' and closed down the negotiations.

Finally, after eight weeks of negotiations, on the afternoon of Monday 5 December, Lloyd George presented the Irish delegation with an ultimatum. He had realised that the delegates were deeply divided between those prepared to accept the Treaty for the sake of peace, and those still opposed to it. He arranged with Sir James Craig in Belfast that he would get a message to him no later than 6 December with news of whether or not the Irish delegates had signed the Treaty. He announced on the afternoon of the 5th that he had two letters written and ready to be despatched post-haste by train and boat to Belfast. One letter told Craig of a peaceful outcome to the long dragged-out talks, the other told of a breakdown. Of this last letter Lloyd George announced, 'If I send this letter it is war, and war within three days. Which letter am I to send?'

At 7.15 p.m. that evening, the Irish delegates withdrew to consider the situation. They were still divided, and were unable to contact De Valera, who was away in Limerick. Eventually, they decided they would have to sign and Griffith, Collins and Barton returned to Downing Street to sign the Treaty at ten minutes past two on the morning of 6 December 1921.

In the frenzied and theatrical atmosphere created by Lloyd George, the Irish had accepted Dominion status and an oath which gave 'allegiance' to the Irish Free State and 'fidelity' to the Crown. It was enough for Lloyd George to satisfy the British Parliament: it was not enough for Collins and his colleagues to satisfy the Irish. As Collins walked through the foggy London night, he reflected:

When you have sweated, toiled, had mad dreams, hopeless nightmares, you find yourself in London's streets, cold and dank in the night air . . . Think — what have I got for Ireland? Something which she has wanted these past seven hundred years. Will anyone be satisfied at the bargain? Will anyone? I tell you this – early this morning I signed my death warrant. I thought at the time how odd, how ridiculous – a bullet may just as well have done the job five years ago.

For the British Government, it seemed that the Irish affair had eventually been resolved. After centuries of conflict and bitterness that had destroyed many politicians and many ministries, Lloyd George felt that he had finally solved England's Irish problem. Westminster thought that Ireland could now be forgotten; it was to be nearly fifty years before troubles in Ireland once again seriously worried a British Cabinet. But the Treaty was to tear Irish society asunder and in six months Ireland was engulfed in civil war. In Northern Ireland, the Treaty did not prevent the sectarian divisions from erupting again, and 1922 saw the worst rioting yet in Belfast, clearly demonstrating that the North had inherited a deeply divided community.

3: LEGACY

No democratic society can exist without consensus, without an agreement by the overwhelming majority that the State itself is legitimate. No matter how great are other disagreements, there must be an acceptance of the legitimacy and authority of the institutions of the State, within which those disagreements can be discussed, resolved or constrained. In a democratic society, there must also be the possibility of alternative government; the opposition must have the potential of being able to take power. The Province of Northern Ireland failed to meet either of these criteria.

From the start, political parties in Ireland were not aligned on the normal spectrum of politics of Left and Right, but between Catholic Nationalists who wanted a United Ireland, and Protestant Unionists who wanted to remain part of the United Kingdom. Political allegiance depended on religion and its counterpart, the constitutional issue; allegiances so strong that there were few in the electorate who would change. Society and politics were both ossified and polarised, with the Protestant Unionists in power. The idea that Unionists might win over a substantial number of Catholic votes was so remote that there was little point in policies that would woo Catholics, while Catholics, in a minority of one to two, had so little chance of gaining influence or power by electoral means that they would constantly be tempted to seek other ways to redress their grievances. While sectarian politics survived, Northern Ireland would remain, in effect, a one-party state with the Catholics no more than a lobby on the periphery of power.

The Province of Northern Ireland could hardly have come into being in less propitious circumstances; 40% of the work-force were out of work, there had been sectarian disorder in the North for a year, and there was a war going on over the border. The Protestants were afraid of a Catholic Republican rising led by the IRA, and the Catholics felt threatened by pogroms.

The signing of the Treaty in December 1921 did not end the violence in Ireland. A civil war broke out in the South, in 1922, between those prepared to accept the Treaty and those opposed to it (see page 104). A year of bloody and bitter fighting followed. Those who supported the Treaty, the Free State party, led now by William Cosgrave, won, with very considerable support from the British who threatened to re-conquer Ireland if it were declared a Republic. The Civil War in the South also prevented Republicans from intervening in the North on behalf of their cherished ideal of a united Ireland. However, the Treaty provoked further disturbances in the North. The Catholics, a majority of the overall population of Ireland but left now as a minority, felt a deep sense of bitterness and betrayal at the Partition of the country. They mounted a campaign of disobedience against the new state, refusing to co-operate with its institutions of government. In the elections for the Northern Ireland Parliament, held in May 1921, six Sinn Fein candidates and six Nationalists were elected (out of a total of 52 seats) and declared that they would not attend the Parliament. Catholics refused to sit on the Lynn Committee which was set up to examine the structure of education in Northern Ireland. Some Catholic teachers refused their salaries for a while, and schools refused to accept grants. Areas with an overwhelming Republican majority openly declared allegiance to the South, and Nationalist local authorities pledged support for the Dail. So the Unionists were faced by a Nationalist boycott that threatened to make the State politically unworkable, and a Boundary Commission that might award substantial areas of Nationalist Ulster to the Free State and make it economically unviable. Yet again they felt under siege.

This was the context of the bitter sectarian violence being unleashed against the Catholic community. Between July 1920 and July 1922, 453 people were killed in Belfast alone: 257 Catholics, 157 Protestants and 2 of unknown religion amongst the civilian population, and 37 members of the security forces. Over 10,000 Catholics had been expelled from their jobs, and well over 500 Catholic businesses had been wrecked. Clashes occurred in the same streets, those which marked the divide between the Protestant and Catholic working-class areas, as they had in the nineteenth century, and would in the late 1960s and 1970s (see map on page 202). In the rest of the Province, 106 people had beeen killed: 46 Catholic and 15 Protestant civilians, and 45 members of the security forces. What amounted to open warfare had been conducted in some of the border territories. In south-west Co. Fermanagh, a triangle of territory was commandeered from Northern Ireland by the IRA. When the British Army was sent in to crush the rebels, a battle took place at the border town of Pettigo, in which nine men were killed.

To meet the Catholic–Nationalist rebellion, a new force had been recruited in the North to assist the police. This was the Ulster Special Constabulary (see page 106). It consisted of three grades of constable: full-time A-Specials part-time B-Specials, and a rather loose category of C-Specials. The Specials were exclusively Protestant, and were largely recruited from the Ulster Volunteer Force, the rebel citizen army raised to resist Home Rule before the First World War. By 1922, one in every five of the adult male Protestant population was in the Specials. They were hated and feared by the Catholic population, for whom they represented all that was repressive in the Protestant State. Many of the weapons for the Special Constabulary were provided by the British Government, which had increased its garrison in Northern Ireland to sixteen battalions. The security forces were determined to beat off the rebel attacks and preserve the integrity of the State.

In the spring of 1922, another powerful weapon was added to the State's arsenal against its recalcitrant minority — the Civil Authorities (Special Powers) Act (see page 110). It gave the Minister of Home Affairs power 'to take all such steps and issue all such orders as may be necessary for preserving peace and maintaining order'. In other words, the Minister of Home Affairs was authorised to do *anything* he felt necessary to maintain order. The Act meant that there was no residual civil, political and legal personal liberty held by the individual as of right — that is to say, rights which the State was not

PARTITION

The First World War had been fought to 'protect small nations' — at least this was the phrase used by the English who entered the War in order to defend the neutrality of Belgium. But the War soon became, for the Allies, a war to destroy German militarism and to dismantle the German Empire. When President Woodrow Wilson brought the United States into the War, the crusading mission to liberate small nations from imperial hegemony was revitalised. So, at the Treaty of Versailles and the other post-War Treaties, the Allies supervised the break up of the old Hapsburg Empire and brought into existence the separate states of Austria, Hungary, Czechoslovakia and Yugoslavia; they recreated the state of Poland; they carved up the German Empire in Africa and the Far East and the Turkish Empire in the Middle East, handing out 'mandates' to the victorious powers to rule over the conquered territories.

The Irish assumed that their own struggle for freedom from the Imperial Parliament at Westminster would become a part of this peace settlement. If England could acknowledge the right to independence of the Czechoslovak people in Central Europe, then surely they would recognise the right to independence of the Irish. But these hopes were soon dashed. England refused to admit that Ireland was a nation. The Irishmen who went to the Versailles Conference were ignored and Ireland was denied membership of the new League of Nations.

Lloyd George, who was fully involved with the peace conferences and the problems of reconstruction at home, allowed the situation in Ireland to drift through 1919. But early in 1920 the Cabinet turned its attention once again to the unresolved problem of Ireland.

Partition seemed to be a gentlemanly way of reconciling irreconcilables. It was adopted as a technique by British governments on several occasions throughout the century. In Palestine it was recommended from 1936 onwards as a way of creating an Arab state of Palestine and a Jewish state of Israel. When the sun finally set on the Indian Raj in 1947, the principle of partition was used to bring into existence a predominantly Moslem state, Pakistan, and predominantly Hindu state, India. In Ireland, it was used to separate a Unionist North from a Nationalist South. But partition has never been totally successful in its objectives; in all these three cases it has left a legacy of conflict and bitterness and a tradition of instability. What seems perfectly fair and rational to diplomats over a map in a government office in Whitehall, might not seem at all reasonable in Co Fermanagh, Jerusalem, or the Punjab.

Partition of Ireland seemed to the Government at Westminster in 1920 to be the only way to prevent the Civil War that had threatened to break out in 1914. The Irish Nationalists had made it quite clear that they would settle for nothing less than independence from Britain, and repeal of the Act of Union. The Ulster Unionists had made it equally clear that they were prepared to go to any lengths to maintain the Union and to stay out of a United Ireland governed from Dublin. The political division was exacerbated by the religious divide between the Protestants in the North and the Catholics of the South, and was further reinforced by the economic divisions between the industrial North-East of Ireland, closely linked to the economy of Britain, and the predominantly agricultural South. Partition seemed to be a way of recognising these differences in a compromise settlement to the problem.

But no line drawn across a map can ever solve complex political problems. Not all the population inside the province of Northern Ireland was Protestant and Unionist. Approximately one in three was Catholic, most of whom preferred to offer allegiance to an Irish Republic in the South. The Unionists accepted a six-county Northern Ireland, knowing that they would have to live with a substantial minority who refused even to accept the right of the state to exist. Nevertheless, it seemed the minimum territory that would provide an economically viable political power base.

To the Republican ideal of a united Ireland, partition was a bitter blow. To make it a little sweeter, a Boundary Commission was set up to examine the border. Its terms of reference were 'to determine in accordance with the wishes of the inhabitants so far as may be compatible with economic and geographic conditions, the boundaries between Northern Ireland and the rest of Ireland.'

It seems that Lloyd George made two sets of promises about this Commission. To Collins and Griffith, he said that substantial parts of counties Fermanagh and Tyrone and parts of South Armagh and South Down were likely to be transferred to the Free State. This guarantee was one of the reasons why they were prepared to accept the Treaty in December 1921. But in the weeks before the signing of the Treaty, Lloyd George suggested to Craig that the Commission would *not* fundamentally alter the lines of the border by taking territory from the province of Northern Ireland. The Commission was to consist of three members, one from the North, one from the Free State, and a British representative in the chair. Craig refused to have anything to do with the Commission, and would not nominate a member.

The Free State, absorbed by Civil War, did not push the matter. Lloyd George himself resigned in October 1922, and was succeeded by Bonar Law, one of the strongest supporters of the Unionist resistance to Home Rule before the Great War. The situation dragged on until 1924, when Ramsay MacDonald's first Labour Government was pressured into action by the Free State Premier, William Cosgrave. The North still refused to name a member, so Britain nominated the Northern representative, and the Commission finally met in November 1924. The Commission's findings came to nothing. Announced at the end of 1925 in an atmosphere of great controversy, it proposed minor changes to the border, with the reallocation of territory from the Free State to the North, as well as vice versa. So, both sides agreed they were better off as they were, and accepted the border as it was. The Council of Ireland, another proposal from the Government of Ireland Act, was also dropped. The Unionists got what they wanted with the recognition of their separate existence, and the partition of Ireland became a central fact of Irish politics. It must be said that, at the time, partition was probably not seen as a long-term solution to the problem by the British Cabinet, but more as a stop-gap answer that would suffice until circumstances changed. Even Winston Churchill, who as Colonial Secretary was in charge of the post-Treaty negotiations with Ireland, said he believed that the ultimate objective of all parties, Britain, the Free State and Northern Ireland, must be the unity of Ireland. In July 1922 he wrote to Collins:

How and when this can be achieved I cannot tell, but it is surely the goal towards which we must all look steadfastly . . . from the Imperial point of view there is nothing we should like better than to see North and South join hands in an all-Ireland assembly without prejudice to the existing rights of either . . . The prize is so great that other things should be subordinated to gaining it.

The PHOTOGRAPH shows a village partitioned by the Northern Ireland border. Pettigo, on the boundary between Cos Fermanagh and Donegal, was divided between the Free State and Northern Ireland. From 1923 the Northern Ireland part of the village was called Tullyhommon. The river, running behind the main street in the picture, is the actual border, dividing the fields of farms and separating villages which had always traded and farmed together. Today, these anomalies still exist with the system of EEC subsidies, which can encourage farmers to transport livestock backwards and forwards over the border, and differentiate between the produce of the Republic and that of the United Kingdom, sometimes grown only yards apart.

empowered to deny in the name of good order. The significance of the Act lay not only in its application (and it was regularly used), but also in the environment of repression it created. It clearly spelt out the State's determination to resist the demands of the Republicans, whatever the cost. Along with the B-Specials, it symbolised and identified for Catholics all that was unjust and repressive in the State.

In local government also, the Nationalist minority was checked. The local elections held in 1920 had seen some notable victories for the Nationalists in Ulster. They had won control over Fermanagh and Tyrone County Councils, ten urban councils, including Armagh, Enniskillen, Newry and Strabane, several rural councils and, most significant of all, the City Council of Londonderry. The Corporation of Londonderry had been in the hands of the Protestants since the siege of 1689, which had given the city a central place in Protestant Orange mythology. Nothing epitomised the Ulster Protestant sense of siege more than the walled city of Londonderry, high and proud, looking out over the sprawling Catholic slums of the Bogside. The victory of the Catholics in the Council elections of 1920 was a profound shock to the Unionists, made more painful when the Catholic Mayor and Corporation declared their allegiance to the Dail in Dublin. The reason for the Nationalist victories in the North in 1920 was the use of proportional representation for the first time in the election process. This was an essential feature of the Government of Ireland Act, intended to ensure that in both the North and the South the minority would be given fair representation in the institutions of government.

In late 1921, the Northern Ireland Government rushed a Local Government (Emergency Powers) Bill through Parliament. It demanded that all the Nationalist local authorities should give their allegiance to the legally constituted Unionist Government. Many of them refused and reiterated their allegiance to the Dail in Dublin. The councillors of Co. Fermanagh declared that they did not 'recognise the partition parliament in Belfast' and that they would 'hold no further communication with either Belfast or British local government departments'. Such a statement was a clear declaration of rebellion and the Belfast Government had little alternative. The police took control of the County Council offices and expelled all the officials, and the Council was dissolved. The same thing happened with Tyrone County Council and in the following year with several of the Nationalist Urban Councils, including Armagh, Newry and Strabane. Commissioners were appointed to carry out the functions of the local authorities. They were, of course, all reliable Unionists; one of them was later to become a County Commandant of the B-Specials.

Proportional representation clearly frustrated effective Unionist government, and in the summer of 1922, another Local Government Act abolished it in all local government elections. To complete the process of gaining control over the local authorities, Sir John Leech, a King's Councillor, conducted a judicial commission to establish the new boundaries for local elections. Most of the Nationalists boycotted the Commission, believing that the Boundary Commission would soon reverse its decisions, and whole territories would revert to the Free State. The outcome was a foregone conclusion. With proportional representation abolished, the boundaries of the local authorities were arranged so as to extend the effectiveness of the Loyalist vote. In the local elections that were held in 1924, the Nationalists won control of only 2 out of nearly 80 councils, as against 25 in the 1920 elections.

When the Boundary Commission finally reported in December 1925 its recommendations came to nothing (see page 99). The Dublin Government agreed to recognise the border as it was. Thus the Unionist position in Northern Ireland was secured. But at great loss. Proportional representation, which might have relieved sectarianism, had been dismantled: the loyalty of local government had been assured only by the suppression of democracy in some areas and blatant gerrymandering in others: security was assured only by the raising of a Protestant Special Constabulary and draconian law-and-order legislation. It could be argued that such measures were necessary in the context of a civil war where the state itself was threatened. However, they were all maintained – indeed strengthened – when the threat of civil war declined. In 1929, proportional representation was abolished for the Belfast Parliament, and in 1933 the Special Powers Act was made permanent. The state's liberties became based on those necessary in civil war.

Constitutionally, of course, this legislation was approved by Westminster, in the sense that the Cabinet could instruct the Crown to withold assent. (It was once used to hold up the abolition of proportional representation. The Government backed down quickly in the face of Unionist pressure.) The ultimate authority in Northern Ireland, and therefore the final responsibility for the State, was at Westminster. But with the tortuous Irish problem now apparently settled, the Westminster Government turned its attention to other matters. A parliamentary convention soon developed that Northern Ireland's internal affairs were not discussed in Parliament. The British Government's interest in the Province can be judged by the fact that in the Parliamentary Session of 1934-35, not untypical, discussion of the affairs of Northern Ireland took only one hour and fifty minutes of parliamentary time.

In the form of devolved government set up by the Government of Ireland Act of 1920, Westminster retained control of war and peace, foreign policy, general taxation, external trade and currency. The Northern Ireland Government had to pay its share of these in what was known as the 'Imperial Contribution'. But not having control over the principal sources of revenue, like income tax, excise and customs, the Belfast Government could never effectively manipulate the sums of money it was to have available in order to pursue the policies it chose. Although its economy worked in parallel with the rest of Britain, Northern Ireland was the poorest region in the UK; the level of unemployment, for instance, was by far the highest of any part of the UK. So, while parity in taxation meant parity in the public services, there were bound to be problems. Northern Ireland could not be seen to be treating its citizens worse than all the other citizens of the United Kingdom. In maintaining parity, a disproportionate share of the Province's income went in socal benefits, starving of funds such needs as housing, sanitation, transport and school building. The answer, after 1926, was that the British Government paid over

101

'equalisation grants' to the Northern Ireland Government, to even out any imbalance on the average spending per head between the two governments. But when Britain was engulfed in economic depression, these grants dried up, and from 1932 no money was paid from the London Treasury to Belfast during three years that saw great distress and disorder in Northern Ireland. In 1938, the British Exchequer finally agreed to subsidise those social services in Northern Ireland that showed a deficit.

So, in the years when determined social, economic and housing policies might have defused sectarianism and lowered social tensions, the Belfast Government was consistently short of cash and unsure of its revenue. The problems created by devolved government were never fully resolved and the Northern Ireland Government found it impossible to address the fundamental economic problems it faced. As the years passed, it fell even further behind the UK in the provision of services, most especially in the building of new houses and in tackling ill-health.

All of these underlying difficulties were not helped by the temperament of the Unionist politicians who ruled in Northern Ireland (see page 103). Drawing on an area not much larger than Yorkshire, and a population of only one and a half million, smaller than the conurbation of Birmingham, the quality of administration was not high. Without the challenge of a serious opposition capable of replacing it, it grew complacent. The government was parochial, part-time and amateur. The Belfast House of Commons met three afternoons a week; ministerial office in the early years was part-time. The Cabinet consisted of men from the same Ulster Unionist background who grew old in power together. It was a government of businessmen and land-owners. Yet the difficulties that the government faced, both political and economic, would have taxed an administration of the highest calibre, for it had to seek a way to win over its dissident Catholic minority and tackle the area's structural economic problems. The Government of Belfast, which became known as Stormont when it opened its grandiose Parliamentary buildings in a Protestant Belfast suburb in 1932, was to prove either unable or unwilling to come to terms with these fundamental issues.

The size of the Province of Northern Ireland had been conditioned primarily by political issues rather than by economic factors. Londonderry, for example, was cut off from the hinterland, Donegal, that it naturally served. Furthermore, the industrial base of the Province, in the conurbation around Belfast, was also vulnerable. It was over-dependent on ship-building, its associated engineering industry, and linen. It had a small domestic market, and was dependent on imported fuel. Northern Ireland had few of the raw materials it needed to supply its heavy industry.

When the slump hit Europe, few industries were to be as depressed as ship-building, and Belfast suffered very great hardship. In 1932 and 1933, Harland and Wolff did not launch a single ship. Numbers employed in the shipyards fell from 20,000 in 1924 to 2,000 in 1933. In the following year, Workman and Clark, the 'little shipyard' in Belfast, closed down for good. As the Protestant workers had a near monopoly of the jobs in the shipyards, this meant that they were hit particularly badly. Between 1930 and 1939,

NORTHERN IRELAND GOVERNMENT

From the establishment of the Northern Ireland Government in 1921 to the imposition of Direct Rule from Westminster in 1972, the characteristics of the successive Northern Ireland cabinets show remarkable consistency. Up to 1969, every member of the Cabinet was a Protestant and a member of the Unionist Party, and all but three were members of the Orange Order. Of the six members of the first Cabinet in 1921, four of them were still in office fourteen years later. Twenty years' tenure of Cabinet office was not unusual.

Furthermore, the men who formed the first Northern Ireland Government were almost exclusively from a narrow social hierarchy. They were land and factory owners. Sir James Craig, Prime Minister, was a landowner; Hugh Pollock, Minister of Finance, was a leading businessman and President of the Belfast Chamber of Commerce; The Marquis of Londonderry, Minister of Education, was a leading landowner in Ireland and in north-east England (he left Northern Ireland politics in 1925 to become leader of the House of Lords); Edward Archdale, Minister for Agriculture and Commerce, was a landowner; John Andrews, Minister for Labour, was chairman of a linen manufacturers and

director of a ropeworks factory and a railway company; Richard Dawson Bates, Minister for Home Affairs, was a solicitor and had been Secretary to the Ulster Unionist Council since 1906. All the members of this first Cabinet had been closely involved with the Ulster Unionist opposition to Home Rule in the years leading up to 1914.

This singularity of age and background meant that all the ministers shared a common vision and political stance; they tended to view all questions about the Constitution, the administration of justice and the role of the Government in the economy from a narrow Ulster Unionist perspective. They all shared the same fears of Catholicism and Socialism. After all, they had gone into Ulster politics to protect and maintain the Union with Britain. It was this over-riding principle that guided their actions in the years to come. Anything that threatened this Union was a threat to the state itself.

The PHOTOGRAPH above shows the Northern Ireland Cabinet in the early 1920s. From left to right: Richard Dawson Bates, The Marquis of Londonderry, Sir James Craig, Hugh Pollock, Edward Archdale, John Andrews.

CIVIL WAR IN IRELAND

The Civil War in Ireland was fought between the hard-line Republicans led by De Valera with the IRA as their army, and the pro-Treatyites in the Provisional Government led by Collins, Griffith and Cosgrave, with the National Army of the new Free State as their fighting force backed by Britain. Like all civil wars, it produced great bitterness, and deeply divided Irish society, which had already suffered the ravages of the war with Britain. Families were split apart, localities were divided down the middle, and hatred bred violence on both sides. Even today in Ireland, nearly sixty years later, the Civil War is a touchy subject, usually to be ignored completely or quickly glossed over.

The signing of the Treaty with Britain in December 1921 was not fully accepted by any part of the Sinn Fein movement. The dominion status still meant that Irish ministers had to swear an oath of allegiance to the Crown and Ireland remained a part of the British Empire. The partition of the country dashed hopes of a united Ireland and separated the industrial North from the South. The debate on the Treaty in the Dail ended with only a narrow vote of approval, 64 votes to 57. De Valera and the opponents of the Treaty withdrew. In April, the Four Courts building in Dublin was seized and held by Republicans, a blatant illustration of the divide in Ireland. The British Government made it clear that it would not tolerate a victory by the Republicans. The Cabinet concluded on 5 April 'the British Government could not allow the Republican flag to fly in Ireland. A point might come when it would be necessary to tell Mr Collins that if he were unable to deal with the situation, the British Government would have to do so.' The withdrawal of British troops from Dublin was halted. Churchill, as Colonial Secretary, continued to provide arms and ammunition for the Free State forces; in the course of April, 8,000 rifles and 20 Lewis guns. In May, he wrote to his agent in Dublin, 'You should do everything in your power to persuade Mr Collins to draw arms from the British Government which has a large surplus. I am quite ready to continue the steady flow of arms to trustworthy Free State troops.' On 31 May, Churchill told the House of Commons that if a Republic were established in Ireland, 'it would be the intention of the [British] Government

to hold Dublin as one of the preliminary and essential steps in military operations.'

Then, on 21 June, Sir Henry Wilson, the military adviser to the Northern Ireland Government, was assassinated by Republican sympathisers in London. This was the final straw. Lloyd George told Collins that 'the ambiguous position of the IRA' could no longer be 'tolerated'. Collins was given British artillery on condition that he capture the Four Courts and suppress the IRA. This he did at the end of June 1922, and the Civil War began.

A rising in Dublin, modelled on the struggle of Easter week 1916, was easily put down by the Provisional Government, and in July and August all the principle Republican strongholds, Sligo, Limerick, Waterford and Cork, were captured by Government troops. The Republicans went underground, and conducted a guerilla war against the Government, launching sporadic ambushes and burning the houses of pro-Treatyites. Michael Collins was killed in one of these ambushes on 22 August. The Provisional Government responded by viciously repressing the Republicans. Dozens were shot, and each ambush was followed by cruel reprisals. The left-wing element in Republicanism was revealed, with the establishment of soviets or communes in certain areas. These were also put down with violence. The Free State was formally declared on 6 December 1922, and over the next few months the Government gained the upper hand. Thousands were shut up in state prisons and the executions

continued. In April, Liam Lynch, the military leader of the IRA, was killed; on 24 May 1923, a ceasefire was declared.

The birth pangs of the Irish Free State had various consequences in Northern Ireland. British Government support for the regimes of which it approved was very much more marked in Belfast than in Dublin. British troops in the North were increased to 16 battalions or 9,000 men. A Special Constabulary was established to defend the Northern Ireland State, and by June 1922 it had been supplied with 50,000 weapons by the British Government.

The turbulence in the South was manifested by bitter sectarian conflict in the North, reaching a crescendo in the late spring and summer of 1922, as the South was engulfed in Civil War. Murderous attacks were made upon the Catholic ghettos: 436 Catholic families were driven out of Belfast in the first week of June alone. With the Dublin Government entirely occupied with its own problems, the Boundary issue fell into abeyance.

The first PHOTOGRAPH shows smoke billowing from the Four Courts building in Dublin at the end of June 1922. It was Collins's attack upon the Four Courts with artillery supplied by the British that is usually thought to have marked the beginning of the Civil War.

The second Photograph shows rioting in the York Street area of Belfast in the summer of 1921. Sectarian battles recurred in Belfast throughout 1920 and 1921, culminating in the pogroms of 1922.

THE B-SPECIALS

In 1920, when war was raging in Ireland between the security forces and the IRA, fears were naturally aroused in the North that the conflict would overflow into Ulster. So in the spring a small number of Loyalist leaders, including Colonel Crawford, who had organised the Larne Gun-Running in 1914, began to organise groups of armed Loyalist vigilantes. Many of these vigilantes had been members of the Ulster Volunteer Force in the 1913–14 period. Richard Dawson Bates, Secretary of the Ulster Unionist Council from 1905–21, pressed Carson to re-organise the UVF to cope with the current crisis in Ireland. In the context of rioting and anti-Catholic pogroms following the Orange marches of July 1920, the British Cabinet discussed the possibility of raising a local force in the North, to release regular Crown forces for the war in the South and to provide a cheap and efficient way of policing the North. On 29 July, the Cabinet sub-committee on Irish affairs voted to establish an Ulster Special Constabulary for this purpose.

More and more ex-UVF units began drilling during the summer of 1920, and finally, in October, plans were announced for the formation of the Ulster Special Constabulary. Although this Special Constabulary was nominally open to all 'well-disposed citizens', it was evident in the climate of late 1920 that this would mean an overwhelmingly Loyalist recruitment, and perhaps little more than the legalisation of the UVF. Sure enough, ex-UVF members soon enrolled in large numbers. Many of the B-Special commanders had been the UVF organisers in the same area.

The USC was divided into three groups: the A-Specials, who were full-time and were used to reinforce the police; the B-Specials who were fully armed but part-time and were used for local patrol duty; and the C-Specials, who had no regular duties but formed large units that could be quickly mobilised.

Within a year there were 3,500 A-Specials and 15,000 B-Specials, with an indeterminate number of C-Specials. The A and B Specials were paid for by the British Government, who also supplied them with weapons. These men were almost entirely Protestant Loyalists, although there was a very small number of Catholic ex-servicemen in the A-Specials.

At the end of 1921, the Government of Northern Ireland assumed control over the Specials, and saw in them the ideal Loyalist force to defend the new state. In the early months of 1922, as tension in the North erupted in violent sectarian clashes in Belfast and Londonderry, the Specials were reinforced, until by June they were about 50,000 strong, well armed and supplied with ammunition from London. The Civil War in the South generally helped to ease the situation, although the Government was still very worried by the possibility of violence spilling into the North, and the Specials were kept mobilised to patrol the border. In December 1925, when the Boundary issue was settled with the Free State Government, the A- and C-Specials were disbanded, although the B-Specials were retained. Many of the disbanded A-Specials joined the police, and constituted about half of the Royal Ulster Constabulary. In 1926 the Firearms Act was amended to enable most of the ex-C-Specials to keep their guns, too.

Throughout the 1930s, '40s and '50s, the B-Specials remained one of the key weapons in the armoury of the Northern Ireland Government. The Special Powers Act specifically gave the Minister of Home Affairs the right to invest in them the same authority as the police whenever he thought the occasion called for it. Their local grass-roots knowledge and familiarity with the comings and goings in their own towns and villages made them particularly feared by the Catholics, and invaluable to the Government during periods like that of the IRA campaign of the late 1950s.

The B-Specials were called out during the Civil Rights disturbances of 1968–69, and their attacks upon the Civil Rights demonstrators gave them a new notoriety. Their willingness to use their weapons led to ugly incidents at Derry in January 1969 and at Dungiven and Dungannon in August. The order for the full mobilisation of the B-Specials at the height of events in Derry in August 1969 produced waves of panic amongst the Catholic population, and an increased determination to hold out behind their barricades. At Armagh, on the night of 14 August, the B-Specials fired into a rioting crowd, killing a man. But the late 1960s were not the 1920s, and the B-Specials could no longer be tolerated as the militant armed defence force of the Northern Ireland Government. The Cameron Commission in September 1969 called them 'a partisan and paramilitary force' and the Hunt Report on the police in the following month unequivocally proposed the disbandment of the Specials. This accordingly took place, despite protest and rioting in hard-core Loyalist areas.

A new local part-time armed force, called the Ulster Defence Regiment, was launched in 1970 with a less sectarian image, coming under the control of the British Army. Initially, the UDR held only small arms, and reflected a more even balance of the

population. By mid-1971, about 18% of the UDR were Catholics, but many of them resigned after the introduction of internment in 1971. Loyalist demands that they should be armed with more sophisticated modern weapons were acceded to. Today, the UDR is, like the force it replaced, almost totally Protestant and Loyalist. Only about one in forty of its members is Catholic.

The PHOTOGRAPH above shows a group of B-Specials in the Strabane region of Co. Tyrone in the mid-1920s. Note the display of weaponry, which includes a Lewis gun and the standard British Army issue, the Lee Enfield rifle.

The second photograph, taken in 1922, shows a group of A-Specials practising taking cover in the event of an ambush.

unemployment never fell below 20%; it averaged 25%, one in four of the working population. In 1932, the year in which the equalisation subsidies from Westminster were stopped, there were 76,000 out of work – 28% of the workforce; of these, nearly 45,000 were in Belfast alone.

The principle of unemployment insurance had been established by Lloyd George in 1911, and radically extended in 1920. In Britain this meant that most manual workers were liable to pay a small sum of insurance each week, and an insured worker, without a job, could claim unemployment benefit from a Labour Exchange. This whole new idea of 'insurance' was an integral part of the twentieth-century concept of the Welfare State. Conditions in Northern Ireland, however, were unlike those in the rest of Britain (see page 118). Fewer workers paid unemployment insurance, and most of those without work were treated in the same way as the rest of the destitute, sick, aged and infirm, and insane. Most of them were forced back on to the Victorian Poor Law Acts administered by Poor Law Guardians, financed from local rates. This meant either accepting Outdoor Relief, or going into the Workhouse. But the local Guardians, like the Unionist politicians who appointed them, were reluctant to raise rates to pay for the unemployed. With little to go around, life for the unemployed in Northern Ireland was grim.

In October 1932, both Protestants and Catholics took to the streets in protest at low levels of relief (see page 112). Rioting broke out, and after a week the Poor Law Guardians agreed to large increases in the rates of relief. Early in 1933, after the Irish Railway Company had applied to the Government to reduce its workers' wages, there were more strikes. Labour showed its strength, and the predominantly Protestant railwaymen stayed out on strike for nearly two months. Eventually, the employers obtained only a part of the cut they had proposed. But such working-class solidarity was short-lived. While the constitutional issue, loyalty to the State, remained the dominant political question, it proved impossible to realign politics on more customary lines. In the 1933 Stormont election, for instance, despite the labour unity of the previous months, the Northern Ireland Labour Party failed to make any real gains, taking only 2 of the 52 seats. Movements trying to organise across the sectarian lines, on the basis of low wages, social conditions, or bad housing, could always be split on the issue of the State itself, on their position regarding the constitution. When such alignments occurred, as in the 1932 Outdoor Relief Workers' strike, particularly if they threatened the power-base of the Unionist Party, that is the Protestant working class, then the Unionists raised the issue of loyalty to the State, the only banner behind which all Protestants would be certain to march.

In the wake of the demonstrations of labour strength, there followed a wave of sectarian speeches. Sir Basil Brooke, then Minister of Agriculture and later Prime Minister, said at the 12 July 1933 orations: 'Catholics were out to destroy Ulster in all their might and power.' In August, Sir Joseph Davison, the Grand Master of the Orange Order, said: 'It is time Protestant employers of Northern Ireland realised that whenever a Roman Catholic is brought into their employment, it means one Protestant vote less . . . and I suggest the slogan should be: Protestants employ Protestants.'

This was a blatant call to sectarian division. But it was not entirely one-sided. The Catholic Cardinal MacRory claimed that the Protestant Church was not part of the true Church of Christ. Meanwhile, the Protestants were anxiously looking at events in the South. In 1932, Fianna Fail won a great election victory under Eamon De Valera, who had been involved in the 1916 Rising, and had been President of the first Dail and the leader of the anti-Treaty faction in the Civil War. De Valera and Fianna Fail gradually dismantled the Treaty that had been signed with Britain, and attacked the dominion status that had kept the South a part of the British Empire. This process culminated in the drafting of a new constitution, which came into effect at the end of 1937. It declared Ireland to be a 'sovereign, independent, democratic state', and in reality this marked Ireland's departure from the Commonwealth. Article Two of this new constitution claimed that 'the national territory consists of the whole island of Ireland, its islands and territorial seas', although Article Three said that 'pending the re-integration of the national territory' the laws enacted under the constitution would apply only to the twenty-six counties. Furthermore, a set of Articles in the constitution seemed to bind the new State to the Catholic Church. Article 44 recognised 'the special position of the Holy Apostolic and Roman Church as the guardian of the Faith professed by the great majority of the citizens'. At the same time it guaranteed religious toleration inside the State. But the Catholic flavour of the new State was unmistakeable. One Article recognised 'the Family as the natural primary and fundamental unit group of society', and guaranteed marriage as the basis of family life, stating that 'no law shall be enacted providing for the grant of a dissolution of marriage'.

Enshrined in the South's constitution was the demand for a united Ireland, the denial of the right of Northern Ireland to remain in the United Kingdom, and an unequivocal assertion of its Roman Catholicism. Protestants were naturally worried by this emphatic statement of the South's posture on the key issues of religion and the legitimacy of the border. It created an atmosphere in which sectarian appeals could flourish.

In the wake of the Orange marches of July 1935, sectarian rioting broke out once again (see page 115). Eleven were killed and nearly six hundred injured. In a now familiar pattern, Catholics were expelled from the shipyards and the linen mills, and some five hundred Catholic families had to abandon their homes. British troops had to be called in to restore order. A Catholic demand for an enquiry was rejected at Westminster. But an investigation by the National Council of Civil Liberties concluded:

the Northern Irish Government has used Special Powers towards securing the domination of one particular political faction and, at the same time, towards curtailing the lawful activities of its opponents. The driving of legitimate movements underground into illegality, the intimidating or branding as law-breakers of their adherents, however innocent of crime, has tended to encourage violence and bigotry on the part of the Government's supporters as well as to beget in its opponents an intolerance of the "law and order" thus maintained. The Government's policy is thus driving its opponents into the ways of extremists.

The Report was denounced as Communist-inspired.

THE SPECIAL POWERS ACT

At the peak of the sectarian violence in Belfast surrounding the birth of the Northern Ireland state, the Government introduced the Civil Authorities (Special Powers) Bill. The bill became law early in April 1922 and was intended to last for only a year, but the decline of violence did not bring the end of the Act; it was renewed annually until 1928, then for a period of five years, and in 1933 it was made permanent. The Act was repeatedly invoked, until 1972. It gave the Northern Ireland Minister of Home Affairs draconian powers to restrict the liberty of citizens. He was empowered to outlaw organisations, to detain people without charge or trial, to impose curfews and restrict movement, to prohibit inquests, and to order searches and arrests without warrants. It gave the Minister even more general powers to make any further regulations to preserve the peace as he saw fit, and to authorise any policeman or special constable to carry out these powers. Despite the severity of these controls, the passing of the Act did not relieve the tensions in Belfast. More people died in the city during the three months after the Act came into effect than during the course of either of the previous two years.

The clauses of the Act speak for themselves:

THE CIVIL AUTHORITIES (SPECIAL POWERS) ACT
(NORTHERN IRELAND) 1922

1. (1) The civil authority shall have power, in respect of persons, matters and things within the jurisdiction of the Government of Northern Ireland, to take all such steps and issue all such orders as may be necessary for preserving the peace and maintaining order . . .

(2) For the purposes of this Act the civil authority shall be the Minister of Home Affairs for Northern Ireland . . .

2. (4) If any person does any act of such a nature as to be calculated to be prejudicial to the preservation of the peace or maintenance of order in Northern Ireland and not specifically provided for in the regulations, he shall be deemed to be guilty of an offence against the regulations.

3. (1) A person alleged to be guilty of an offence against the regulations may be tried by a court of summary jurisdiction . . . (and 4.) . . . shall be liable to be sentenced to imprisonment with or without hard labour for a term not exceeding two years or to a fine

not exceeding one hundred pounds or to both such imprisonment and fine . . .

5. Where after trial by any court a person is convicted of any crime or offence to which this section applies, the court may, in addition to any other punishment which may lawfully be imposed, order such person, if a male, to be once privately whipped . . .

SCHEDULE

REGULATIONS FOR PEACE AND ORDER IN
NORTHERN IRELAND

1. The civil authority may by order require every person within any area specified in the order to remain within doors between such hours as may be specified in the order. . . .

3. (1) The civil authority may make orders prohibiting or restricting in any area:

(a) The holding or taking part in meetings, assemblies . . . or processions in public places;

(b) The use or wearing or possession of uniforms or badges . . . indicating membership of any association or body specified in the order;

(e) The having, keeping, or using of a motor or other cycle, or motor car by any person, other than a member of a police force, without a permit from the civil authority . . .

8. It shall be lawful for the civil authority and any person duly authorised by him, where for the purposes of this Act it is necessary so to do:

(d) To cause any buildings or structures to be destroyed, or any property to be moved from one place to another, or to be destroyed;

(f) To do any other act involving interference with private rights of property which is necessary for the purpose of this Act.

16. If any person attempts or does any act calculated or likely to cause mutiny, sedition, or disaffection in any police force or among the civilian population, or to impede delay or restrict any work necessary for the preservation of the peace or maintenance of order he shall be guilty of an offence against these regulations.

23. Any person authorised for the purpose by the civil authority, or any police constable or member of any of His Majesty's forces on duty when the occasion for the arrest arises, may arrest without warrant any person whose behaviour is of such a nature as to give reasonable grounds for suspecting that he has acted or is acting or is about to act in a manner prejudicial to the preservation of the peace or maintenance of order . . .

25. No person shall by word of mouth or in writing, or in any newspaper, periodical, book, circular, or other printed publication:

(a) Spread false reports or make false statements;

(b) Spread reports or make statements intended or likely . . . to interfere with the success of any police or other force . . .

(c) . . . and no person shall produce any performance on any stage, or exhibit any picture or cinematograph film, or commit any act which is intended or likely to cause any disaffection, interference or prejudice as aforesaid . . .

26. The civil authority may by notice prohibit the circulation of any newspaper for any specified period . . .

From 1935 to 1936 the National Council of Civil Liberties conducted a Commission of Inquiry into the workings of the Special Powers Act. The Commission consisted of a King's Counsel, a solicitor, two barristers-at-law and the Head of an Oxford College. The Commission concluded:

Whether the legislation be viewed as a whole or in its particular applications, it is impossible to escape the conclusion that there are two pillars upon which the whole structure of Special Powers rests. These are:

1. The present derogation from the sovereignty of Parliament by the surrender, to such a degree, of its law-making powers to the Executive.

2. The annihilation of the rule of law by the substitution of the arbitrary power of the Executive for the legally defined and protected rights of the subject.

Jurists have hitherto regarded the sovereignty of Parliament and the rule of law as the two cardinal principles of the British Constitution. The Northern Irish Government in abrogating them has ravished the heritage for which generations of Britons have fought and suffered. The Special Powers Acts, the basis of a legal dictatorship, are a vital link in the chain which has been forged around the freedom of the community of Northern Ireland.

The Commission, in the light of these conclusions, believes that the operation of the Special Powers Act has the most widespread effect upon political life in Northern Ireland. The existing conditions of Rule – secured by the supercession of representative government and the abrogation of the rule of law and the liberty of the subject, the bases of Special Powers – cannot be described otherwise than as totally un-British.

It is clear to the Commission that the way to the re-establishment of constitutional government, the prerequisites of law and order in democratic communities, can be paved only by the repeal of the Special Powers Acts. Wherever the pillars of constitutional rule, Parliamentary sovereignty and the rule of law are overthrown there exist the essential conditions of dictatorship.

The PHOTOGRAPH shows an RUC patrol on the border in December 1957, during the IRA campaign.

The great depression that followed the Wall Street Crash in the United States was soon reflected in the economies of Europe. It hit the urban industrial workers the hardest, and in Northern Ireland this meant the workers in the mills, ship-building and the heavy engineering industries. Companies went out of business and workers were laid off.

In Northern Ireland, the circumstances of unemployment were such that a large number of those without work did not qualify for the dole – unemployment benefits paid out at Labour Exchanges – but were thrown on to the Victorian system of Outdoor Relief organised by the Poor Law Guardians. They were reliant upon the 'charity' of the Poor Law, and not the insurance of the dole. Men had to do two and a half days' 'task work' to get relief. If there was no 'task work' to be done, or for single men and single women, who did not qualify, the only alternative was to go into the workhouse which still had all the stigma of humiliation attached to it. The scheme was administered by Boards of Guardians who were described by Belfast journalist Jimmy Kelly, in an interview for *The Troubles* as:

a very Dickensian body of low-grade politicians whose outlook on unemployed people was that they were layabouts and they had no sympathy whatsoever with them. . . . In fact the Government at this time seemed to be completely insensible to this approaching tragedy because these people had no other place to go except to the workhouse.

Not only were there more people in Northern Ireland on Outdoor Relief than in Britain but also the Poor Law rates were generally lower in Belfast than in the rest of the United Kingdom. In Britain, a married couple with one child could hope to get between 21 shillings and 27 shillings (£1.05 and £1.35) per week on the dole. In Belfast the same family would stand to get 12 shillings (60p) per week on Outdoor Relief. By the end of September 1932 various workers' committees agreed that conditions had got bad enough, and it was decided to call a strike of Outdoor Relief workers.

On 4 October tens of thousands of unemployed marched in protest demanding 'work and wages not charity'. The next day 7,000 unemployed marched to the workhouse on the Lisburn Road. Saidie Patterson, then an unemployed mill worker and union organiser, said in an interview for *The Troubles:*

There was no work so we decided that we would march to the workhouse on the Lisburn Road and march we did. Many marched in their bare feet . . . and when we got outside the workhouse we sat down. It was a step in the right direction. The Falls and the Shankill united.

On the next day, another march was led to the workhouse. Here as a gesture of protest, 300 single men demanded that they be admitted destitute to the workhouse, knowing that it would actually cost the authorities *more* to keep them there than to pay them relief. Once inside the workhouse, riotous scenes ensued. The men started singing and refused to go to bed at the statutory time of 8 pm. The RUC was called in, and arrested the ring-leaders of the protest. The next morning, another protest broke out when the men demanded eggs with their breakfast. They were all expelled from the workhouse.

A new wave of protest meetings was called for 12 October, all over the Protestant and Catholic working-class districts of Belfast. The Government was terrified at seeing the Protestant and Catholic workers uniting against the Unionist hierarchy. The meetings were banned under the Special Powers Act but when crowds went ahead and assembled, the RUC strongly reinforced for the occasion, was sent

in. In the Protestant areas of the city, they baton-charged the crowds. But in the Catholic ghettos they fired over the heads of the demonstrators and a full-scale riot broke out in the Lower Falls area. Barricades were set up, cobbles were prized out of the streets and thrown at the police, and 'birdcage' covered police wagons were sent in to break up the rioters. A curfew was imposed. But for three days the rioting continued. Two of the strike leaders and about a hundred demonstrators were imprisoned, the rest went into hiding.

The Government had been considerably shaken by these non-sectarian riots, and the Unionist leaders greatly feared a repetition. The Prime Minister, Lord Craigavon, blamed the rioting on Republican agitators when he said:

If they have any designs by the trouble they have created in our city, if they have it in the back of their minds that this is one step towards securing a Republic for all Ireland . . . then I say they are doomed to bitter disappointment.

Nevertheless, the Government was forced into negotiating new rates with the Poor Law Guardians. Approximate parity with the rest of Britain was agreed upon, and a man and wife with one child were now to receive 24 shillings (£1.20) per week. The October Outdoor Relief strike succeeded not only in achieving its desired result, but also in bringing together working-class Protestants and Catholics behind their common grievances against the Unionist Government. It was to be a short-lived unity.

The two PHOTOGRAPHS are from a Movietone News item on the Belfast riots. The silent era of the cinema had ended. The newsreels now united sound and picture and became a potent force for the communication of news. At this time there were five major newsreel companies in Britain, each releasing a ten-minute newsreel twice a week.

The first frame shows children in the Falls Road area breaking up the cobbled streets for ammunition to throw at the police, and the second shows an RUC armoured wagon, called a 'cage car' or 'birdcage'. It was designed for protection from missiles.

The state was still divided, its minority still vulnerable, and little progress had been made in the resolution of the state's fundamental problems. It was ominous.

The background to all these troubles was the social deprivation that plagued Northern Ireland. In Belfast over a quarter of the houses were overcrowded, 9,000 married couples had no homes of their own and lived with other families. Eleven per cent of houses were unfit for habitation or needed major repairs. A housing survey published in 1944 concluded that in the Province as a whole, 100,000 new houses were needed immediately, and 200,000 were required to make any real impact on the province's housing problem. In the rural areas, 87% of houses had no running water in 1939, while in the Fermanagh countryside nearly 60% of houses were overcrowded. Yet, less than 3,500 new houses were built by local authorities in country areas between 1921 and 1939, and in three rural councils in Co. Fermanagh, none was built at all.

Housing conditions were revealed by the health statistics. Consumption, as tuberculosis or TB was called, was rife in Northern Ireland, thousands died of it. The principal reason for its hold in the working-class population was malnutrition. Weakened by a poor diet, bad working conditions and bronchitis, people became vulnerable. In 1938, 46% of those who died in the 15–25 age group were killed by tuberculosis, and of those in the 26–35 age group, 38%. The Poor Law dispensaries and the hospitals for tuberculosis were overworked, understaffed and utterly inadequate to cope with the scale of the problem.

There was also social hardship. A survey in 1938–39 reported that 36% of the population were in absolute poverty – meaning that they had too little to buy the food, clothing and fuel necessary to maintain health and working capacity. The children of the Belfast unemployed were on average two to three inches shorter and ten pounds lighter than their middle-class contemporaries. The death rate was still the worst in the United Kingdom, 25% higher in Northern Ireland than in England and Wales. In 1938 more mothers died in childbirth (5.5 per 1,000) than in 1922 (4.7 per 1,000). In housing, public health, sanitation and medical services, there had been virtually no progress in twenty years.

When war broke out in 1939, the reaction in Northern Ireland was predictable. For the Unionists it was an opportunity to cement the British connection with a demonstration of the Province's loyalty to the Crown. Lord Craigavon, in a famous broadcast, put it simply when he said: 'We are the King's men.' For militant Republicans, English difficulties were Ireland's opportunity. There was sporadic IRA activity in both Ireland and England, although it did not amount to much. The IRA fostered contacts with the Germans. This too came to nothing, but it was enough to upset the British and enrage the Loyalists. It was a reminder that there were still those prepared to fight for a United Ireland even if it meant attacking Britain whilst she was fully occupied in total war with Hitler's Germany. The Dublin Government of De Valera maintained a sympathetic neutrality throughout the War, but refused to join the Allies in their struggle to destroy Nazism. Ireland's strategic importance was emphasised once again in the crucial use of the ports in the

1935 RIOTS

Despite the display of solidarity between Protestant and Catholic workers during the hard times of unemployment and the hunger marches of 1932, religious tension still existed in the community. The scarcity of jobs and consistently high levels of unemployment made for severe frictions in Northern Ireland society. For the Unionist Party leadership it was vital to keep the loyalty of the Protestant working classes, and Orange speeches fanned sectarian flames. Protestant employers were exhorted to take on only Protestant workers. In July 1933 the *Fermanagh Times* reported a speech by Basil Brooke, later to become Prime Minister in Northern Ireland, appealing to Loyalists 'wherever possible to employ good Protestant lads and lassies.' In the *Londonderry Sentinel* in March 1934 he said:

I recommend those people who are Loyalists not to employ Roman Catholics, 99% of whom are disloyal . . . If you don't act properly now, before we know where we are we shall find ourselves in the minority instead of the majority.

The Ulster Protestant League was formed in 1931 with one of its objectives being 'to safeguard the employment of Protestants.' It was a sectarian organisation whose virulently anti-Catholic platform frequently led to violence. In November 1933, a Catholic publican was shot dead in York Street, Belfast, the first sectarian murder since 1922. Sectarian disputes escalated through 1934 to a crescendo in the summer of 1935. A big Ulster Protestant League rally on 18 June was followed by two weeks of disorders, and led the Minister of Home Affairs to ban all parades in the city. But this would have prohibited the annual Orange parades, and the outraged Orange Order put pressure on the Government to relent. They gave in, the ban was lifted, and the parades went ahead.

Predictably, bloody scenes ensued. Shooting began in the York Street area. The Catholics claimed that the Orangemen broke out of the march and attacked Catholic homes. The Orangemen claimed that Catholics fired into the parade. Who fired the first shots is impossible to determine now, but Belfast was in an uproar, and within days serious rioting had spread from York Street and had broken out all over the city, in the Short Strand, in Sandy Row and Peter's Hill. Catholics in the shipyards were expelled from their jobs, and Catholic girls were expelled from the York Street and Crumlin Road linen mills.

The RUC could not control the situation, and British troops were called in to try to restore order. They erected metal barricades as a sort of peace line along the ends of the Catholic streets around York Street, as they were to do in 1969. Whilst trying to control a Loyalist crowd in the Docks, they shot and killed two Protestants.

The fighting continued for three weeks, although some of the barricades were not taken down for months. Eleven people were killed and nearly 600 injured. There were 133 cases of arson and 367 of malicious damage.

The PHOTOGRAPH shows British troops passing burnt-out houses in the York Street region of Belfast.

North, Belfast, Larne and Londonderry, as naval bases in the Battle of the Atlantic. When the Germans were defeated in 1945, the entire U-boat fleet was surrendered to the port of Londonderry in acknowledgement of the town's contribution to the victory in the Atlantic. From 1942 the Province became a major aircraft base and a principal training ground and assembly area for American troops. All in all, 240,000 American soldiers were billeted in Northern Ireland during the course of the War.

But the War had sealed the loyalty of Northern Ireland in blood again. With one third of the population Nationalist, it was construed unwise to introduce conscription. Nevertheless, 38,000 men and women volunteered, and some 4,500 lost their lives. The civilian population suffered too. Belfast, ill-prepared for total war, suffered four air raids in 1941 (see page 121). On 15 April the city lost more casualties in one night than any other city during the course of the War: 100,000 people abandoned their bombed, blasted and burning city for the safety of the countryside. In adversity, Protestant and Catholic joined briefly in prayer.

In 1943, Churchill was fulsome in his praise for Northern Ireland. He emphasised the strategic role the province had played in keeping open the sea-lanes supplying England. He said: 'Only one great channel of entry remained open. That channel remained open because loyal Ulster gave us the full use of the Northern Irish ports and waters and thus ensured the free working of the Clyde and the Mersey. But for the loyalty of Northern Ireland and its devotion . . . we should have been confronted with slavery and death . . .' At the end of the War, Churchill reiterated this gratitude to Ulster and expressed anger with Eire's neutrality. He restated England's strategic need for Ireland that had echoed down the centuries: 'Owing to the action of the Dublin Government . . . the approaches which the Southern Irish ports and airfields could so easily have guarded were closed by hostile aircraft and U-boats. This was indeed a deadly moment in our life, and if it had not been for the loyalty and friendship of Northern Ireland, we should have been forced to come to close quarters with Mr De Valera or perish forever from the earth.'

It was in this atmosphere of gratitude, and in the immediate context of the Dublin Government's declaration of an independent Republic in the South, that the British Government passed the Ireland Act of 1949. The Act guaranteed 'that in no event will Northern Ireland or any part thereof cease to be a part of His Majesty's dominions and of the United Kingdom, without the consent of the Parliament of Northern Ireland'. This cemented the bond with Britain as powerfully as any die-hard Unionist could have hoped for. The Union was now formalised in a Westminster statute. This was a pivotal point. The clause has been consistently and effectively used by Unionists in the political battles of the current phase of the troubles.

Even during the War, the inequalitites between Britain and Northern Ireland remained marked. Although the numbers employed in ship-building increased three-fold to 21,000, those in aircraft manufacture four-fold to 23,000, and agriculture was fully stretched feeding a hungry British market, the unemployment rate fell only to 5%. Indeed, 60,000 people went to work in Britain, where there was a surplus of jobs. Social conditions too remained grim. In the wake of the bombing, when relief was given to those made homeless in the slums, it revealed to those from the better-off suburbs the extent of the deprivation. One Presbyterian clergyman said: 'I have been working for 19 years in Belfast and I never saw the like of them before. If something is not done to remedy this rank inequality there will be revolution after the War.'

When the War was over, as a result of investigations into health, housing, education, roads and sanitation, the considerable discrepancy between Northern Ireland and the rest of the United Kingdom became clear. The new Labour Government of 1945 assured the province that it would enjoy the same levels of social benefits as the mainland, and that Britain would provide the additional money necessary to achieve this in the form of increased subsidies. This was the period which saw the creation of the Welfare State as we know it in the United Kingdom. The whole apparatus of social welfare, free medical aid, free schooling and national insurance, was set up in the pioneering years of the post-war Labour Government. The result was that, as Professor F.S.L. Lyons has put it: 'Within a decade Northern Ireland passed from the status of an exceptionally backward area to full membership of the Welfare State.'

This improvement produced a wide gap between the North and the South of Ireland, which for three decades was to be a formidable agrument in the North, at all levels of society, against unification under Dublin. In education, for instance, the North, with only half the population of the Republic, had more children in secondary schools than the South; 95,000 and 85,000 respectively in 1964. In 1969, unemployment benefit for a single man was £3.25 in the Republic and £4.50 in Northern Ireland – 40% higher. Only a convinced Nationalist would not think twice before advocating the abolition of the border.

Northern Ireland now had the same housing, welfare, social and health services as Britain. By 1963, 112,000 houses had been built, insufficient to destroy the shortage left over from the pre-War period, inadequate for a long term solution to the housing problem, but nevertheless a good start. A special Tuberculosis Authority was set up to deal with the particular health problems of the province. This, combined with the post-War development of new drugs to combat the disease, resulted in a striking fall in mortality, and a marked improvement in health. The impact of the Welfare State was substantial. Not only did it extend the powers of local government (which administered many of the new policies) but also it raised expectations.

This social revolution was the result of Westminster's initiative. It was opposed by the Unionist politicians, whose natural conservatism led them to dislike the increased intervention of the state in the affairs of the community. But when legislation at Stormont was required, they acquiesced. Britain, after all, was paying the bill. Stormont's obsessions remained the maintenance of the Union and the control of the internal tensions of a deeply divided community. The more fundamental problems, for which the symptoms were there for all those who were prepared to look, remained the ultimate responsibility of Westminster, which had neither the time nor inclination to confront them.

UNEMPLOYMENT

were registered out of work; 29.5% of the workers, as against the highest British figure of 23.8% in Wales and 12.8% for Britain as a whole. The post-War period saw a great improvement, and throughout the 1950s and 1960s the figure in Northern Ireland as a whole averaged between 5% and 10%. By mid-1969, on the eve of the beginning of the recent troubles, 6.8% of the workers were out of work, nearly three times the level of the rest of Britain, which was at 2.28%.

One of the main problems, even at relatively prosperous times, was the unevenness of unemployment. It was nearly always worse in the West than the East, worse in Londonderry than Belfast. The number out of work in Catholic areas was nearly always double that of Protestant areas. But, also, male unemployment was especially severe in the areas where female labour in the linen mills had always been well established. The 1924 census of production showed that over half of all those in work were employed in the linen and textile finishing industries, and a good many of these were women. And although the traditional linen industry has largely died out in Northern Ireland, the new man-made fibre and clothing factories established since the 1950s have often maintained this unusual

The photographs on these pages were taken in Londonderry in December 1955, by Bert Hardy, a photo-journalist working for the pictorial magazine *Picture Post*. By the mid-1950s, the menace of unemployment had been largely forgotten in Britain. The hunger marches and the dole queues were a thing of the past; England was about to enter a period in which she had 'never had it so good'. Britain didn't want to be reminded of those grim memories of the past. But in one part of the United Kingdom, unemployment was still a threat hanging over everyone's livelihood. When *Picture Post* carried this spread in 1955, one man in five was out of work in Londonderry.

Unemployment had been one of the major problems of Northern Ireland. It lurked beneath all the other difficulties of the province. When the Northern Ireland Government was formed in June 1921, at the worst point of the post-War depression, there were 103,000 men unemployed in Northern Ireland, over 40% of the insured male working population. But this figure was exceptional, and it soon settled at about half of this rate, or 20 to 25% of the working population. The worst relative position was reached in February 1938, when 92,000

state of affairs – as, for instance, in the shirt factories of Londonderry.

In the summer of 1980 there were 70,000 without jobs in Northern Ireland, the highest figure for forty years. This represents an average of 12% of the working population, as against 6% without jobs in the rest of Britain. But this average figure still conceals great inequalities. In some of the Catholic districts, unemployment is today as high as 50%.

Throughout its history, unemployment in Northern Ireland has run parallel to the position in Britain, but has always been worse. When people go on the dole on the mainland, even more are suffering in Northern Ireland.

Bert Hardy captured in these photos something of the impoverished feel of Londonderry, caught at a time of prosperity in Britain but deprivation in Northern Ireland. These images give a glimpse of life on the dole in a community where there was little prospect of improved job prospects. The man in the heavy overcoat in the first photograph has been out of work for six years.

Photography had now moved on from the days of Robert French and Robert Welch; new cameras using roll film with 36 exposures had replaced the old 'single shot' cameras. They were smaller and more portable. Cameramen began to move in to those situations in life from which they had been excluded before. The pictorial magazines like *Picture Post* and *Illustrated*, and later *Life*, gave a great boost to photo-journalism. But few photographers were as able, as Bert Hardy was, to capture those candid moments that speak far more than mountains of words or tables of statistics could ever hope to do.

% of the workforce unemployed in	Great Britain (i.e. England, Scotland and Wales)	Northern Ireland
December 1922	14.1%	22.9%
February 1938	12.8%	29.5%
December 1955	1.0%	6.7%
July 1980	6.5%	12.1%

Note: In 1948, with the implementation of the full National Insurance scheme, the method of calculating the numbers of unemployed slightly changed. However, this does not affect a comparison between figures for the same period.

The post-War period saw the revival of constitutional Republicanism. Anti-Partition candidates stood in the 1949 Stormont election. It was a heated contest, marred by sectarian disorder. The politics of Northern Ireland moved towards the streets again. Nationalist rallies and marches were banned under the Special Powers Act. Crowds confronted the police; there were minor but ominous clashes. The Government responded by passing the Public Order Act in 1951, requiring 48 hours' notice for all parades except traditional ones (presumably Orange marches). In 1954, the Flags and Emblems Act was passed, which made it illegal to interfere with the display of the Union Jack and empowered the police to remove any flag or emblem that they considered might lead to a breach of the peace. The most likely offender was the Irish Tricolour. Republican politics moved from the constitutional to the extra-parliamentary, and the IRA reorganised. In 1955, Sinn Fein, the political wing of the IRA, put up twelve candidates in the Westminster election, and received over 150,000 votes (56% of the Catholic vote). Half of the Sinn Fein candidates were in prison for an arms raid, including the two who were elected for the constituencies of mid-Ulster and Fermanagh – South Tyrone. The IRA launched a new campaign in the North in December 1956. Customs posts were destroyed, RUC barracks attacked, and property blown up in the border areas. All this was part of an overall strategy aimed at driving the Crown forces out of the rural areas of Northern Ireland where the Nationalists were in a majority, by making them ungovernable, as they had done in the Black-and-Tan War. But in the late 1950s, unlike the early 1920s, the IRA did not have that tacit support of the populace which is necessary to mount an effective guerilla campaign. This demonstration of militant Republicanism yet again only served to harden the Unionist determination to cut the cancer from the state. Internment without trial was introduced both sides of the border, and the security forces co-operated in the suppression of the IRA. The number of B-Special patrols was stepped up, and their detailed, local knowledge proved especially effective in locating IRA activity. The campaign cost nineteen lives, caused considerable damage to property and was a complete failure. As support for Sinn Fein withered, Nationalist politics returned to constitutionalism. It looked as though the Republicans of the North had finally turned their backs on violence and would now rely on other means to redress their grievances.

But for those Catholics who tried to work inside the constitution, their problem was their ineffectiveness. Northern Ireland was run by Unionist Protestants. The Unionist Party, with its close links with the Orange Order and its central creed of Protestantism, had held power continuously since 1921, with no prospect of losing office. No Catholic had ever held ministerial office, in fact only a tiny handful of Stormont Cabinet Ministers were not members of the Orange Order (see page 126). The Northern Ireland Civil Service was overwhelmingly Protestant too. In June 1969, only 23 Catholics were employed in the 319 jobs in the administrative grades – i.e: 7%. Only 13 (6%) of the 209 jobs in the professional and technical grades were held by Catholics. In 1961, only 12% of the RUC was Catholic. The B-Specials were entirely Protestant. Such bias against Catholics was manifest at all levels within

THE BELFAST BLITZ

Belfast housed important war industries, the Harland and Wolff shipyards, working at full capacity in the War, and the Short Brothers aircraft factory. But nearly all the anti-aircraft guns in Northern Ireland were sent to Britain on the outbreak of the War to assist the air defence of the mainland. Little had been done by the elderly Unionist government to protect Belfast or Londonderry. Lord Craigavon, the Prime Minister, died in 1940, and was succeeded by 69-year-old John Andrews. But very little changed.

The Blitz of London began in earnest in September 1940, when Hitler ordered Luftwaffe bombers to attack the docks of the East End. In October and November, these bombing raids intensified and spread out to the provinces. On the night of 14 November, the centre of Coventry was devastated by fire bombs, and over the next few weeks raids were made on the other provincial cities of England. In the spring of 1941, these raids reached a new crescendo. In March, on consecutive nights, massive raids were made on Clydeside with its important shipyards. In April, the West Midlands suffered another series of attacks. On the night of 7 April, the first bombs fell on Belfast, and 13 people were killed. But this was only a hint of what was to come.

On 15 April 1941, the Germans made a huge raid against Belfast, and left 745 dead in one night. Large areas of the centre of the city were devastated. Belfast's lack of shelters and air-raid precautions were made tragically apparent. On the night of 4 May, there was a further raid on the shipyards of East Belfast, leaving another 150 dead. Finally, late in May, Hitler lifted his attacks against the United Kingdom and prepared to turn his fury against Russia.

A terrible price had been paid in Northern Ireland: 942 people killed, 56,000 houses damaged, extensive damage to the shipyards. The Irish Free State remained neutral throughout the War, but sent fire engines from Dublin and Dundalk to help in Belfast after the 4 May raid, a gesture that was much appreciated in the North. In the Falls and the Shankill, the people united briefly again to work in soup kitchens and relief centres for the homeless. Northern Ireland had once again shown its loyalty to Britain in her time of need.

EDUCATION

Education is a good example of the difficulties and the failings of the Northern Ireland state. At the birth of the state in 1921, the problems facing the organisation of schooling were immense. The provision of schools was hopelessly inadequate. Many Ulster schools were tiny, frequently with no more than thirty pupils. Many buildings were in a terrible state: old, decaying, insanitary and cold. In Belfast, the number of schools had fallen disasterously behind the expansion of population, and it was estimated that there was no room at all for some 12,000 children. Ireland had been the only part of the United Kingdom where schooling was not compulsory, and in 1922 it was estimated that one child in four was absent from school at any one time. Schools were poorly equipped with books, and the standards of teaching were low, as salaries were too small to attract suitably qualified candidates.

The Lynn Committee on education was established by the new State in 1921. Almost all interested bodies were represented on the Committee, except the Roman Catholic Church, which boycotted it. The result of the Committee's findings was the 1923 Education Act, a courageous attempt at wholesale reconstruction of the educational system in Northern Ireland. Schooling was made compulsory. All local authorities were given the duty to provide elementary schools, and the principle of secular education was adopted, stemming from the clause in the Government of Ireland Act which guaranteed religious toleration for all denominations. But such fine intentions soon met with determined resistance from the churches. Catholics have always believed that education is a function for the Church. The Protestant Churches and the powerful Orange Order put pressure on the Government to insist upon Bible education in elementary schools. It was against these frustrations that the first Minister of Education, Lord Londonderry, the only administrator of a really high calibre in the Northern Ireland Cabinet, resigned in 1925 and left Ulster politics altogether, for the more tranquil life of the House of Lords.

In the face of such overwhelming opposition, the Government soon gave way and agreed to provide Bible instruction in schools if the parents of no less than ten children applied for it. This made for schools which were, as the Prime Minister, Craig, put it, 'safe for Protestant children'. Most Catholic schools stayed outside the state system, so Catholics were forced to pay rates to support schools they detested. Despite the intransigence of the Roman Church, the Government went some way to

levelling out this imbalance in 1930 when it agreed to provide grants for voluntary schools, even if they did not come under the control of the local educational authorities.

Over the decades some limited progress took place. The number of trained teachers increased considerably. The number of school places increased to cope with declining truancy, but the concentration of schools into larger units made for a decrease in the total number of schools in the six counties. The scale of new building, though impressive for a time of financial difficulty, was nowhere near sufficient. The books and stationery provided were enough for only one child in ten. Medical services and meals in schools were still very primitive, and often non-existent.

Secondary education was almost entirely denominational. Protestant and Catholic governing bodies managed their own grammar schools, and government grants were usually based on examination results. But many pupils got no further than elementary schooling because their parents could not afford to transfer them from free elementary schools to fee-paying secondary schools. However, some progress was made. In 1921 there were just over 6,000 pupils in secondary schools in Northern Ireland, which rose to 11,500 in 1938. Furthermore, an improvement in teachers' salaries and conditions made for a considerable rise in teaching standards.

Higher education was almost the exclusive prerogative of the rich who could afford the fees. Between 1934 and 1938, all the local authorities of Northern Ireland provided a total of only 24 scholarships a year for children to go on to university.

Educational progress after the War was stimulated by Britain. The 1947 Education Act provided for the changeover in education from elementary to secondary schooling at the age of eleven. It gave educational authorities extensive obligations to provide medical treatment, transport, milk and meals, books and stationery, all free of charge. The position of the voluntary schools, most of which were Catholic, was still a point of controversy. They refused to come fully under the state system, but to remain outside would have meant a considerable reduction in standards of education during times of inflation. The Government therefore decided to increase the grants available, whilst respecting the independence of the schools. The outcry that this provoked, especially amongst the Orange Order, caused the Education Minister to resign in 1949. Nevertheless, real advances were made in the post-War decades; from 1947 to 1964, 250 new

primary schools were built, and most of the provisions of the Act were realised by the local authorities.

In the mid-1960s, the Unionist Government was very slow to encourage comprehensive schooling on the British model. The problem of the voluntary schools was, again, paramount, as they said they would opt out of such a system and become private fee-paying institutions. Despite enormous advances over the previous half-century, schooling in Northern Ireland still largely remained about a generation behind education in Britain by the 1970s.

Education represents almost a microcosm of the problems facing Northern Ireland. Constantly harassed by the lack of funds, progress has been slow but real. Frequently at loggerheads with the religious leaders of both sides, and faced with the powerful opposition of the Orange Order, the Government has been forced to walk a tightrope between the demands of free state education, and private denominational schooling. Although common schooling offers perhaps the best opportunity for healing the wounds of the past and creating unity in the community, it has proved almost impossible to attain in Northern Ireland. Educational partition is still the order of the day in the vast majority of Northern Ireland schools, just as it was sixty years ago. Separate schooling is a melancholy example of the sectarian divide that permeates Northern Ireland society.

The PHOTOGRAPH shows a classroom in the Brow of the Hill School in the heart of Derry's 'Bogside' area, in 1929. The school was a Catholic foundation run by the Christian Brothers, catering for the poor of the Bogside, although the pupils in this photo look very scrubbed and healthy.

government. In March 1969, for example, Fermanagh County Council (governing an area with a slight Catholic majority) employed 338 Protestants and only 32 Catholics. And this was not exceptional. It can be argued, of course, that many Catholics saw these forms of employment as a betrayal of their Nationalist creed, which demanded allegiance to the Republic and a refusal to serve the Northern state. But this implies a huge and unyielding Republican sentiment at all levels of the Catholic community. It was clearly the case that Catholics were never encouraged to take up public service. At the Ministry of Home Affairs, Richard Dawson Bates, Minister from 1921 to 1943, refused to allow Catholic appointments. In 1927, Edward Archdale, the Minister of Agriculture, boasted that his Ministry only contained four Catholics. Significantly, the number of Catholics in the higher reaches of the Northern Ireland Civil Service actually *fell* during the 1920s and 1930s, as Catholics appointed by the British at the time of partition retired. In 1959, the Unionist Party considered a proposal to admit Catholics as members of the Party. Sir George Clark, the Grand Master of the Orange Order, said, 'It is difficult to see how a Catholic with the vast differences in our religious outlook, could be either acceptable within the Unionist Party as a member, or, for that matter, bring himself unconditionally to support its ideals.' Such discrimination, whatever the cause, would in any case hardly be conducive to good government, and was bound to provoke suspicion and grievance.

Evidence on discrimination in the private sector is sketchy. Undeniably, some employers practised it. Sir Joseph Davison, Grand Master of the Orange Order, said in 1933, 'When will the Protestant employers of Northern Ireland recognise their duty to their Protestant brothers and sisters and employ them to the exclusion of the Roman Catholics.' In 1970, Harland and Wolff employed only 400 Catholics in a workforce of 10,000. With the unemployment rate of Catholics twice as high as that of Protestants, it is hard to believe that discrimination was not operating at some level of society. If, for example, it could be shown that discrimination was not operating in the labour market, and that Catholics were less well qualified, it would merely suggest discrimination in the educational system.

There was also discrimination in electoral procedures. A quarter of the population who voted on the basis of universal suffrage in national elections could not vote in local elections. This was due to the property qualification. To qualify for the vote in local elections, one needed to be a house-owner or a tenant, or the wife of an owner or tenant. Those who owned business premises of a rateable value of over ten pounds could vote for every ten pounds of the rateable value their premises attracted, up to a maximum of six votes. This discriminated on behalf of businessmen and against the poor. In Belfast alone, some 10,000 married couples, living with others, were without a vote. Some of the disenfranchised were Protestant, but many were Catholics. Of those disenfranchised in 1969, three-quarters were Catholics.

But the Unionists used another device for ensuring that they would retain control of local authorities, known as gerrymandering. This was a system of drawing up the boundaries of local districts and wards so that the final results grossly distorted the political division of the electorate in favour of one side. In

Co. Fermanagh for instance, a slight majority of the population were Catholic (in 1961, 53% Catholic and 47% Protestant), but because of the arrangement of the local constituencies, the areas of Catholic population were all concentrated together in a few wards, whereas the Protestant population was spread more thinly over a larger number of wards. The result was that the Catholic population elected 17 Nationalist councillors, and the Protestants elected 36 Unionist councillors. So, despite the slight Catholic majority, the county was permanently in the hands of a Unionist council. Londonderry provided the most blatant example of this technique (see page 129). In gerrymandered Derry, a Catholic vote was in effect worth less than half of a Protestant vote. As a result of these techniques applied in areas of Catholic majority, only Newry and Strabane elected Nationalist councils.

Gerrymandering, together with an electorate voting consistently along religious and constitutional lines, meant that elections became foregone conclusions. Between 1923 and 1955, 96% of Rural Council seats, 94% of County Council seats, and 60% of Urban and Borough elections went uncontested. With local politics virtually moribund, it was natural that Unionist councillors should favour their own supporters. Again in Co. Fermanagh, for instance, 1,589 new houses were built between 1945 and 1969; 1,021 of them were allocated to Protestants and 568 to Catholics. The rigid mould in which local government found itself also accounts for the predominance of Protestants in Council employment. Where gerrymandering was crucial in preserving the status quo, as in Derry, electoral considerations influenced housing policy.

Unlike the rest of the United Kingdom, local authorities in Northern Ireland did not allocate council houses on a 'points' system, whereby those on the waiting list for housing were given points according to the size of family, the conditions of their present home, and so on. Housing was at the discretion of the local authority, and this made for glaring injustices, as when single men and women were allocated houses whilst whole families were condemned to go on living in squalid and over-crowded accommodation. In 1969, the Cameron Commission reported that 'Council housing policy has also been distorted for political ends in the Unionist-controlled areas.' It noted 'a determination to keep Unionist control of the Council to the detriment of the majority as . . . evidenced by a past manipulation of ward boundaries and the allocation of Council houses to achieve the same ends'. Such considerations, plus the fact that in local government, housing meant votes, were unlikely to produce an efficient and effective housing policy. It also encouraged the growth of ghetto areas.

However, these injustices, the siege mentality that sustained them, the sense of grievance they were generating, the historical context in which it had grown up . . . all went unreported. Neither television nor the Press reported it before the violence broke out, partly through ignorance, partly through indolence, partly because established institutions hampered those who tried (see page 131). Northern Ireland's affairs were Northern Ireland's affair, it was thought by those who took their cue from Westminster. Those working for Civil Rights described it as the 'paper wall'; few would listen, fewer still would

ORANGEISM AND THE STATE

In April 1934, Lord Craigavon, the Prime Minister of Northern Ireland, commented in the Northern Ireland Parliament at Stormont:

I have always said that I am an Orangeman first and a politician and a member of this parliament afterwards . . . The Hon. Member must remember that in the South they boasted of a Catholic state. . . . All I boast is that we are a Protestant Parliament and Protestant state.

Two years later, after troops had been called in to put down the sectarian riots of 1935, Craigavon said at an Orange rally:

Orangeism, Protestantism and the Loyalist cause are more strongly entrenched than ever and equally so is the Government of Stormont.

The Northern Ireland province was an Orange State. The influence of the Orange Order was felt at all levels of Northern Ireland society. In the early twentieth century, it was estimated that some two-thirds of the adult male Protestant population were members of the Order. It was organised hierarchically into 'Loyal Orange Lodges', belonging to a district, then a county, and finally the province. The Order was dedicated to maintaining the Protestant religion and the Protestant ascendancy, and from its origins in the 1790s had been firmly associated with Unionism.

Furthermore, because of its basis in local, district lodges, the Orange Order transcended conventional divisions of class. The Order acted as a link between the small farmers and the aristocratic landowners, between the mill workers and the linen owners, between the shipyard craftsmen and their foremen and bosses. All these groups came together in

regular parades and ceremonies to defend their religion and their privilege. This feature of the Order gave it a unique role in the political life of Northern Ireland. It proved essential to the structure of Unionism, by providing a bond between the bosses and landlords in the government and the Protestant working classes.

There were two principal issues on which the Orange Order acted as a pressure group: education and employment. The Order was always determined to safeguard the Protestantism of the educational system, and the Education Act of 1923 was drawn up by the Government in close liaison with prominent Orangemen. This, alongside the determination of the hierarchy in the Catholic Church that education should be the domain of religious organisations, meant that schooling in Northern Ireland became almost entirely segregated. Catholic boys and girls went to one set of schools, and Protestants to another. With some important exceptions in the larger cities, this system has survived until today.

In the area of employment, the Orange Order was determined to see that the best jobs – and when there were only few prospects of employment, the only jobs – went to Protestants. Repeatedly, Orange leaders appealed to employers to give jobs 'to good Protestant lads and lasses'. At times this same theme was taken up by leading Government members who were also Orangemen, and in the 1930s when jobs were very scarce and each vacancy was sought after by several men looking for work, it made for great tensions and repeated unrest (see pages 108-9).

All this added up to make the Orange Order a powerful force in the land. Membership of the Order amongst Protestants was vital for social cachet, and sometimes to ensure employment. Orange leaders and Government ministers enjoyed a mutually profitable relationship. The leaders were frequently taken into the confidence of ministers, and in return could use the Order, with its regular rallies and speeches, to support the Government. Government ministers were often anxious to settle sensitive questions before the round of parades and rallies in July, in order to avoid denunciations from Orange platforms throughout the six counties. The Order helped to maintain the divisiveness of the state, and to ensure the security of its government as long as it remained true to Orange principles.

But, of course, the Order was primarily a religious organisation in a land where religion and politics were indivisible. Much of the vigour of Orange activities came from a profound and deeply felt

Protestant spirit in the North. This helped to give the Order an almost sacred place in the hearts of Ulster Protestants. The marches and the rituals of the Order, culminating in the parades of 12 July, had a political potency, but were also laden with the fervour of religious fundamentalism. One tale indicates this quite vividly:

Witness the story of a stranger who asked an Orangemen, 'What is the twelfth anyway?' The Orangeman looked at him in horror and amazement: 'Ye never heard of the Twelfth?! Away home, man, and read yer Bible!'

The first PHOTOGRAPH illustrates the extraordinary Orange enthusiasm shown in working-class Belfast. The banners and bunting with their Loyalist and anti-Catholic slogans were erected at the end of Brown Street just off the Shankill Road for the 1951 Orange Day celebrations.

The second photograph shows Sir Basil Brooke, Viscount Brookeborough, addressing an Orange rally sometime in the 1960s. Brookeborough was a wealthy Co. Fermanagh land-owner and Prime Minister of Northern Ireland for twenty years, from 1943 to 1963.

publish. So far as we can establish, only *This Week* reported (twice), on national television, the political situation in the North in the years before 1968. While amongst the national newspapers, effective coverage of the situation, like the *Sunday Times* series of articles called 'John Bull's Other Island', was rare. In Westminster, apart from a handful of Labour MPs who were continually rebuffed, there was the same conspiracy of silence. This was the twentieth century, and in England it seemed unimaginable that religious divisions could lead to violence in Ireland again. It was also the 'sixties, a time in which it was thought that economic growth would alleviate the affliction of poverty, slums and social unrest. There was great optimism. Nothing was seen to be so serious as to defy solution.

Terence O'Neill, a Liberal Unionist who became Prime Minister of Northern Ireland in 1963, epitomised the optimism of the times. He offered the promise of gradual and sustained reform; the chance of transforming the province's ailing economy with new industries; the possibility of at least an economic *rapprochement* with the South. In this area, there did seem to be a positive identity of economic interests in the early 'sixties, between the declining economy of Northern Ireland and the under-developed economy of the Republic. Both economies desperately needed foreign investment to encourage growth, and O'Neill was driven, by the need for at least some sort of economic co-operation between Dublin and Belfast, into meeting the Prime Minister of the Republic, Sean Lemass. They first met in Belfast in January 1965, before O'Neill had gained approval from his Cabinet colleagues for such a meeting which, despite its economic good sense, profoundly shocked many of his supporters. Meetings between Cabinet ministers for trade and agriculture followed these initial exploratory talks between O'Neill and Lemass. But as O'Neill moved towards reform, he split the Unionist Party, while at the same time was unable to give the Catholics all that they expected. For, by the 'sixties, new forces were at work in Northern Ireland society which were to frustrate O'Neill's initiative.

When the Province was poor, local authorities had little to dispense. But within the Welfare State, they were the administrators of considerable largesse. With spending greater, their control was more important. Furthermore, welfare had raised Catholic expectations of what the state could and should provide. In demanding a fairer distribution of welfare, and the reform of the electoral system along English lines, the Civil Rights movement of the 'sixties challenged not only the Unionist power-base, but also its right of selective patronage and, it seemed to some, its very ability to maintain its political control over Northern Ireland.

O'Neill adopted a style of accommodation. He visited the Catholic schools and was photographed talking with nuns. He visited the Prime Minister of the Republic and was seen promoting relations with the South. In Unionists hearts, all this raised not only the dangers of embracing the Catholics, fears for the security of the border and the spectre of a united Ireland once again, fifty years after Padraig Pearse had led his rebels to martyrdom in 1916, but also it seemed to threaten the whole of the Protestant way of life – and this in a climate in which the separate existence of the Protestant Church was brought into

GERRYMANDERING

Gerrymandering was the process by which the Unionists held power by manipulating the electoral boundaries of localities where there was a Catholic majority in the population. It dates from 1924 and the Judicial Commission into electoral boundaries conducted by Sir John Leech.

The County Borough of Londonderry provided a clear example of this technique. Here, in 1967, over 60% of the adult population was Catholic, yet 60% of the seats on the Corporation were occupied by Unionists. The universal adult suffrage that applied in Parliamentary elections did not apply in local elections. Firstly, the restricted franchise, or the property qualification, reduced the number of Catholic voters to a greater extent than it did the Protestants – by 28% in the case of Catholics; 14.5% in the case of Protestants.

In each of Londonderry's three wards there was a straight vote to elect blocks of either Protestant Unionist or Catholic Nationalist councillors. The principle of the gerrymander was that electoral boundaries were drawn in such a way that Unionists were returned by fairly small majorities, whereas Nationalists were elected by huge majorities, thus wasting much of the Catholic vote.

In the North Ward, a Protestant majority of 1,416 (3,946 Protestant voters to 2,530 Catholics) elected 8 Unionist councillors. In the Waterside Ward, a Protestant majority of 1,845, (3,697 Protestants to 1,852 Catholics) elected 4 Unionists.

However, in the South Ward, which contained the Catholic ghetto of the Bogside and the solidly Catholic housing estate of the Creggan, there was a massive Catholic majority of 8,909 (10,047 Catholic votes to 1,138 Protestants) which resulted in the election of only 8 Nationalists.

Thus, despite the overall Catholic majoirty, the gerrymander produced 12 Unionist and only 8 Nationalist councillors in the City Corporation. These voting figures are taken from the report of the Cameron Commission, which was appointed in 1969 by the Government of Northern Ireland to investigate the causes of the 1968 and 1969 outbreaks of violence and civil disturbance. Its report criticised the argument used to justify the electoral system as rationalising 'a determination to achieve and maintain Unionist electoral control.' In the Cameron Report's conclusion, there was further condemnation of . . .

deliberate manipulation of local government electoral boundaries . . . in order to achieve and maintain Unionist control of local authorities and so to deny to Catholics influence in local government proportionate to their numbers.

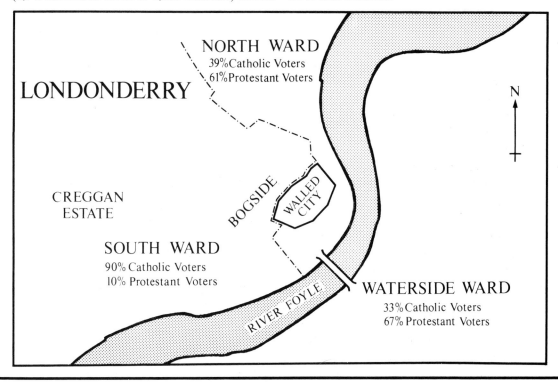

LONDONDERRY

NORTH WARD
39% Catholic Voters
61% Protestant Voters

N

CREGGAN
ESTATE

BOGSIDE

WALLED CITY

SOUTH WARD
90% Catholic Voters
10% Protestant Voters

RIVER FOYLE

WATERSIDE WARD
33% Catholic Voters
67% Protestant Voters

question by the world-wide movement called Ecumenism, the bringing together of the Christian Churches. Such fears produced eloquent expression in the powerful personality of Ian Paisley, who marshalled the hard-line Unionists behind the traditional slogans of 'No Surrender' and 'Not an Inch'.

Even economic reform itself became a source of division. O'Neill's programme for reviving the economy was attacked for favouring the Protestant East of the province as against the Catholic West. Economically, it could be argued that it was sensible to place all the new industries in a region where the economic infrastructure already existed to service these industries, but politically, this became deeply contentious. There were protests at the motorway plans and the siting of new factories in the East. Both Protestant and Catholic marched in protest at the decision to build Ulster's new university at Protestant Coleraine rather than Derry, the Province's second city.

When Civil Rights were frustrated, the movement turned to civil disobedience. This was seen as disloyalty to the state, and reminiscent of Nationalist behaviour in 1921. When Catholic Civil Rights marches were routed through Protestant areas, it was seen as a challenge, for to march through an area in Northern Ireland is to claim it. Militant Protestants resisted them with force and threats of force. When the mainly Catholic students of Belfast, products of an educational system that had allowed substantial numbers of working-class Catholics into higher education, went on protest marches in the North, they were met with the clubs and stones of Protestant vigilantes. The inspiration for the students was the Civil Rights movement amongst the blacks of the American South and the student 'revolution' in France. Conservative and anxious Protestants saw this as a threat of not only Republicanism but also Communism. As the campaign escalated through 1968, the police lost control, and their violence was displayed before the world on television. And into a worsening situation was unleashed another new phenomenon in the province – a young militant proletariat. Sullen and neglected, these were the children of the ever-growing unskilled Catholic working class that had been excluded from political life and the social rewards of work. Unlike their parents, they were uncowed, and the student protest raised in their consciousness the idea that something could and must be done. As confrontations grew increasingly violent, these were the men and boys who would first throw stones, then petrol bombs, and finally, as the Catholic community in Belfast was threatened by a pogrom and the province stood on the verge of civil war, take to the gun. As British troops moved in to the province to prevent that civil war, Northern Ireland was back in the headlines.

A state is a set of institutions, in which the debate about the kind of society wanted, and how that society might be achieved, is conducted. In Northern Ireland, society was so divided that the state became fragile and beleaguered, or at least felt itself to be, and its main business became its own preservation. It could not allow full political discussion of the Province's very considerable problems, since it feared that such discussion might undermine the legitimacy of the state itself. So fundamental problems were obscured, remained unsolved, and finally erupted in violence. Yet such a discussion and its resolution was, and is in the end, its only hope of survival.

THE MEDIA
AND NORTHERN IRELAND

Just as the 'Westminster Rule' in politics meant that the affairs of Northern Ireland were not discussed at the Westminster Parliament, so in the affairs of broadcasting, the reporting of events in Northern Ireland was left to the local broadcasting institutions, the BBC, and, from 1959, Ulster Television (UTV), the local ITV station. In a society divided as deeply as Northern Ireland, even down to the question of whether or not the State had a right to exist, the task of the broadcasters was a difficult one. Should the broadcasting institutions attempt to reflect the divisions of the community, or should they try to reconcile the two communities, to create a consensus? These were delicate subjects that aroused much passion. From the early days of BBC Radio in the 1920s, even the playing of the National Anthem became a political act, and so a bone of contention.

The media institutions decided that they must try to create consensus in the community. Up to 1948 the BBC would not allow mention of partition, as this would suggest disunity. The duty of television, both BBC and ITV, as far as the Government and the broadcasters themselves saw it, was to emphasise the common ground between the communities and to ignore or to downplay the areas of differences. The issue of discrimination, for instance, was almost never discussed in the media. When the Cameron Report was published in 1969, analysing the process of discrimination and gerrymandering by which the Unionist Party had maintained its control over the politics of the community, it seems that many people in Northern Ireland heard for the first time the facts about the situation in the community. The broadcasters had ignored even such a fundamental issue as this. The Annan Report into the future of broadcasting, in the late 1970s, looked back over the way the broadcasting institutions had reported current affairs in Northern Ireland. It reported:

The BBC said that before 1965 they had tried in their reports on Northern Ireland to maintain a consensus and build up the middle ground, but when that policy failed they abandoned it . . . In our view the BBC operated a mistaken policy in their coverage of events in Northern Ireland up until the middle of the 1960s by ignoring both the problems of civil rights and some unsuccessful IRA action in the early 'sixties. Broadcasters cannot be impartial about illicit organisations. Nevertheless these organisations are a political force in Northern Ireland and it would be unrealistic of the broadcasters not to take account of them.

In the rest of the United Kingdom, ignorance about the affairs of Northern Ireland was further compounded by the silence of the media. Broadcasters were encouraged to leave the reporting of Northern Ireland to the locals, who, it was said, knew the region and its particular difficulties best of all. Whenever a reporter or a film-maker did go to Northern Ireland, he or she was encouraged to promote those aspects of life which, again, suggested reconciliation. This hostility to investigative journalism meant that most reporters were loath to go to Northern Ireland to report on affairs and bring controversy down on themselves.

When the situation became more tense in the middle 'sixties, the broadcasters faced new problems. Under the various Television Acts for Independent Television, and the Charter for the BBC, the companies were obliged not to transmit anything that would be an incitement to violence. It was generally agreed by broadcasters and politicians alike that some of the speeches of, for instance, Ian Paisley, would have provoked violence in the community. This further encouraged the media to keep silent, but ITV found a way out of the difficulty by occasionally allowing current affairs reports, for instance some Rediffusion *This Week* programmes about Northern Ireland, to be shown in Britain but not to be screened in Ulster.

This silence meant that when the problems of Northern Ireland did finally burst on to the television screens of Britain, with the violence at the Civil Rights marches in late 1968, it came as a bombshell to many – a sudden reminder that the long-forgotten problems of Northern Ireland had not been solved.

4: REBELLION

The Unionists had been frozen in power for forty years, but the sixties brought stirrings outside Unionism which inexorably forced the establishment to yield. As successive Unionist Prime Ministers searched for an accommodation with the Catholics, they alienated their power-base in the Unionist Party. Each attempt to placate the minority failed because Catholic demands outpaced the rate of concessions made to them and Loyalists were outraged by the treachery of their leaders. As the middle ground of politics collapsed, passive opposition turned into strident agitation, causing Unionists to use the machinery of state to quell it. When that failed, confrontation between the two communities intensified. On to the streets came people who would seek to dismember the state by force of arms; the advent of the Provisional IRA was the outcome of half a century of discriminatory and sectarian rule.

In March 1963, after 20 years as Prime Minister, the 75-year-old Viscount Brookeborough handed over the leadership of the Unionist Party and of Northern Ireland to Captain Terence O'Neill. To many, it looked as though the old style of Unionism was giving way to the new, and that a more enterprising and liberal phase in Northern Ireland's history was beginning.

Educated at Eton and in the Irish Guards, O'Neill was a member of the ruling class with a pedigree stretching back to the Plantation. He was aloof and paternal, and he kept faith with the Orange Order by joining its elite fraternity, the Royal Black Preceptory, and the Apprentice Boys of Londonderry. Nevertheless, he was more liberal than his predecessors. His recent experience as Minister of Finance under Brookeborough from 1956 to 1963 had clearly revealed to him Northern Ireland's financial dependence on Westminster.

Northern Ireland's economic base required re-shaping, and there was an urgent need for more jobs. Sixties Britain enjoyed a new spirit of confidence, and great faith in modernisation. Wilson's Labour government brought an emphasis on new technology, along with increased development grants for the deprived regions of the UK. All this had its effect on Northern Ireland, where new factories opened, and for the first time economic links were developed with the Dublin government. But this change made the Unionists anxious, for it seemed to them that their traditional power-base of working-class Protestant support was being eroded from under them.

It was in this context that Ian Paisley became a major force in Northern Ireland politics. The son of a Baptist pastor who had served in Carson's Ulster Volunteer Force, Paisley was a fundamentalist Gospel campaigner who emerged as a powerful street orator in the tradition of the nineteenth-century Bible-thumpers, Roaring Hanna and Henry Cooke. 'I have hated God's enemies with a perfect hate,' he proclaimed, and he opposed theological liberals who would betray Protestants to 'the forces of popery and the scarlet whore drunk on the blood of churches'. At a time when the Christian Churches were coming together by seeking common ground, Paisley represented the implacable opposition of the Ulster Protestants to ecumenism. But he also symbolised hard-core Ulster Loyalism, and over the next few years he was to challenge the Unionist Party leadership every time he saw it straying from the path of traditional Unionism. He was able to focus the anxiety of those Loyalists who felt that current shifts in religious attitudes were combining with the new economic trends to loosen the hold of traditional Unionism. Paisley appointed himself the conscience of the Loyalist people and embarked on a series of protests in which he expressed his loathing for the Roman Church. He declared, 'I would be proud to do time for Protestant liberty.'

In the early sixties, Paisley played a leading role in a group known as Ulster Protestant Action, which was organised 'to keep Protestant and loyal workers in employment in times of depression in preference to their Catholic fellow workers.' In the General Election campaign of 1964, Paisley once again appeared as the voice of militant Loyalism when he demanded the removal of the tricolour flag from the window of the offices of the Republican Party, Sinn Fein, in Divis Street in West Belfast. The RUC acceded to Paisley's demands and twice broke in to tear down the flag. This ignited the worst riots in the Falls Road since 1935 (see page 135).

O'Neill's appeasing style of Unionism alienated many of his supporters. The traditional Unionist attitude of 'No Surrender' was never far below the surface of Unionist politics. Unionists felt that because so many Catholics opposed the existence of the Northern Ireland state and would be only too willing to take up arms to destroy it, they were all fundamentally untrustworthy. They genuinely felt that to give an inch to the Catholics would encourage them to take a mile. Hence, O'Neill's flirtations with Romanism, like his trips to Dublin and his visits to Catholic schools and hospitals, made him increasingly suspect in the eyes of many Unionists. He seemed to be courting the very forces that were determined to undermine the state; he was giving encouragement to the disloyal.

Nineteen sixty-six became a pivotal year in the tension that was beginning to permeate Northern Ireland (see page 136). It was the year of the fiftieth anniversary of the Dublin Easter Rising, and to Nationalists the planned commemoration parades rekindled the glories of the blood-sacrifice of 1916. The Catholics took pride in recalling 1916, but in reviving the ideal of a united Ireland they were acutely aware of their inferior status in Northern Ireland. In Loyalist minds, 1916 re-awakened the ghost of the IRA. Although it was currently dormant, the IRA had waged three campaigns since the State was formed and it was feared that at any time it could re-emerge.

Sensitive to any nuance of Republicanism, hard-line Loyalists, led by Paisley, called for a prohibition on all 1916 commemoration parades. The Government responded by banning all trains from the South for the period of the anniversary celebrations, and mobilised the B-Specials. To show their disapproval of ecumenism, Paisley and his followers marched to protest at the 'Romeward' trend of the Presbyterian Church, and when they clashed with Catholics, rioting followed. Some extreme Loyalists expressed their apprehensions in a more direct way, by forming a group which took its name from Carson's famous paramilitary force, the Ulster Volunteer Force. Its members sensed the mounting expectations of the minority. They were determined both to prevent change and to discourage the minority from seeking to achieve a united Ireland through its traditional physical force movement, the IRA. The UVF hunt for IRA leaders in Belfast in the summer of 1966 led to a series of ugly sectarian murders, on the eve of the Queen's visit to commemorate the Ulster sacrifice at the Battle of the Somme. The Government replied with strong condemnation of this Loyalist backlash. Although Paisley's UPA had close links with the UVF, he firmly denounced any association with the acts of violence.

These events were causing the people of Northern Ireland to examine their heritage. The commemorations; the new Unionist liberalism and Paisley's resolute opposition to it; rumours about the impending emergence of the IRA; the revival of the UVF; all these factors were leading Northern Ireland to confront its history.

The expectations of the Catholic minority had risen. The welfare improvements and the advances in education following the Second World War had left their mark. A much larger Catholic middle class had emerged by the mid-sixties which, according to the Cameron Commission of 1969, was 'less ready to acquiesce in the acceptance . . . of assumed (or established) inferiority and discrimination.' There were more Catholics going through higher education: by the early sixties one student in five at Queen's University in Belfast was Catholic. But despite the expansion in the numbers of Catholics in the professional classes, Catholic students found themselves graduating into a community which still treated them as second-class citizens. At the other end of the social spectrum, the number of Catholic unskilled workers had actually increased since the establishment of the State, despite all the advances of the twentieth century. In 1911, one Catholic in five was classed 'unskilled'; in 1971, the proportion had risen to one in four. The prospects for the mass of unskilled Catholic workers were grim. They faced discrimination in housing and in the search for jobs. Discrimination bred disaffection, and despite the liberalising zeal of O'Neill's Government, none of these root causes of Catholic grievance were tackled.

Cautiously, the minority began to make demands for their civil rights. In January 1964, a group of middle-class and professional Catholics established the Campaign for Social Justice and, backed by Nationalists and the Northern Ireland Labour Party, they conceived a programme for civil rights reforms. In 1966, O'Neill's Government agreed to the abolition of the business vote for local elections, but rejected all other points in the civil rights programme.

In February 1967, some members of the Campaign for Social Justice and the Republican Clubs, together with students and workers, formed the Northern Ireland Civil Rights Association (NICRA). Their aim was to force

In the 1964 General Election campaign the keenest and bitterest fight in Northern Ireland was over the marginal constituency of West Belfast. Here it looked as though the Unionist Party candidate, James Kilfedder, might be defeated. There were three other candidates, from the Northern Ireland Labour Party, Republican Labour and Sinn Fein. With a split Protestant vote, the Unionist Party might well lose to the Labour Party. A rallying call for the Protestants to unite was urgently needed.

At the Sinn Fein Election Headquarters in Divis Street at the city end of the Falls Road, a Republican tricolour was put on display in the window. Under the Flags and Emblems Act of 1954 the flying of a tricolour was an illegal act, but the police had given up interfering with Tricolours in hard-core Catholic districts. But on Sunday 27 September, Ian Paisley said that the flying of the flag was an insult to all Loyalists, and demanded that either the police remove it, or he would lead a procession to Divis Street and remove the flag himself. On the Monday, a group of RUC men visited the Sinn Fein Office and took away the Tricolour. The Minister of Home Affairs asked Paisley to call off his procession, but Paisley insisted on his right to hold a rally at the City Hall. He said to the *Belfast Telegraph*:

In defence of the elementary right of free speech and free assembly our Protestant rally must go on. No Surrender.

On the evening of Tuesday the 29th, at the same time as Paisley was holding his rally at City Hall, a group of between one and two thousand Republicans met outside the Sinn Fein Divis Street office and blocked the street singing Irish songs. They insisted that the Republican Tricolour should be replaced.

On the following day, Wednesday 30 September, the Tricolour was flown again, and the RUC was sent in. But this time a huge crowd gathered and shouted at the police, refusing to disperse once the incident was over.

On Thursday 1 October the tricolour was replaced again. By now tensions had risen to the extent that when the RUC, spurred on by Paisley's demands, went in to remove it, the Falls Road erupted into violence. Rioting continued for nearly twenty-four hours. The RUC brought in armoured cars and baton-charged the crowd. The crowd responded by producing petrol bombs which were thrown back at the police. A bus and an RUC wagon were burnt out. By the Friday evening the police had crushed the resistance; 21 policemen and 50 civilians were in hospital. Over 50 Catholics were arrested. The Prime Minister, Captain Terence O'Neill, blamed the IRA for using a General Election to provoke disorder in Northern Ireland. The *Belfast Telegraph* noted it was 'the worst outbreak of disorder in Belfast for thirty years.'

The appeal for Protestant unity was entirely successful. Ten days after the rioting, the electors of West Belfast went to the polls and returned James Kilfedder, the Unionist candidate, to Westminster. Although the Unionist Party share of the vote decreased, only 24% of the electorate voted for the Northern Ireland Labour candidate and a tiny 6% voted for Sinn Fein. So, with the opposition vote split, the Unionist Party easily secured a victory. However, in the next General Election campaign, fought in 1966, the Unionist Party lost its traditional control over West Belfast when Gerry Fitt was elected as Independent Irish Labour MP for the constituency.

The PHOTOGRAPH shows the tricolour displayed in the Sinn Fein office in Divis Street.

The year 1966 marked the fiftieth anniversary of the two 'blood sacrifices' of 1916, the Easter Rising in Dublin and the Ulster losses on the first day of the Battle of the Somme. With the temperature rising in Belfast it looked as though the year would be a violent one.

Ian Paisley was playing a leading part in the escalation of tension. Throughout 1965 he had built up a considerable following by denouncing O'Neill's liberalism, and in February 1966 founded his virulently anti-Catholic and anti-left-wing newspaper the *Protestant Telegraph*. In April he formed the Ulster Constitution Defence Committee to co-ordinate the popular Loyalist backlash against liberalisation. April also saw celebrations throughout Ireland of the Easter Rising. Paisley called for the Government to ban all Republican parades in Northern Ireland. Once again, by acting as the voice of militant Unionism he was forcing the Government into a difficult position. Either they had to confront a large body of their own supporters – by ignoring Paisley – or give in to him and perhaps provoke violence from the Catholic minority. The demands came at a sensitive time in the North, so the Government partly gave in to them, allowing

Republican commemoration marches to go ahead, but banning all trains from the South for the period of the celebrations, and mobilising the B-Specials. A Republican parade passed off quietly in Belfast. On the same day, Paisley held a Loyalist counter-demonstration in the city.

A few weeks later the General Assembly of the Presbyterian Church met in Belfast, and elders from congregations of all Presbyterian churches assembled to discuss policy. The Christian churches throughout the world were coming together to seek common ground, but many Ulster Protestants were fearful of this ecumenical movement, as it seemed to them to hint of compromise with Rome. Paisley and his supporters were, therefore, very opposed to the Presbyterian Church agreeing to unite with other Protestant churches in a dialogue with Roman Catholicism. On 6 June, Paisley led a protest march to the General Assembly. Paisley and his supporters carried banners proclaiming 'No Unity' protesting against 'the Romanising tendencies of the Presbyterian Church.' At Cromac Square they met a group of Catholic counter-marchers. A short riot ensued in which, according to the *Belfast Newsletter*, RUC 'riot squads charged a mob which formed a human

barricade at Cromac Square to prevent Paisley's protest to the Presbyterian General Assembly getting through.' The Government was deeply embarrassed by the violence. The Home Affairs Minister apologised to the General Assembly, and in a speech at Stormont, O'Neill lashed out at what he called the 'Nazi gangsterism' of Paisley and his supporters. 'We must take a stand now,' he declared. Paisley was arrested, and later sent to jail for three months.

A group of Paisley's more militant supporters had formed the Ulster Volunteer Force, named after the original UVF of 1912–14, and wrote to the local papers saying that they would 'declare war against the IRA and its splinter groups.' They declared that 'known IRA men will be executed mercilessly and without hesitation.' The UVF embarked on a fruitless search for leading IRA man, Leo Martin. A series of attacks led to the deaths of Matilda Gould, an elderly Protestant woman who died of burns received during a petrol bomb attack on a Catholic pub next door, and John Scullion, a Catholic who was shot whilst walking down Clonard Street off the Falls Road. On 26 June, three Catholic barmen, mistakenly identified as IRA leaders, were shot as they left a pub in Malvern Street near the Shankill Road. One of them died later. The Government declared the UVF illegal under the Special Powers Act, and three UVF men were convicted of murder and imprisoned for life. One of them, Gusty Spence, the leader of the UVF, later became revered by extreme Loyalists as a folk-hero – a prophet who had anticipated the Catholic threat and had the vision to do something about it. It emerged that Paisley's UPA had close links with the UVF, although Paisley himself denied all knowledge of them and disclaimed responsibility for the violence.

Only a week after the Malvern Street shootings, the Queen and the Duke of Edinburgh arrived in Belfast to commemorate the Ulster losses at the Battle of the Somme. During their two-day visit, a concrete block was thrown at the Queen's car denting the bonnet. The incident caused further embarrassment to the Government.

Tension was high at the Orange parades on 12 July of that year. For the Orangemen, it was time to reassert their ascendancy after the trials of the recent few months. The marches all passed off peacefully, but the movement against O'Neill's liberal policies continued to gather momentum. Resolutions were passed against the 'Romeward trend' of the Protestant Churches, and government ministers taking part in the parades were heckled by Paisleyites.

O'Neill and his Cabinet colleagues became increasingly worried about the image of Northern Ireland abroad. It looked as though the ugly sectarian legacies of the past were being revived in the narrow backstreets of Belfast.

The PHOTOGRAPHS show the Belfast Easter Parade entering Milltown Cemetery, Falls Road, on 12 April 1966, and Belfast Orangemen marching, 12 July 1966.

the Unionists to remove some of the injustices, and to extend to Northern Ireland the civil rights enjoyed by the rest of Britain. The demands were: (1) One man, one vote. (2) The removal of gerrymandered boundaries. (3) Laws against discrimination by local government, and the provision of machinery to deal with complaints. (4) Allocation of council housing on a points system. (5) Repeal of the Special Powers Act. (6) Disbanding of the B-Specials.

These apparently simple requests were totally unacceptable to the Unionist Party. If O'Neill had been able to attack the core of the discrimination which caused the minority to make these demands, he might have succeeded in prolonging the Unionist leadership. But he did not, and his failure, under pressure from the right wing of his party, was to set Northern Ireland on a course heading for disintegration.

The advent of NICRA and its demands alarmed the Unionists, especially as it was non-sectarian and included Socialists, Nationalists and Republicans. They tried to counter the movement by representing it as a Catholic attempt to undermine the existence of the State, and so they invoked Orange opposition. That opposition became tangible when the Minister of Home Affairs, William Craig, banned Republican Clubs in March 1967, provoking two student marches from Queen's University.

To people in Northern Ireland, marching has an almost tribal significance. Since the plantations of the seventeenth century, the occupation and control of territory by one side or the other have been fundamental to the sectarian divisions that have existed. People have been imbued with a sense of territory quite unlike that found elsewhere in Britain, where religious affiliations play no part in determining where people live or where they walk. The traditional Orange marches have always been ritualistic assertions of the Protestant ascendancy. By parading through the towns and villages of Northern Ireland, the Protestants demonstrate that to march through an area is to establish a claim over it, a reminder to the Catholics of the latter's subordinate status.

No one understood this better than Paisley, and when the students marched from the University, he gathered his followers in Shaftesbury Square for a meeting. In this way, they interposed themselves between the students and their goal, Belfast City Hall, and successfully thwarted the march. This use of obstruction was a technique which Paisley was to employ repeatedly whenever Catholics marched outside their enclaves. A fact of life in Northern Ireland was that Loyalists could march or assemble anywhere they pleased, and by blocking the path of a student or Civil Rights march they forced the police into re-routing the march, thus once again asserting the Unionist ascendancy in the State.

Nevertheless, the campaign proceeded. In early 1968, the Derry Housing Action Committee was formed, to encourage squatting and the disruption of traffic and Corporation meetings in the City. The Unionist-controlled local authorities of Northern Ireland allocated council housing along sectarian lines (see page 125). For instance, in the rural district of Dungannon, Co. Tyrone, Catholics felt excluded from the new housing that was being built. A small protest organised by the Campaign for Social Justice in 1963 had gone almost unnoticed, but in October 1967 at Caledon, near Dungannon, Civil

138

Rights organisers encouraged homeless Catholic families to squat in newly-built council houses. In June 1968, the local authority evicted these families and allocated one of the houses to a 19-year-old single Protestant girl who happened to be the secretary of a Unionist Parliamentary candidate. Austin Currie, a Nationalist MP at Stormont, occupied the house to publicise this overt act of discrimination. Currie was evicted on 20 June, but scored a considerable victory in drawing attention to the discrimination in housing policies.

A march was called by the Campaign for Social Justice to protest against the housing policies of Dungannon Council, and hesitantly backed by the Civil Rights Association. On 24 August, about 2,500 Civil Rights supporters marched from Coalisland to Dungannon, and although there was threat of a Loyalist counter-demonstration, the march passed off quietly. The success of the demonstration caused many who had previously been uninvolved with political activity to see marching and demonstrating behind Civil Rights banners as a peaceful way of registering their frustrations and complaints against discrimination.

After the success of the Dungannon march, the various community groups asked the Civil Rights Association to hold a march in Derry, the city that not only held a pride of place in Protestant mythology, but also epitomised Catholic grievance through the gerrymandering that produced a Unionist Council despite a Catholic majority. Although the march was banned, it went ahead anyway on 5 October 1968, and resulted in violent scenes when the police baton-charged the demonstrators (see page 142). The march proved to be a landmark. Not only was it the most violent confrontation yet between the state and the Civil Rights supporters, but also it took place in full view of the television cameras, and the publicity which resulted exposed Northern Ireland's iniquities to a wider gaze. Although the Westminster Government was concerned, it took no action to investigate or intervene in the Province.

On the day following the Derry march, 800 students decided on a march to Belfast City Hall. On the traditional pattern of obstruction, Paisley summoned a counter-demonstration and the RUC halted the students, provoking a three-hour sit-down. Students were outraged that small numbers of Loyalists could so easily frustrate their efforts, and more militant action was called for. This helped to polarise attitudes. As hesitant moderates backed away, the radical element formed People's Democracy. This socialist group was to become the dynamic force behind the demands for civil rights reforms. In an effort to alleviate future clashes with extreme Loyalists, one of the People's Democracy representatives, Bernadette Devlin, went to see Paisley. Although he conceded that there might be injustices, he said, 'I would rather be British than fair.'

Also, in the wake of the police violence of 5 October, the non-violent Derry Citizens' Action Committee was formed. It decided to mount a series of protests against the partisan RUC and Derry Corporation. In November, Craig banned all processions within Derry's walls, but this did not deter a march from taking place on 16 November. Fifteen thousand people brushed aside police barriers to breach the City's walls, and then held a sit-down protest in the Diamond, in the heart of the walled city.

By November 1968, the Government was becoming alarmed. Prime Minister Wilson and Home Secretary Callaghan summoned O'Neill for talks in London, before telling the Commons that unless reforms came quickly, the British Government would need to consider 'a very fundamental reappraisal' of its relations with Northern Ireland. O'Neill was forced into offering a package of reforms to placate the minority, which he announced on 22 November. Local councils would in future allocate council houses on the basis of need, calculated on a points system; an ombudsman would be appointed to investigate grievances; local government would be reformed by the end of 1971; parts of the Special Powers Act would be withdrawn when the Government 'considered this could be done without undue hazard'; and the Londonderry Borough Council would be replaced by a development commission. Although this looked like sweeping reform, much of the package was imprecise and would take years to implement. Only the appointment of a development commission in Derry was expedited with speed. It was too little for the Catholics, but it was more than enough to frighten the Loyalists. To them it seemed a victory for the Catholic minority. It suggested that the pillars of the Protestant ascendancy were no longer secure, that they could be pulled down under pressure from the Catholics and the Westminster Government.

Paisley and the Ulster Protestant Volunteers stepped up their obstructionist tactics wherever People's Democracy and Civil Rights activists marched or met. At the end of November a legal civil rights march in Armagh was stopped by the RUC after an illegal counter-demonstration by Paisleyites. Much Catholic support for O'Neill's reforms was lost by this sectarian policing. The right flank of the Unionists thought that appeasement had gone far enough. They increased the pressure on him, but O'Neill repulsed the challenge by sacking Craig in December, thus provoking more hostility from the Right. By the end of 1968, the Stormont regime was in the throes of a leadership crisis, exacerbated by the continuing demands of the Catholics and the call from the Loyalists to bring the dissidents to heel.

Although the Civil Rights and People's Democracy campaigns had been coloured by the radical events of 1968, their leaders were inspired by the struggle for civil rights in the southern states of the USA, for many Catholics saw parallels between themselves and the Blacks of the USA. They took as a blueprint the 1966 Alabama Civil Rights march, and decided to adapt it to Northern Ireland by beginning the new year with a long march from Belfast to Derry. The activists were by no means unanimous. The Civil Rights Association and the Derry Citizens' Action Committee were against the march, feeling that it would be provocative coming so soon after O'Neill's reforms. To march across Northern Ireland through Protestant territory would be a test of the Government's intentions; either the march would be protected from the reaction of the extreme Right, or it would be exposed to the fury of Orange militancy. The march was blocked by Paisleyites and re-routed by the RUC at various stages, to prevent it moving through Loyalist villages and towns. There was constant physical harassment from

Nineteen sixty-eight was the year of protest and near revolution. In the United States, the Vietnam War was tearing American society apart as it dragged on into a new agonising phase, with the Tet Offensive and an increase in the bombing of the North. Rioting accompanied the Democratic Party Convention in Chicago, and in Washington, hundreds of thousands joined the peace marches to the Pentagon. In Paris, during May, workers and students took control of their factories and universities and nearly succeeded in uniting to bring down the Fifth Republic of De Gaulle. In England, the public was horrified to see scenes of violence when boisterous anti-war demonstrations took place outside the American Embassy in Grosvenor Square. Disenchanted youthful protest reverberated around Europe, and the USA and university campuses echoed to the chants of 'Ho-Ho-Ho-Chi-Minh' or 'Hey-Hey-L-B-J, How many kids have you killed to-day?'. The mood of the year was best represented in the universal protest song 'We Shall Overcome'.

It is hardly surprising that this atmosphere of protest and unrest should have affected Northern Ireland, for no community exists in a vacuum. The influence of revolutionary events elsewhere in the world was seen in Ireland in the 1640s, the 1790s, in 1848, in 1867 and now, once again, in the late 1960s. As world events grew more tumultuous, protest in Northern Ireland was nearing a climax.

The PHOTOGRAPHS show an anti-war demonstration in Grosvenor Square in July, and a clash between students and police in Paris in May.

DERRY, 5 OCTOBER 1968

The Northern Ireland Civil Rights movement had been gaining ground throughout the mid-1960s. When a march from Coalisland to Dungannon in August 1968 passed off without violence, it convinced many that marching behind Civil Rights banners was a good way of peacefully demonstrating their opposition to the Unionist regime.

Derry was an obvious focus for Civil Rights protests. It was the most graphic example of a gerrymandered city council in Northern Ireland (see page 129).

Notice was given to the authorities that a Civil Rights march was to take place on Saturday 5 October and would pass from the Waterside to the Diamond, at the centre of the walled city. The Unionists were furious at this. No Catholic march had been allowed into the sacrosanct territory of the Diamond for nearly twenty years. The Apprentice Boys of Londonderry duly gave notice of an 'Annual Initiation' parade to take place over the same route on the same day, although no such 'annual' event was known in Derry. This was the excuse that the Home Affairs Minister, William Craig, wanted. On the certainty that violence would break out between the two marches, he banned them both. The local Derry action groups announced that the Civil Rights march would go ahead despite the ban and over two thousand marchers met on the day.

Craig had brought up large RUC reinforcements for the day and had given them orders that they were not to allow the marchers to cross the river into the walled city. Accordingly, when the marchers assembled in Duke Street in the Waterside, they found their way blocked by a line of police. On the Craigavon Bridge the police had brought up two watercannon. After a brief meeting, the marchers turned to withdraw but found a line of police behind them, blocking their retreat. It was at this moment that, as the film of the march shows, the RUC baton-charged the demonstrators and Gerry Fitt, Nationalist MP at Westminster, and Eddie McAteer, the leader of the Nationalist Party at Stormont, were both hit across the head. The RUC District Inspector in charge of the march, according to the Cameron Commission 'used his blackthorn [stick] with needless violence'. When the march was finally dispersed, small scale rioting erupted at the Diamond and resulted in groups of stone-throwing youths being forced down into the Bogside by the police. Altogether 77 civilians were treated for wounds, mostly for bruises and lacerations of their heads, and 11 police were injured.

The march and the police attack upon it had all taken place in full view of the television cameras. Horrified viewers in Britain and Ireland saw on their television screens policemen brutally laying in to a demonstration that was calling for 'One Man, One Vote'. That such a thing could happen in the United Kingdom was a profound shock to many, including the Home Secretary, James Callaghan, who later wrote that 'pictures of the extraordinary scenes of violence and fighting were flashed around the world. Ulster had arrived in the headlines.' Certainly, it was the best publicity that the Civil Rights movement could have hoped for.

The 1960s had seen great leaps forward in film technology. The most significant advance had been the replacement of heavy, cumbersome 35mm film cameras with light-weight portable 16mm cameras and sound-recording equipment. This gave an entirely new 'feel' to the television news film as against, for instance, the cinema newsreels. Cameramen could actually be a part of events, they could walk in marches, mingle with crowds, run with demonstrators. Matching this was the ability to process quickly and transmit the newsfilm. In the late 1960s, Vietnam was called the first war to be fought out on television, with scenes of the war being watched in living rooms throughout America every evening. Events in Northern Ireland over the next few years were to unfold in front of the television cameras of the world. In Britain, this saturation with almost daily scenes of horror and violence must in large part be responsible for the considerable revulsion that is felt for the 'impossible' problem of Northern Ireland.

The PHOTOGRAPHS on the opposite page are still frames from film taken during the course of the Civil Rights march in Derry on 5 October. They are some of the images that flashed around the world and brought Northern Ireland back into the headlines again. The top four frames were taken by a cameraman working for Irish Television (RTE) and the bottom two frames were taken by a cameraman working for the Northern Ireland ITV Company, Ulster Television (UTV). Frame 1 shows Gerry Fitt, Westminster MP, and Eddie McAteer, Stormont MP, marching under a Civil Rights banner. Frame 2 shows the police lunging at the marchers. Frame 3 shows the RUC District Inspector using his blackthorn stick on a fallen marcher. Frame 4 shows a man hit by the police after appealing for reason. Frame 5 shows the police watercannon being used on Craigavon Bridge — firing, in fact, at members of the public who were not taking part in the march. The last frame shows Gerry Fitt with a blood-stained shirt, after having been hit by the police.

1

2

3

4

5

6

the Paisleyites and off-duty B-Specials.

The march reached its climax on the morning of the fourth day, on the road between Claudy and Derry. Here, the marchers were escorted to Burntollet Bridge by the RUC. It was a trap, for the Loyalists were waiting on the hillside above the bridge. The marchers were ambushed, they were stoned, clubbed and driven into the River Faughan. Many of the two hundred attackers were off-duty B-Specials, and even the RUC joined in. The Cameron Report called this 'a disgraceful episode'. The battered survivors were attacked twice more before they reached Derry to a rapturous welcome from the Catholics.

That night, the RUC visited its wrath on Catholic Derry. As the Cameron Commission found: 'a number of policemen were guilty of misconduct which involved assault and battery, malicious damage to property in streets in the predominantly Catholic Bogside . . . and the use of provocative sectarian and political slogans.' Even the moderates who had opposed the march now rallied in defence of the Bogside. Barricades were built, the RUC was kept out of the area for a week, and 'Free Derry' was born. Many of the inhabitants no longer had any faith in Stormont and decided that in future they would have to defend themselves.

O'Neill desperately tried to prevent the middle ground from collapsing, but he had to appease his Unionist supporters and so further alienated the Catholics. Any support which he might have won from moderate Catholics for his liberal policies was lost when he accused the marchers of provoking the violence which had accompanied their journey. He said: 'Enough is enough. We have heard sufficient for now about Civil Rights; let us hear a little about civil responsibility.' The Cameron Report commented that 'For the moderates this march had disastrous effects' and said it polarized the communities through which it marched. For many of the marchers, Burntollet was the turning point. There was to be no going back. The influence of the militant Left flourished. Protest had been pushed beyond the demands for Civil Rights reforms into socialism with People's Democracy. Violence had been used on the marchers, and now within a week of Burntollet, the marchers themselves replied in kind.

Eighty per cent of the population of Newry was Catholic, and a march was planned in the town for 11 January. Robert Porter, William Craig's replacement as Minister for Home Affairs, outlawed a section of the route, and the marchers' patience evaporated. Three police tenders, separating the marchers from the RUC, were burned, and there was some disorder. Violence was answered with violence, and the Unionists claimed that Republicans had infiltrated the Civil Rights Movement and were using it as a front to destroy the State.

The Right was indignant when Paisley and Bunting were jailed for organising the illegal demonstration that had taken place in the previous November. Hardliners in the Unionist Party were convinced that too much had been conceded, and there were those who felt that the architect of limited liberalism, O'Neill, must go. Brian Faulkner, Minister of Commerce, resigned in protest at the lack of 'strong government'.

In March and April, there was a series of bomb outrages which caused millions of pounds worth of damage to electricity supply lines and water-works. British soldiers were brought in to protect vital installations. The explosions were assumed to be the work of the IRA, for they echoed the style of the border campaign of the 1950s and the bombings were thought to be the logical outcome of Republican infiltration into Civil Rights. But it later emerged that they were the work of the illegal extreme Loyalist group, the UVF. In December 1969, Samuel Stevenson of the UVF (a former B-Special) was convicted of causing the explosions. He admitted that his object had been to bring down O'Neill and advance Paisley's cause. Within a month of the explosions, another group of extreme Loyalists, led by John McKeague, formed the Shankill Defence Association, with the aim of safeguarding Protestant interests in that area of the city.

The deepening divisions were reflected in the mid-Ulster by-election of April 1969, when over 90% of the electorate turned out and 21-year-old Bernadette Devlin, the militant People's Democracy activist, abhorred by the Loyalists, was elected to Westminster. The bitterness being generated in Northern Ireland came to the surface in Derry. On 19 April, rioting broke out in the town. The RUC occupied the Bogside and beat up several Catholics, one of whom, Sam Devenny, later died. Rioters used petrol bombs, and the Bogside remained in uproar until the RUC was withdrawn.

O'Neill's liberal tendencies now brought him into direct conflict with the Unionist Party power-base. A series of meetings was held at the Party headquarters in Glengall Street. Ministers were consulted as to their loyalties. On 28 April, O'Neill pre-empted the moves that were afoot and resigned. His passing was regretted neither by the Loyalists, whose supremacy had been undermined by his actions, nor by the minority whose hopes had been so falsely raised. The following words, reported in the *Belfast Telegraph*, were spoken on radio by O'Neill after his resignation:

The basic fear of the Protestants in Northern Ireland is that they will be outbred by the Roman Catholics. It is as simple as that. It is frightfully hard to explain to a Protestant that if you give Roman Catholics a good job and a good house they will live like Protestants, because they will see neighbours with cars and television sets. They will refuse to have 18 children, but if the Roman Catholic is jobless and lives in a most ghastly hovel, he will rear 18 children on national assistance. It is impossible to explain this to a militant Protestant because he is so keen to deny civil rights to his Roman Catholic neighbours. He cannot understand, in fact, that if you treat Roman Catholics with due consideration and kindness they will live like Protestants in spite of the authoritative nature of their church.

James Chichester-Clark was chosen to take over the Unionist leadership. With a similar lineage to his cousin O'Neill, he was less astute and less liberal. Indeed, shortly before his succession, he had resigned from O'Neill's cabinet in protest at the intended reform of local government. But his appointment was a compromise since he was not as hard-line as the alternative candidates for the leadership, Faulkner and Craig.

THE BATTLE OF THE BOGSIDE

In the volatile atmosphere of Derry, Chichester-Clark's Stormont Government was asking for trouble by allowing the Apprentice Boys of the city to parade, despite the attempts of people like local Stormont MP John Hume to moderate the situation and defuse tempers. Accordingly, on 12 August 1969, when 15,000 Apprentice Boys paraded to commemorate the 280th Anniversary of the lifting of the siege imposed on the town by King James II in 1689, fighting broke out.

The parade began peacefully enough, but at about 2.30 p.m. as it passed through the walled city that looked down on the Bogside ghetto, stone-throwing began between groups of Catholics and Protestants. Ivan Cooper, a Stormont MP, was hit in the face and knocked unconscious. The police responded by forcing the Catholics down into the Bogside district. Barricades appeared and petrol bombs were thrown. As police reinforcements arrived and took up positions around the entrance to the ghetto, the 'battle' of the Bogside began.

With memories of January, when the police had gone on the rampage, and April when the Bogsiders had barricaded themselves against a police 'invasion', the Catholics feared violence from the police if they were allowed to advance into the Bogside. The police were afraid that if the Catholics broke out of the Bogside, they would attack the Protestant ghettos of the city. For both sides, it became crucial to hold their ground. In the early evening, as the police drew up armoured cars and watercannon and began to advance on the barricades of the Bogsiders, the whole community rallied to the defence of their territory.

The police now produced a new weapon; they fired CS gas into the Bogside. This was the first time in the United Kingdom it had been used, sanctioned by the Home Secretary James Callaghan in his meeting with Chichester-Clark the week before. Riot-control CS gas had been first produced in 1928. Exposure to it causes tears and a very strong burning sensation in the eyes, often making them close involuntarily. It also produces severe pains in the nose, throat and chest, and can lead to vomiting and nausea. The British had first used CS gas to disperse rioters in Cyprus in 1956, and it had been used on several other occasions in troublesome colonies, but never in the UK. Its usage in Northern Ireland produced an outcry and the Home Secretary set up a Committee under Sir Harold Himsworth to investigate the gas. Its first report concluded that no healthy person would be made ill or any sick person made

permanently worse by exposure to the gas. But a further report by the same Committee a year later recommended much stricter control over the use of CS gas in built-up areas.

By the morning of Wednesday 13 April, the Battle of the Bogside had settled down into an almost ritualistic pattern of violence. The Bogsiders' stones and petrol bombs were answered by police CS gas. The forces of law and order of the Protestant state were in direct confrontation with the rebellious Catholic minority.

The mood in the Bogside was defiant. The area was declared 'Free Derry', and the Derry Citizens Defence Association organised elaborate defensive preparations. First-aid depots were established, a fire brigade was organised, the old and the ill were evacuated from dangerous areas, and instructions were handed out on how to cope with CS gas. The Republican Tricolour was flown from the roofs of high flats. On the evening of the 13th, the Defence Association stated that they were prepared for a long siege and would not dismantle the barricades until the RUC was withdrawn and Stormont abolished. The Unionist Government mobilised the B-Specials to free more policemen for duty in Derry.

That evening, Jack Lynch, the Prime Minister of the Republic, broadcast a speech on television from Dublin. He declared:

. . . the present situation is the inevitable outcome of the policies pursued for decades by successive Stormont governments. It is clear, also, that the Irish Government can no longer stand by and see innocent people injured and perhaps worse. It is obvious that the RUC is no longer accepted as an impartial force. Neither would the employment of British troops be acceptable nor would they be likely to restore peaceful conditions, certainly not in the long-term . . . Recognising, however, that the reunification of the national territory can provide the only permanent solution for the problem . . .

Lynch called for urgent talks with the British Government.

This powerful statement was a reminder of the claim by the Dublin Government to a united Ireland. For the Unionists, it seemed a blatant call of rebellion to the dissident minority. At 11 pm that evening, James Callaghan was called by alarmed officials to the Home Office. He wrote later: 'We had to consider the possibility that within the next twenty-four hours we might face both civil war in the North and an invasion from the South.' The province of Northern Ireland seemed on the verge of disintegrating.

The first PHOTOGRAPH shows Catholic crowds throwing stones at the RUC on Wednesday the 13th, in the ritualistic violence of the Battle of the Bogside. The second and third photographs show the protagonists in the battle. The youth holds a home-made petrol bomb in a milk bottle (the local dairies reported the loss of 43,000 milk bottles during the course of the week). The policeman holds a gun for firing CS gas cartridges into the crowds.

Photographs 1 and 2 were taken by photojournalist Clive Limpkin.

Chichester-Clark succeeded to the premiership in time for the Orange marching season. British military representatives were alarmed that the marches were to go ahead as usual, for traditionally the temperature was raised by the summer displays of Orange triumphalism. Following the parades of 12 July, trouble flared between sectarian groups at various places throughout Northern Ireland; at Unity Flats in Belfast, in Dungiven, and in Derry, where 40 people were injured. Troops were put on standby as rioting continued, but the minority's rage was fuelled by the mobilisation and deployment for riot duty of the B-Specials. Ominously, in Belfast, minority families living in mixed areas began to move out, and there was an increase in sectarian intimidation (see page 153).

At Westminster a Cabinet Committee was formed to consider the menacing situation in Northern Ireland, consisting of Harold Wilson, James Callaghan, Dennis Healey, Roy Jenkins, Michael Stewart, Richard Crossman and Lord Gardiner. Traditionally, Northern Ireland's affairs were never discussed at Westminster. Since the early 1960s a small group of Labour MPs, including Paul Rose and Stan Orme, had been trying to arouse the interest of their colleagues in defusing the potentially explosive mixture in Ulster society, but without success. There was little public interest in the Province, distanced from the mainland by geography and by history. Between 1964 and 1969, the Home Secretary spent only one half-day in Northern Ireland. Whitehall had no senior civil servant devoting full-time attention to the Province. Until October 1968, Northern Ireland's affairs had been dealt with by the General Department of the Home Office, which also had responsibility for the regulation of British summertime, London taxicabs, liquor licensing and the protection of birds and animals. As James Callaghan later wrote about becoming Home Secretary in December 1967: 'There seemed to me at that time no reason to disturb the arrangements that I found on arrival. Besides, there were many other things to preoccupy me.'

In the summer of 1969, Northern Ireland began to preoccupy the Westminster Government more and more. The Cabinet Committee considered various options, and civil servants drew up alternative plans for imposing Direct Rule, or for sending troops onto the streets. The idea of imposing Direct Rule was rejected, because it was felt that the Northern Ireland civil service would not co-operate, and the Ministry of Defence calculated that it would need twenty or thirty thousand troops to enforce Direct Rule if the Protestants resisted. Moreover, the Cabinet was reluctant to send in troops until all other methods had been exhausted by the civil powers. There was a debate about the legal basis on which troops could be sent in, and the use of the military in an active role in Northern Ireland was thought to have far-reaching constitutional consequences. Crossman and Jenkins were reputedly very opposed to the idea, but it was felt that some sort of 'peace-keeping' intervention might become necessary to save lives. Callaghan later recorded: 'The advice that came to me from all sides was on no account to get sucked in to the Irish bog.' At the end of July, the Cabinet finalised its business before breaking for the summer holidays. Wilson and Callaghan were left in charge of affairs.

On 2 August there were more disturbances at Unity Flats in Belfast, and these spread to the Shankill Road. The RUC was pushed to its limit to control the rioting. The B-Specials were put on stand-by, and on the next day 60 soldiers were sent in to a police barracks in Belfast to await further orders. Two days later, Sir Harold Black, the Secretary to the Northern Ireland Cabinet, flew to London to meet his counterpart Sir Philip Allen, the Permanent Secretary at the Home Office. On 8 August, Chichester-Clark met Callaghan in London. He wanted an increase in the security forces to augment his civil power. Reluctantly, Callaghan agreed that a limited use of troops as a peace-keeping force in an emergency would not involve constitutional repercussions.

Chichester-Clark, like O'Neill before him, was under great pressure from the hard-liners in his party. The Apprentice Boys' annual parade in Londonderry was approaching. Although Civil Rights marches had been banned for over a year from the centre of the city, there was no such ban on traditional Orange parades. Callaghan wanted to prohibit all future marches, but Chichester-Clark convinced him that preventing the Apprentice Boys' Parade from going ahead would gravely offend Loyalists, ruin him politically and ensure that he was succeeded by Faulkner, who was even further to the Right. Callaghan baulked at this prospect, and so Chichester-Clark's government allowed the Apprentice Boys' Parade to go ahead, despite predictions that violence would ensue. The Parade turned out to be a landmark in the history of Northern Ireland. It ignited the different factions and ferocious fighting broke out between the police and the Catholics. The march set off what became known as the 'Battle of the Bogside' (see page 146). The RUC laid siege to the Bogside, and the residents fought them with stones and petrol bombs from behind their barricades. For the first time, the RUC used CS gas to try to control the rioters.

On 14 August, after 48 hours continuous 'battle', the Northern Ireland Government finally asked Westminster for help. Wilson and Callaghan agreed that troops should be sent in to Derry (see page 150). The troops were sent in as a temporary, emergency measure. It was felt that the longer the troops stayed, the greater would be the political involvement of Westminster, whereas a speedy restoration of law and order might not affect Stormont's position. In the late afternoon of Thursday 14th, the British soldiers entered the city.

The Catholics of the Bogside felt they had won a great victory, not only because they had kept out the RUC, but also because they had forced the British Army to intervene. Now London was involved, but so too was Dublin. The anxiety felt in the South about the fate of their fellow-Catholics in the North was expressed by Taoiseach (Prime Minister) Lynch, addressing the nation on television (see page 147). He declared that the Republic could not 'stand by' while Catholics were attacked over the border. He called for a United Nations peace-keeping force to be sent to Northern Ireland. The Irish Army set up field hospitals and refugee camps along the border to provide aid for the refugees from the North. In the frantic days of mid-August, it even seemed possible that the Irish Army might invade the North to establish a

At 5 p.m. on Thursday 14 August 1969, 400 soldiers of the 1st Battalion Prince of Wales Own Yorkshire Regiment crossed the Craigavon Bridge and entered the heart of Derry.

The decision to send in troops to restore order in a part of the United Kingdom had not been taken easily. In July, the Cabinet Committee on Northern Ireland had opposed the idea, but agreed that a peace-keeping force might have to be sent in on a temporary basis in order to prevent the loss of lives.

At 1.30 p.m. on the 14th, the Inspector-General of the RUC, Anthony Peacocke, telephoned the Home Affairs Minister at Belfast, Robert Porter, to ask for military help. After a short meeting, Chichester-Clark called Downing Street at 3 p.m. and made the official request. However, officials at the Home Office had already decided that the sending in of troops was inevitable. The Home Secretary, James Callaghan, had been recalled from a break in Sussex. The Prime Minister, Harold Wilson, was on holiday in the Scilly Isles. The Leader of the Opposition,

Edward Heath, who would normally have been consulted before making such a momentous decision, was sailing in the Fastnet Race off the south-west coast of Ireland. Callaghan flew to Cornwall for an urgent meeting with the Prime Minister, who flew in from the Scilly Isles. A brief discussion on the situation took place. They found they had no maps of Northern Ireland with them and a Group Captain was sent away to fetch an atlas which everyone studied. Callaghan proposed that soldiers should be sent in and Wilson agreed. When he was back in the air returning to London, Callaghan received the formal request for troops from Chichester-Clark, relayed from the Home Office. He cabled back 'Permission granted' and within minutes the 400 soldiers that had been alerted on stand-by were moving into the streets of Derry.

To the Catholics of the Bogside, the arrival of the troops was a cause of jubilation. The soldiers were welcomed like a liberating army. It seemed to the Catholics that it was a sign of the defeat of the RUC

and of the Stormont Government. With the British Army on the streets of Northern Ireland, it was felt that the Westminster Government would have to take over the management of affairs and the injustices of Unionist rule would be removed.

The first problem facing the British Army lay not in Derry, but in Belfast, where on the night of 14 August, there was the most severe rioting yet. When crowds assembled, the tension mounted, and the police, heavily understrength and exhausted, responded by turning out Shorland armoured cars with Browning machine-guns. During the next twenty-four hours, ten civilians were killed and some Catholic streets burned almost entirely to the ground. The Catholics accused the police of standing by and allowing the Protestant mob to attack them. The Scarman Tribunal reported that in the Conway Street area 'the police on duty in these streets were seriously at fault in that, though there in some strength, they failed to control the Protestant mob or to prevent the arson and the looting.' The use of the B-Specials only further aggravated the situation and attracted more fusilades of stones from the Catholics.

As the rioting continued during the next day, another request was made by Chichester-Clark to send troops into the burning city. Callaghan agreed, but it took some hours for soldiers to arrive in the city. After brief consultations between the commanding officers and the police whom they were relieving, the army took up positions along the Falls Road and Divis Street, hoping to interpose themselves between the Protestant and Catholic factions. The soldiers were few in numbers and were confused by the sectarian topography in Belfast. They were ill-equipped and ill-prepared for their role. The first two PHOTOGRAPHS show troops in the Falls Road on Saturday 16 August, the day after they were sent in. The soldiers look bemused. Their heavy weaponry was clearly unsuitable for the demands of preventing civil rioting. Their webbed helmets were more suitable to the jungles of Malaya than the backstreets of an industrial city in the United Kingdom.

Unlike July 1935, when troops were also used to restore order after riots had broken out in Belfast, this time the soldiers were not quickly withdrawn. The hostilities aroused were so great that the reintroduction of the police would probably have provoked further bloodshed. The troops were there, and they were there to stay. Slowly, of course, the army tried to adapt to its new role. The tactics they employed, the intelligence they gathered and their presence on the streets, all evolved to meet the needs of what they called 'low intensity' civil operations. Major General Frank Kitson developed a whole new policy for coping with civilian 'insurgents'. The British Army is consulted throughout the world for its tactics in combating civil disturbances.

The third PHOTOGRAPH shows soldiers marching into the Catholic district of Ballymurphy in 1970. By now, their uniforms and equipment had changed, they carry riot sticks and fibre-glass shields and their helmets are fitted with protective visors.

When the first 400 troops had moved into Derry, a spokesman in Whitehall predicted that they would be back in their barracks by the weekend. But, eleven years after these first soldiers were sent in as an emergency measure, there are still 12,500 British troops in Northern Ireland.

The PHOTOGRAPH below was taken in Derry on 31 July 1972 during 'Operation Motorman', when troops went in to remove the barricades of the 'No-Go' area.

SECTARIAN WARFARE

The top PHOTOGRAPH was taken in Belfast on 16 August 1969, the day after the troops had arrived.

It shows the scene in Percy Street, at the point of the 'line' between the Catholic and the Protestant enclaves. The Catholic homes on the right of the picture were entirely destroyed during the rioting. The mixed terrace on the corner of Percy Street and Beverley Street was partially destroyed. According the the Scarman Tribunal, a Protestant mob containing twenty B-Specials clashed with a Catholic mob shortly before midnight at the junction of Percy Street and Beverley Street. At one point, the B-Specials recruited ten or fifteen 'reliable men', and these civilian volunteers along with the B-Specials and several members of the Shankill Defence Association armed with sticks and broom handles, charged the Catholic mob in an attempt to drive them out of the Protestant district and back into the Catholic stronghold of Divis Street. Petrol bombs were thrown and several houses were burnt out.

The second PHOTOGRAPH shows Farringdon Gardens, a Protestant street on the edge of the Catholic Ardoyne district in August 1971, during the rioting that followed the introduction of internment. The Protestant families of the street felt under threat from their Catholic neighbours and can be seen evacuating their homes. The Protestants burnt their own houses on leaving in order to prevent them from being occupied by Catholic families.

The increased concentration of Protestant and Catholic families in their own sectarian areas was a feature of the troubles in Belfast. Another way in which this took place was through the enforcement of 'swaps'. As intimidation intensified, Catholic families isolated in Protestant enclaves and Protestant families in Catholic territory were forcibly evicted, and retreated into their own ghettos. In 1969, the Shankill Defence Association had been prominent in intimidating Catholics into leaving their homes, and later Catholic vigilantes forced Protestant people to move out. These forcible 'swaps' were another sad feature of the urbanised sectarian warfare that rocked Belfast from 1969 onwards.

united Ireland. Events in Derry totally polarised the communities. Even the moderates were driven to extremes. As the Bogsiders appealed to their fellow Catholics elsewhere in Northern Ireland to relieve the pressure on them in Derry, fighting erupted in other towns. On the evening of 14 August, there was a riot in Dungiven, and in Armagh a man was shot dead by the B-Specials. But the worst rioting of all was still to come.

While it was strategically possible for Catholics to defend their corner in Derry, the same cannot be said of Belfast. The topography of the city is more complex than any other part of Northern Ireland. Apart from a series of dense estates in West Belfast, Catholics live in enclaves situated in different parts of the city, each surrounded by concentrations of exclusively Protestant working-class people. In most cases, the Catholic ghettos contained some mixed streets, and a small Protestant minority within them.

On the night of 14 August, after the British Army had brought an eerie calm to Derry, Belfast was ripped apart by vicious sectarian clashes, the worst since 1922. The pressures had been building up for some time, and with the atmosphere so tense from the news in Derry, anything seemed possible. In Divis Street, Ardoyne and Clonard, the Protestants and the Catholics did battle. The B-Specials were mobilised in Belfast, and that produced waves of panic amongst the Catholics. Furthermore, the RUC brought out Shorland armoured cars that were equipped with Browning machine guns, and used them quite randomly, as it seemed to the Catholics. The Browning had been the standard machine gun of the US Army. It fired ten or eleven high-velocity bullets every second, and could only be fired in bursts. It had a range of 2½ miles. When it was used as a riot control weapon in the narrow backstreets of Belfast, its firepower proved lethal. The police were given instructions to fire at 'identifiable targets', but in the course of the night of 14 August, it was not at all clear what this meant. Firing began at about forty minutes past midnight in the Divis Flats area, between the Protestant Shankill and the Catholic Falls Road. Forensic evidence later established that a large area of the buildings had been sprayed with machine-gun fire. A soldier at home on leave was killed on his balcony, and a nine-year-old boy was killed as he lay asleep in his bed. Other bullets sped across the city embedding themselves in buildings miles away. Loyalist mobs from the Shankill Road invaded Clonard, off the Falls Road, and burned dozens of Catholic houses to the ground. A 15-year-old boy died defending Bombay Street. The Catholics believed the B-Specials were all part of these gangs and had returned to attack them. Their fears were articulated by the Superior of the Catholic Monastery in Clonard who said in giving evidence to the Scarman Tribunal later: 'I was terribly agitated and worked up and terribly afraid there was going to be a holocaust and that the whole area was going to be wiped out. I was absolutely convinced that this was an attempt not merely to wipe out the Monastery but the whole area.'

Fleeing Catholics sought shelter in schools and community centres in the city, and some crossed the border to the refugee centres in the Republic. At the end of the rioting, which continued through the 15th, 10 people had been killed, 145 injured and nearly 200 houses, mostly Catholic, burnt out.

The resources of General Freeland, the Army GOC in Northern Ireland were fully absorbed in Derry. He had received no reinforcements, as the Government still wanted to minimise the military involvement. Eventually, troops arrived in Belfast late on the 15th, but they were few in numbers and had little idea of which side was which. However, by lining up in the main streets they succeeded in interposing themselves between the two sides and their presence probably averted civil war. As an enforced and uneasy peace followed, families resettled within the sanctuary of their own areas, and vigilantes roamed the streets — embryonic paramilitaries who were soon to dominate the conflict between the communities.

At first, the soldiers were regarded with wary relief by the embattled Catholics. Belfast paused while the politicians worked feverishly to draft some reform proposals to placate the dissident minority. The military urged all speed for a solution, aware that its role as peace-makers would soon become untenable unless a constructive political solution was forthcoming. General Freeland observed that 'the honeymoon period cannot obviously continue forever . . . but unless there is a solution or some hope for the future — and this is where the politicians have got to come in — the soldiers are not going to be welcomed on the streets for ever and ever.'

Wilson, Callaghan, Healey, Chichester-Clark and Porter met in London on 19 August and issued a joint communiqué, the Downing Street Declaration. They stressed the need to keep up the momentum of reform but made it clear that, at this stage, there would be no change in Northern Ireland's constitutional status. Citizens of Northern Ireland were to receive 'equality of treatment and freedom from discrimination', and the B-Specials would be phased out. The Unionists wanted to retain them for riot control duty, but Westminster wanted to disband them. Two committees were appointed, one under Lord Hunt was to examine the structure of Northern Ireland's police force; the other, under Mr Justice Scarman, was to inquire into the disorders between April and August 1969.

On the ground in Belfast the bemused military tried to gauge the sectarian geography of the city, inbred in the locals but incomprehensible to outsiders. They gradually fixed the physical divisions between the streets and alleyways along sectarian lines, constructing barriers to separate them. This 'Peace Line' was a construction of barbed wire and high corrugated metal screens. To the Catholics, it seemed no guarantee of protection and their barricades stayed up. Despite assurances from their leaders that their position was not being undermined, Loyalists looked at the Peace Line and the barricades blocking Catholic streets and felt that the existence of these obstacles was proof of the Government's unwillingness or inability to go in and bring the rebels to order. They answered the slight by raising barricades of their own which were removed only when the army succeeded in persuading the Catholics to remove theirs.

In the tense respite that followed the August battles, the armed forces, now swollen to 6,000 men, kept the two sides apart. Moderate Catholics were given some hope by the publication of the Hunt Report, which recommended the replacement of the B-Specials by a new force, the Ulster

Defence Regiment. The Loyalists were shattered, and their anger was compounded by the Tory Party Conference, which endorsed the moves to placate the Catholics. It seemed that they were alone in their fight to cling on to the Union, and savage riots erupted on the Shankill Road at the Unity Flats in October 1969. Inflamed Protestants were a potent force. Most of Northern Ireland's 102,000 licensed guns were in their hands, but for the first time, the army and the police turned on them. Ironically, one of the three killed was RUC Constable Arbuckle, shot not by dissident Republicans, but by the very people seeking to prevent the emasculation of the RUC.

Callaghan visited Northern Ireland and beseeched people to 'stop this nonsense on the streets'. Unionists were coerced into implementing Westminster's required changes relating to employment, housing and local government. Mistakenly, Callaghan felt that this would mean improvement. However, the new measures were administrative changes rather than political reforms, and, in any case, it would take years before the planned changes could reach fruition. Crucially, the power structure in Northern Ireland remained intact and unaltered.

It was at this time that the IRA, dormant for many years, once again entered the political equation. The events of August 1969 had caught the IRA entirely unprepared; it had only a handful of weapons and was unable to defend the Catholic communities (see page 166). Graffiti sneered from the walls: 'IRA — I Ran Away'. The resulting frustrations accelerated the split which was already coming in the Republican movement, between those who wished to pursue a political campaign as a pre-requisite to physical force (later to become known as The Officials) and those who felt the immediate armed resistance was the only way to respond to the present crisis, (later to become known as The Provisionals). In the early months of 1970, the Provisional IRA began to gather weapons, and to train volunteers.

During early 1970, the relationship between the British Army and the Catholics began to deteriorate sharply. The cups of tea offered to the soldiers in August ceased, and the Catholics began to see the army no longer as an impartial presence, but as an occupying force that was there to protect Orangeism and maintain the Unionist establishment in power. The army knew that the Provisionals were organising, and they began to make extensive arms searches in West Belfast. These arms searches succeeded only in further antagonising Catholics, and as a result of one search there was widespread rioting in Ballymurphy. The Provisionals unsuccessfully tried to curb the rioting since they were not yet prepared for a confrontation with the army. Rioting only led to an increase in the army presence and the army's raids resulted in bigger arms hauls and more arrests of Provisionals.

As this spiral got worse, the new RUC Chief, Sir Arthur Young, appointed directly by Callaghan, became worried by the obtrusiveness of the army. He wanted the army's role on the streets to be taken over by the police, and he hoped that his re-styled force, expanded but relieved of the B-Specials, would be more acceptable to the minority. The army was designed and trained to be aggressive whereas a police force was more normal and more passive in its role. To Young, the police represented visible law and order which the military did not, but Freeland was afraid that the RUC might run amok again and endanger the army's relationship with the Catholics. So Young's proposal for unarmed RUC riot squads was rejected. Thus, Britain's direct involvement in the affairs of Northern Ireland was alienating both sections of the population — the Catholics, hemmed in by the military who were squatting in their districts in order to preserve the system which was responsible for their grievances; and the Protestants who were forced back by a violent army and felt themselves betrayed by reformers at Westminster.

The response of the Provisional IRA to the increasing number of raids was to launch a bombing campaign against commercial targets, in order to stretch the security forces. Protestants were incensed by the Provisional campaign, especially as their citizens and businesses were the main casualties. The Shankill Defence Association, along with Paisley, exhorted Loyalists to take the offensive, and rioting proliferated through May and June. Preoccupied as it was with the forthcoming General Election in June, Westminster seemed to be losing interest.

The Conservative Government of Edward Heath took office in June 1970, and almost immediately, the jailing of Bernadette Devlin MP, on 26 June, for riotous behaviour during the Battle of the Bogside, caused heavy disturbances and injuries to nearly three hundred people in Derry.

Despite the calamity of the previous summer, and against Army advice, the new administration imposed no restrictions on the Orange marching season, which was imminent. The celebrations commemorating the Ulster contribution to the Battle of the Somme were allowed to go ahead. The Catholics waited for the marchers to pass and in the Springfield Road and Ardoyne areas of Belfast, where the route touched Catholic territory, fighting broke out and three people died.

On the other side of the city, the tiny enclave called the Short Strand, where 6,000 Catholics were surrounded by 60,000 Protestants, was attacked by the UVF. For the first time, armed Provisionals appeared on the streets to challenge the UVF. The gun battle which followed lasted all night. The army claimed later that it had been too stretched by the fighting elsewhere to have anything left in reserve for the protection of Short Strand, but to the Catholics, the army had stood off again just, they claimed, as it had done in August 1969 when Bombay Street was burnt out. The Battle in Short Strand was of crucial importance, for the ghetto had been at the mercy of the UVF until the Provisionals stepped out of the shadows to defend their people. For a section of the Catholic working-class, its representatives in the continuing struggle henceforth would be the Provisionals. The night of 27 June 1970 ended in Short Strand with five dead, four of them Protestants.

At the time Labour lost office, Wilson and Callaghan had been leaning towards Direct Rule. Tory policy was different. Their emphasis was to be on 'firm measures', despite the misgivings of the civil servants. When the new Home Secretary, Reginald Maudling, paid a short visit to Northern Ireland in the wake of the riots, his confusion and ignorance were apparent. The first positive move the Tories made was to introduce the most repressive piece of

At 4.30 a.m. on 9 August 1971, British troops swooped on houses all over Northern Ireland and detained 342 people from a list they had drawn up with the RUC Special Branch. A rattle of dustbin lids on the pavements gave the warning that echoed through the small streets of Belfast to alert sleeping households to the raids.

The Special Powers Act of 1922 permitted the Unionist Government to jail anyone indefinitely without the legal necessity of proving them guilty in a trial. It was to be used almost exclusively against IRA suspects and Republican sympathisers. In May 1922, 300 men were 'lifted', and within months 500 people were interned. The last die-hard internees were released in 1924.

Internment was re-introduced in December 1938, after the bombing of customs posts on the Ulster border. Men were kept in detention throughout the Second World War as sporadic IRA bombing attacks hit mainland Britain and Northern Ireland. Those IRA men who were caught and sent to prison were interned as soon as their sentences ended. There was no refuge for Republicans on the run in the South either. The De Valera Government took a strong line, passing the Emergency Powers (Amendment) Act in January 1940, which gave them too the power to intern without trial. Internees were released at the end of the War.

Ten days after the start of the next IRA campaign in December 1956, internment was introduced in the North again. The authorities in the South followed suit, and this dual attack on IRA membership contributed significantly to the eventual failure of the

whole operation. Detention without trial was therefore highly regarded by Unionist politicians as a way of containing and suppressing the Republican element in the North.

In 1971, the Unionists did not realise that if there were no simultaneous introduction of internment in the South, detention without trial in the North would not have the same effect, and despite the warnings of the British Army, they also did not realise how bitterly the minority community would resent this draconian measure. No paramilitary Loyalists were arrested, nor were their sympathisers, but neither were many members of the Provisional IRA, for in anticipation of the swoop, they had flown.

As the army had foreseen, the 'lifting' of the internees caused an immediate and violent response: 22 people died in the riots of the next four days. In Derry, the Bogside and the Creggan became 'No-Go' areas, and a huge rent and rates strike was called by Republican families in protest.

Within 48 hours of the initial arrests, 116 men had been released. They told stories of having been beaten up, thrown backwards out of helicopters they believed to be high in the air, forced to run barefoot between rows of baton-wielding soldiers and across broken glass and barbed wire. In 1975, the Home Secretary, Merlyn Rees, told Parliament in a written answer that over £300,000 compensation had been paid in 473 cases of detainees and ex-internees claiming redress for false arrest, false imprisonment, assault and battery.

The stories of the treatment of the internees fuelled the anger of Republican sympathisers, but it was the experience of a further twelve detainees (and two more a month later) who became known as the 'guinea-pigs' that focused world attention on Northern Ireland and resulted in Britain being taken to the Court of Human Rights in Strasbourg, charged with torture, but found guilty of 'inhuman and degrading treatment'. The twelve guinea-pigs had experienced an in-depth interrogation method known as 'sensory deprivation', its aim being to confuse the senses by cutting off any outside stimulii, so that an artificial psychosis or episode of insanity would occur and thus make the prisoner responsive to questioning. Each man was hooded, made to wear loose-fitting overalls, kept in isolation, and put in a fixed position against the wall, with arms and legs spread out. Any movement attracted beating or kicking from the guards. They were deprived of sleep and food and subjected to a constant background noise (known as 'white noise'), that cut off any other sound. In between these extended periods of standing at the

wall, the men were subjected to prolonged bouts of interrogation. This treatment continued for up to seven days.

The complaints about the experiences of the hooded men induced the British Government to appoint a Commission of Inquiry headed by Sir Edmund Compton to look into the allegations of physical brutality; mental cruelty was put outside their terms of reference. The Compton Commission reported:

Where we have concluded that physical ill-treatment took place, we are not making a finding of brutality on the part of those who handled these complainants. We consider that brutality is an inhuman or savage form of cruelty, and that cruelty implies a disposition to inflict suffering, coupled with indifference to, or pleasure in, the victim's pain. We do not think that happened here.

As the stories of the guinea-pigs' harrowing treatment became even more widely known through publicity in the Press and on television, the Parker Commission was appointed to review interrogation methods, and denied there were any long lasting mental effects from the use of the techniques.

Lord Gardiner published a Minority Report to the Parker Commission in which he said: 'there has been no dissent from the view that the procedures are illegal alike by the law of England and the law of Northern Ireland.' This was underlined by Article 17 of the 1948 Geneva Convention:

No physical or mental torture, nor any other form of coercion, may be inflicted upon prisoners of war to secure from them information of any kind whatever. Prisoners who refuse to answer may not be threatened, insulted, or exposed to any unpleasant or disadvantageous treatment of any kind.

The fourteen men who experienced sensory deprivation have been paid altogether, £188,250 in damages.

The PHOTOGRAPH shows women beating dustbin lids on the pavement, the traditional sign to warn the community that troops are in the area. Every year on 9 August, at 4.30 a.m., Internment is remembered in Catholic districts by a ritualistic banging of dustbin lids.

Most of those interned in late 1971 were taken to Long Kesh Internment Camp, on the site of a disused airfield. The AERIAL PHOTOGRAPH shows Long Kesh camp in October 1971. Long Kesh is today the location of the notorious H-Blocks.

legislation since the Special Powers Act of 1922. Within four days of the June riots, they introduced the Criminal Justice (Temporary Provisions) Act which made mandatory the imposition of a six-month jail sentence for rioting. This encouraged popular support for the Provisionals, since the army was the instrument used to enforce the Act and make the arrests. At the same time, the Incitement to Religious Hatred Act was passed with the intention of countering Loyalist sectarian bigotry.

The army's response to the sectarian mayhem was to get tough. On 3 July, a systematic search for arms in Balkan Street in the Lower Falls Road led to widespread allegations of damage to property by the soldiers, and their behaviour detonated the local people. The troops were cut off by rioters, and reinforcements used CS Gas to disperse the aggressors, and imposed a curfew which lasted 36 hours. Four people were killed, and the army's conduct ensured the hostility of the Catholic ghettos. Recruitment into the Provisional IRA soared.

During the course of the searches in the Lower Falls, the army had found a total of 30 rifles, 24 shotguns and 52 pistols, and army policy became centred on curtailing the Provisionals' ability to move arms and explosives around Belfast and Derry. The Provisionals extended their bombing campaign to the border with explosions in the Crossmaglen area of South Armagh in August 1970, and this pattern continued throughout the seventies. The army replied initially by blowing up roads in the border area making them impassable except on foot. This, of course, outraged the local population, North and South, and caused severe disruption to the local farming communities. As the Provisional IRA bombing campaign continued, more and more civilians were killed by mis-timed explosions and inadequate warnings.

Despite Lynch's hints at the peak of the Battle of the Bogside, the Dublin Government had overtly done little to intervene in the North. Recent evidence that has come to light, however, shows that it became Government policy to supply arms and money discreetly to the North. In late 1969, a few Catholics from the North were given military training in the South, and in February 1970, the Irish Minister of Defence issued a directive to the Irish Army Chief of Staff to make weapons and gas masks available and 'to train the forces for incursion into Northern Ireland.' Disclosures about arms shipments to the North became public in May 1970 and in the ensuing controversy, although Lynch denied knowledge of the plans, it emerged that arms and money had been supplied to the Provisional IRA via well-connected businessmen and politicians in the South. Two ministers were sacked, including the Minister of Finance, Charles Haughey. Together with others, the sacked ministers were charged with smuggling arms to the North. Those who stood trial were acquitted, but the regime was split on what to do about the North. The Government retreated from its Republican position, and active pursuit of unity was replaced by lip-service to the ideal and an increase in the level of co-operation with Westminster's attempts to subdue the Provisional IRA. Entry into the EEC became the dominant political aspiration of Southern politicians. Ironically, it was Haughey who replaced Lynch as leader of Fianna Fail and Prime Minister in December 1979.

The introduction of internment in August 1971 brought the Catholic community of Northern Ireland into open rebellion. In the Creggan and the Bogside areas of Derry, the barricades went up again, and these Catholic enclaves almost seceded from the state for a year. All the non-Unionist political parties came together and called for a rent and rates strike, and in a short space of time about 26,000 families were taking part in the strike. On 16 August, 8,000 workers in Derry went on a one-day strike in protest. Street committees and resistance councils were formed to co-ordinate the rent and rates strike and to organise protests. In Derry, 30 prominent Catholics resigned their positions on public bodies, including the City Commission which had replaced the City Corporation in 1969. In mid-August, 100 councillors in Co. Tyrone withdrew from their elected seats and other Catholic councillors resigned from their local councils over the next few days. Catholic MPs withdrew from Stormont and refused to discuss with either Belfast or London representatives the role of the Catholic minority in Northern Ireland affairs until internment was ended. Internment had united middle-class and working-class Catholics in mass alienation from the state, and had driven the Catholic community into a policy of civil disobedience designed to undermine the workings of government.

All this had grave echoes of 1921–22, when the Catholic community, by refusing to accept the existence of the state, had tried to paralyse its institutions of government. In 1921, many local councils had declared their allegiance to Dail Eireann in Dublin. In 1971, about fifty 'moderate' Nationalist MPs formed an 'alternative' assembly at Dungiven. The Assembly met twice, and at its first session, on 26 October, John Hume said:

Today we do not recognise the authority of the Stormont Parliament, and we do not care twopence whether this is treason or not. Ever since then [1921], we have had government without consenus, because the free consensus of all the people has not been given to the system of government, and when you have a situation like that, you have a situation of permanent instability, and when you have permanent instability you have recurring acts of violence, and surely that has been the history of the fifty years of this system of government.

The PHOTOGRAPH shows John Hume making his speech at the Dungiven Assembly.

1

2

3

4

5

6

BLOODY SUNDAY

All marches and parades in Northern Ireland were banned after the introduction of internment in August 1971. However, demonstrations continued to take place to protest at the internment policy, and a Civil Rights Association march was planned for Sunday 30 January 1972, in the city of Derry.

The march was planned to pass from the Creggan Estate to the Guildhall in the centre of the town. The police and the army commanders decided that to attempt to stop the march altogether would be likely to provoke violence, whereas to contain the march in the Bogside and Creggan areas would minimise the danger of rioting and prevent damage to commercial premises and shops in the city centre. Twenty-six barriers were erected at strategic points. In addition, the army commander issued orders that 'An arrest force is to be held centrally behind the check points and launched in a scoop-up operation to arrest as many hooligans and rioters as possible.' Otherwise the army orders specified that the march 'should be dealt with in as low a key as possible for as long as possible.' Among the reinforcements brought in to the city for the day was the 1st Battalion of the Parachute Regiment, known to be one of the toughest regiments in Northern Ireland. They were the troops assigned to the arrest operation units.

The demonstration passed off peacefully enough to begin with, until crowds began to assemble around the army barriers, protesting at the re-routing of the march. Stones were thrown and insults shouted at the soldiers on the barriers. A few minutes before 4 p.m., the army gave orders to launch its arrest operation to round up the hooligans. The Paratroopers went forward, and what took place next is contentious. The army say that as they went forward they came under attack from home-made nail bombs and then from small arms fire. They say they fired back at 'identifiable targets', civilians aiming bombs or weapons at them. Many of those in the march claim that the Paratroopers went in to the march and started shooting. Within a very short space of time 13 Catholic men had been shot dead and another 13 wounded. Seven of those killed were still in their teens.

The British Government ordered a public enquiry into the events to be set up under Lord Chief Justice Widgery. A forensic test was applied to the dead men to see whether they had been carrying arms, but in practice, Lord Widgery found it very difficult to decide one way or the other. He concluded that seven of the dead men had not been firing weapons, four of them possibly had been, and that the result of the tests on the other two were inconclusive. Lord Widgery summarised his conclusions:

3. If the Army had persisted in its 'low key' attitude and had not launched a large scale operation to arrest hooligans, the day might have passed off without serious incident . . .

8. Soldiers who identified armed gunmen fired upon them in accordance with the standing orders in the Yellow Card [the orders issued to each soldier on the use of his firearms]. Each soldier was his own judge of whether he had identified a gunman. Their training made them aggressive and quick in decision and some showed more restraint in opening fire than others. At one end of the scale, some soldiers showed a high degree of responsibility; at the other, notably in Glenfada Park, firing bordered on the reckless . . .

10. None of the deceased or wounded is proved to have been shot whilst handling a firearm or bomb. Some are wholly acquitted of complicity in such action; but there is a strong suspicion that some others had been firing weapons or handling bombs in the course of the afternoon and that yet others had been closely supporting them.

However, the Londonderry City Coroner, Major Hubert O'Neill, said at the end of the Inquest on the 13 deaths, on 21 August 1973:

It strikes me that the Army ran amok that day and they shot without thinking of what they were doing. They were shooting innocent people. These people may have been taking part in a parade that was banned — but I don't think that justifies the firing of live rounds indiscriminately. I say it without reservation — it was sheer unadulterated murder.

The PHOTOGRAPHS opposite are single frames from the film taken during Bloody Sunday by RTE and ITN cameramen. The first three stills are taken from film shot at the army barriers, erected to contain the march within the Creggan and the Bogside. The RTE cameraman (frame 1) was on the side of the Civil Rights marchers; the ITN cameraman (frames 2 & 3) was on the side of the army and frame 3 gives some idea of the abuse the army came under. Once the shooting began, frames 4 (RTE) and 5 (ITN) show the crowd running and frame 6 (ITN) shows some of those rounded up by the Parachute Regiment's 'arrest operation'. Television film and journalists' photographs were used by the Widgery Tribunal as evidence.

Meanwhile, middle-class Catholic politicians in the North came together, and in August 1970 formed a new party, the Social and Democratic Labour Party (SDLP). The party was an amalgam of Republicans, Nationalists and Socialists, brought together by the need to present a united front to the Unionists and a weighty opposition party at Stormont. The SDLP was avowedly non-sectarian but with the principle of 'the eventual reunification of Ireland' as the cornerstone of its policy, it was unlikely to appeal to many Protestants in the North. In fact it soon became representative of moderate Catholic opinion in Northern Ireland, and perhaps the one chance for a constitutional reconciliation between the Catholic and the Protestant communities. Its leader was Gerry Fitt and his deputy was John Hume.

In the North, the Provisional IRA continued to bomb commercial centres, rural power installations and border posts, and by the end of 1970 Chichester-Clark was calling for an all-out onslaught on it. The army ringed ghettos and Catholic alienation increased. The Ballymurphy pattern was repeated, as troops and local people clashed on four consecutive nights in January 1971. By now, the Provisionals were controlling their own districts, and heavy military searches in the Clonard and Kashmir areas in February provoked a bitter reaction from local women. This escalated into serious rioting which spread right across the city to New Lodge and Ardoyne.

The Provisionals now felt able to take the offensive against the army and increased their use of snipers which lead to the shooting of Gunner Curtis in February 1971, the first soldier to die since the army had arrived in 1969. There was an immediate outcry. A group of Stormont MPs called for block searches, curfews and 'punitive expeditions'. Chichester-Clark announced on television that Northern Ireland was 'at war' with the Provisional IRA. To many Protestants, the rise of the Provisional IRA represented what they had always most feared in the Catholic community, the resurgence of the violent Republican tradition determined to overthrow the state.

On 16 March, three soldiers were taken from a Belfast pub and shot dead by the Provisional IRA. Eight thousand Protestant shipyard workers demonstrated, calling for direct action to suppress the IRA, and Loyalists marched to Stormont to demand the recall of the B-Specials and the reintroduction of the ultimate sanction, detention without trial – internment. Chichester-Clark flew to London to urge Westminster to use extreme measures, but he succeeded only in raising another 1,300 troops. This was insufficient to reassure the Loyalists that the disloyal elements could be annihilated. But Westminster would not give in to the Unionist Right and so, at the end of March, Chichester-Clark resigned.

Brian Faulkner succeeded him for what was to be the shortest premiership in the history of the Province. Faulkner was unlike his predecessors. He was not a member of the landed gentry and his father had been described by Brookeborough as 'the little shirt-maker from Comber'. His family linen firm made him a member of the Protestant business class. He had been a hard-line Unionist during the 1950s, and had resigned from O'Neill's reforming government in 1969. On the other hand, as Minister of Development under Chichester-Clark from 1969 to '71, he had initiated mild reforms in housing and local government, and now as Prime Minister he offered what seemed a major initiative to the Catholics of the SDLP by trying to ease them into the governmental machine by way of Stormont committees. He balanced this appeasement of the Catholics by constantly displaying his fidelity to Orangeism. By using this political agility, he hoped to edge towards an accommodation with both extremes. Once again, however, events in the streets were to take over.

In July 1971, there were more riots in Derry, and two men, Seamus Cusack and Desmond Beattie, were shot dead by the army, though neither of them was armed. Loyalists rejoiced in the army's firm action. Paisley's *Protestant Telegraph* said of the IRA: 'The vermin must be suppressed either by internment or effective action by our security forces.' But the minority were outraged, and when the Government refused to hold a public enquiry into the shootings, the SDLP withdrew from Stormont. All hopes for Catholic participation in government were finished, almost before it had begun. Faulkner was being undermined by a rapid collapse of the middle ground, just as O'Neill and then Chichester-Clark had been before him.

Internment had been under consideration as the only alternative to full-scale military operation against the Provisionals for some time before the summer of 1971 (see page 158). Faulkner himself had been convinced of its efficacy since it had been used to quell the 1956–62 IRA campaign. The continued bombings, and the collapse of his attempt to embrace the SDLP, gave Faulkner the opportunity to demand the use of the Special Powers Act to intern suspects without trial. The army was opposed to it, and so were some of the Government, but the Minister of Defence (Lord Carrington) and William Whitelaw were in favour. Lists were prepared, and on 9 August 1971, the army swooped. Some 342 men were arrested in the first raids, but there had been advance knowledge, and the Provisional IRA command structure survived virtually intact.

The Catholic population responded with full-scale insurrection (see page 161). In the immediate wake of internment, there were sectarian clashes along all the flashpoints and, in a replay of 1969, over two hundred houses were gutted as people fled the streets bordering the sectarian divide (see page 153). Between April and July 1971, 4 soldiers and 4 civilians had been killed. In the four months after internment, 30 soldiers, 11 RUC and UDR men and 73 civilians died. By mid-December, 1,576 persons had been interned and 934 released, leaving well over 600 still interned. All but a handful were Catholics.

The total alienation of the Catholic community was ensured by the wave of stories about the brutal ill-treatment of the internees that swept Northern Ireland (see page 158). The Catholics, who increasingly saw the army as oppressors, were only too willing to believe all the stories they heard. That many of the rumours were built on a basis of fact, however, cannot be denied, and the outcry was such that Home Secretary Maudling appointed Sir Edmund Compton to look into the allegations. His committee sat in secret and its terms of reference excluded investigation of psychological ill-treatment. They said that although ill-treatment had taken place there had

165

PROVISIONAL IRA

Ever since Partition, the IRA had been heirs to the tradition represented by the Defenders, the Fenians, the Invincibles and the Irish Republican Brotherhood. Three times the Phoenix had risen, in 1919–21, 1939–43 and 1956–62, in an attempt to subvert Britain's solution of the Irish problem. Each time, the full machinery of the State's emergency provisions had been invoked to suppress it. Armed resistance was followed by internment (on both sides of the border) and a period of quiescence, only for the IRA to re-emerge at a more propitious moment and begin the cycle again. The last IRA campaign had continued intermittently from 1956–1962 (see page 120). It had ended with its leaders interned and with an acknowledged lack of public interest; the IRA had melted away for a reappraisal.

The IRA strategy was redesigned to evolve in three stages. A first period of broad agitation would be combined with a second phase concerned with political persuasion, before proceeding to armed resistance in the final stage. Accordingly, the movement was gradually de-militarised through the 'sixties, to the point where, in 1968, it sold most of its remaining arms to the Free Wales Army. It became an overtly socialist organisation. Thus, when events in Northern Ireland erupted once again, the IRA had neither the arms nor the organisation with which to fight the police or the Loyalists, and when it failed to come to the aid of the Catholic ghettos, it lost much support.

At the end of 1969, a clear split emerged inside the IRA, between those who wanted to continue struggling on the political front alone, and those who thought that the pressing need was to take up the armed struggle to defend the Catholic minority. This division amongst the membership was centred on Belfast, where those dissatisfied with IRA policy set about the task of preparing the armed defence of Catholic districts.

So, each of the hundred or so companies of the IRA in Northern Ireland was visited by representatives of the two viewpoints within the movement and asked to decide. Eighty per cent voted for armed resistance, the traditional Republican position; the rest voted for persevering with the political campaign, consistent with Marxist theory. Those companies in favour of armed resistance formed a Provisional Council, and later, in April 1970, the Army Council Convention ratified this change of policy by the majority of the IRA.

There were now two factions of the IRA, and although the Officials were concerned to pursue the policy of converting Ireland to socialism by means of peaceful persuasion, initially they felt it was necessary to defend their areas and to attack British military targets. Although the two groups agreed to co-operate, feuding broke out almost at once, and this was to continue throughout the early 1970s, and again from late 1974 to 1978, by which time the Officials had been further depleted by the breakaway of the militant Irish Republican Socialist Party (IRSP) and its military wing, the Irish National Liberation Army (INLA).

In early 1970, the Provisional wing began to acquire weapons and to train volunteers. The original structure of brigades was retained. Battalions were made up of companies which were divided into Active Service Units. This conventional military hierarchial structure survived until about 1978, when a formal reorganisation of the Provisional command into autonomous 'cells' took place. Much of the IRA's activity had already evolved into operations loosely based on cells by this time, and the Provisional IRA came to resemble other guerillas.

Throughout 1970 the Provisional IRA carried on a defensive campaign with the aim of protecting the minority population and building up weapons and training. British Army policy at this time concentrated on limiting IRA activity by saturating Republican districts and constantly raiding them for arms. In late 1970, the Provisionals embarked on a bombing campaign which was designed to drive the army out of their areas and to apply economic pressure on Britain, by destroying as much commercial property as possible. Frequently the bombings went wrong. Warnings were often mis-timed and many innocent civilians were killed as a result. A leading Provisional rationalised the errors with the comment: 'the Brits had Sandhurst, the Provisional IRA took bookies' runners and barmen and made them Generals.' However, there have been occasions when bombings have been planned in the certain knowledge that they would kill and maim ordinary citizens.

The bombings intensified throughout 1971 and 1972 as the Provisionals sought to drive out the British Army. By the autumn of 1973, the security forces were becoming increasingly effective in their use of surveillance and intelligence. Arrests increased and the Provisionals countered with greater use of ambush and sniping tactics.

Despite the hostility of the Catholic Church, the middle-classes, and the SDLP, the bombing campaign continued. In 1973 and 1974, the Provisionals intermittently bombed mainland Britain in the hope that such outrages would force British public opinion to opt for withdrawal from the North (see page 175).

The carnage did much to foster the image of the Provisionals as mindless terrorists, rather than as politically motivated guerillas, as they and their supporters would see them.

The Provisionals are partly financed by fund-raising activities in the USA, and links have been forged with guerilla groups elsewhere in the world, especially in the Middle East which has been a source of weapons and explosives.

During a ceasefire from February to October of 1975, the Provisionals moved into social work and community activities. They began to administer some of the commercial life in their districts and since the RUC would only venture into the ghettos escorted by the army, it fell to the Provisionals to police their own areas. General petty crime, much of it committed by youths, has always been dealt with severely. Miscreants are regularly disciplined by 'punishment shootings' in the legs, generally known as 'knee-cappings'. The rationale behind these extreme measures is that the Provisionals feel they must deal with misbehaviour ruthlessly in order to retain credibility as the civil authority in their areas.

From 1976 onwards, the Provisional campaign has been more specialised and sophisticated in its application. Bombing technology has advanced and the use of remote-controlled explosions, expecially in rural areas, has posed a major threat to the security forces – the army, the UDR, prison officers, and members of the political establishment. This struggle between the Provisionals and the security forces has replaced the high incidence of violence of the early 1970s. Consequently, the overall level of violence is lower, with fewer civilian casualties.

Guerilla groups can only operate if they have at least the tacit support of the people they claim to represent. In 1919–21 the IRA guerilla campaign against the British succeeded at least in part because of the support they received in regions of Ireland, like the South and the West. From 1956–62 the IRA campaign failed because of lack of support from the Catholic population of Northern Ireland. Today, the Provisional IRA is able to command the respect of sections of the Catholic community, enabling it to raise recruits and to function in urban and rural areas.

A secret British Army document, known as Document 37, written at the end of 1978, was leaked to the Press in May 1979. In the army's estimation:

The Provisional IRA has the dedication and the sinews of war to raise violence intermittently to at least the level of 1978, certainly for the foreseeable future . . . Any peace will be superficial and brittle. A new campaign may well erupt in the years ahead.

Its opinion of the ordinary volunteers

. . . does not support the view that they are merely mindless hooligans drawn from the unemployed and unemployable. The Provisional IRA now trains and uses its members with some care. The Active Service Units (ASUs) are for the most part manned by terrorists tempered by up to ten years of operational service.

The PHOTOGRAPH, taken by Colman Doyle for Camera Press, shows a Provisional IRA road-block outside one of the 'No-Go' areas of Derry early in 1972. Controlling the traffic in an area was one way of claiming authority over that area.

ULSTER DEFENCE ASSOCIATION

Demands for a strong military Loyalist wing (that finally became the Ulster Defence Association) date from the spring of 1971, after the Provisional IRA bombing campaign started in earnest. Under the auspices of the Shankill Defence Association, gun clubs were formed in Loyalist areas, and the SDA's *Loyalist News* told its readers to prepare for 'a holocaust which will make August '69 look like a Sunday picnic.' As the bombing rose to a new crescendo in July and August, a pamphlet was handed out in the Shankill and Sandy Row stating:

Being convinced that the enemies of the Faith and Freedom are determined to destroy the state of Northern Ireland and thereby enslave the people of God, we call on all members of our Loyalist institutions, and other responsible citizens, to organise themselves immediately into Platoons of 20 under the command of someone capable of acting as Sergeant. Every effort must be made to arm these Platoons with whatever weapons are available.

The explosion of Catholic violence after the introduction of internment in August 1971 gave a new impetus to these Loyalist demands for an active people's militia. A number of Loyalist Defence Associations came together under a central council called the Ulster Defence Association. On 6 September, a huge rally was organised by Billy Hull and his Loyalist Association of Workers. Twenty-five thousand Protestant workers from Harland and Wolff, Short Bros. and Mackie's foundry downed tools and met to listen to Loyalist appeals. Hull proclaimed that 'the age of the rubber bullet is over. It's lead bullets from now on . . . We are British to the core but we won't hesitate to take on even the British if they attempt to sell our country down the river.' This mixture of armed force and militant working-class Loyalism proved a lethal combination.

The Ulster Defence Association became the heirs of the tradition that had been passed down through Unionism, from the hesitant attempts to arm the community after Randolph Churchill's appeals in 1886, to the fully mobilised citizen's army of the Ulster Volunteer Force under Carson in 1912–14. The revival of the UVF in 1966 had been met with governmental proscription, but the UDA had never been declared an illegal organisation and had tended to come more and more out into the open. The parallel with the UVF before the First World War is striking. Just as they had armed and openly drilled throughout the Ulster countryside threatening civil war in 1912–14, so in the early months of 1972 the UDA paramilitaries marched openly in the streets.

At a series of rallies organised by William Craig's Vanguard movement (an umbrella organisation for several Loyalist groups), UDA paramilitaries paraded. On 18 March 1972, some 60,000 Loyalists attended a rally at Belfast's Ormeau Park. Included were a large number of masked and uniformed men and 2,000 former B-Specials. At the end of May, a huge phalanx of hooded UDA men marched in formation through the centre of Belfast.

One of the questions asked of armed Ulster Loyalist groups has always been, who would these 'Loyalists' take up arms against? In 1914 it looked as though the UVF would be prepared to fight the British Army if necessary to prevent the imposition of Home Rule. But in 1972, when respect between the UDA and the British Army seems to have been greater, the UDA began to 'respond' to the crisis by organising a random campaign of sectarian murders. February and March 1972 saw the renewal of the killings of Catholics in Belfast. Another two Catholics were killed in April and four in May, in what had become indiscriminate attacks upon the Catholic community. In addition, several Protestant males who had Catholic girlfriends were murdered.

In June 1972, the Provisional IRA began to retaliate, with equally indiscriminate killings of Protestants. These attacks and reprisals soon escalated to a horrifying degree and spread from the Belfast ghettos to the rest of Northern Ireland. The number of sectarian killings in July totalled 36: 19 Catholics and 17 Protestants. Thereafter, the number declined, but remained in the approximate ratio of three Catholics to each Protestant for several months. Another gruesome aspect of these killings was the increasingly sadistic nature of some of the murders which, included torture, brandings and burnings before death.

The size and distribution of the organisation gave rise to internal disputes, and several leaders were shot. However, this did not seriously weaken the overall position of the UDA amongst the Protestant people. The organisation stabilised with the appointment of Andy Tyrie as its leader in May 1973.

The Loyalists were also angry and frustrated at the authorities' reluctance to move in and break the Catholic 'No-Go' areas in Belfast and Derry. From 13 May 1972 onwards, therefore, the UDA organised their own weekend 'No-Go' areas, with men in combat jackets and hoods manning the barricades. The UDA was clearly copying the Provisional IRA in declaring itself the authority over certain districts, even down to the detail of organising 'People's Taxis' to operate where corporation buses could no longer

travel. Northern Ireland, now governed under Direct Rule from Westminster, seemed to be sliding into anarchy as more and more areas became temporarily or permanently 'out of bounds' to the agents of the state.

This led to increased confrontation between the Army and the UDA. On 7 September, a civilian and a UDA gunman were killed in a gun battle on the Shankill Road and, after further battles in October, the UDA declared 'war' on the British Army. Further show-downs between Loyalist paramilitaries and the Army led to a new wave of internments, until by mid-1974 there were nearly 60 Loyalist prisoners (against 600 Republicans) in Long Kesh.

In mid-1973, the Ulster Freedom Fighters (UFF) emerged as a group whose declared aim was to combat the IRA and defend Loyalist areas. The UFF is thought to be a splinter group from the UDA, engaged in attacks on Republicans. Membership of Protestant paramilitary groups has never been fixed, and some people alternate between one group and another.

It is clear that the UDA gained some of its support by intimidating the Protestant population and its brutal gangster methods cannot be ignored. Nevertheless, the UDA, along with the Loyalist Association of Workers, were genuinely working-class-led bodies inside the Loyalist community, independent of official Unionist Party patronage and suspicious of the middle-class-led Vanguard movement of William Craig. A leading UDA defector said to the *Sunday*

Times in January 1973 that Unionist politicians were 'middle-class smartie-pants poncing down our streets once every five years asking for our votes and then never bothering to come again until the next Election.' One weapon these working-class movements could draw upon was the withdrawal of labour by Protestant Loyalist workers. In May 1974, a strike was called by the Ulster Workers' Council to protest at the Power-Sharing Assembly (see page 176). The details of the strike campaign were worked out in the back garden of the leader of the UDA, Andy Tyrie.

From 1974 onwards, there was a growing rift between the Orange establishment and the UDA. Many working-class Protestants turned to the paramilitaries in preference to the Unionist politicians. Since 1975, the UDA has worked hard at playing down its paramilitary role and concentrating on its political aspirations. Although still at war with the Provisional IRA, the UDA (and the UVF) have left most of the fighting to the security forces. Even so, the Protestant paramilitaries periodically respond to the Provisionals's campaign and throughout 1980, the UVF and the UFF have continued with assassination attempts on leading members of the Provisional IRA.

The photograph is of a UDA parade outside Belfast City Hall on 27 May 1972. Despite a prohibition on the wearing of paramilitary uniforms, the UDA openly paraded in uniform, marching in disciplined ranks.

been no brutality because those inflicting the suffering took no pleasure in it.

On all levels, internment was a disaster. Catholic politicians refused to meet representatives from Stormont or Westminster, and set up an alternative Assembly at Dungiven (see page 161). Internment renewed and reinforced Catholic alienation from the state, and the sense of injustice was profound. Henceforth, many Catholics regarded armed resistance as the only effective response.

Despite the comprehensive hostility, the British Government still persisted in the view that the Catholic population was being coerced and intimidated by the Provisionals into subverting the State. Ministers argued that if only the Provisionals could be smashed militarily, then the Catholics would acquiesce in the continuation of the State. In addition, Faulkner complained that many of the minority's grievances had been put right. Committees had been opened to them, and there was the possibility of more Catholics entering Stormont. Faulkner also proposed a return to Proportional Representation for the first time since it had been discontinued in 1929. However, any Catholic politician who saw Irish unity as an objective would be barred. This was a last throw by the Unionists, but it still ignored the fundamental problem; how could there be a mixed administration when the ethos of the State was built on the notion of the supremacy of the Protestant Unionist majority? Indeed, that supremacy had been the chief reason for the State to come into existence, separate from the rest of Ireland.

The emphatic Catholic reaction to internment also provoked an indignant response from the Loyalists. Paisley called for the formation of a people's militia and, towards the end of 1971, Loyalist groups came together under the umbrella of an organisation called the Ulster Defence Association (see page 168). Along with the UVF, the UDA rapidly became the Loyalist paramilitary answer to the Provisionals. Throughout the remainder of 1971 and in 1972, sectarian assassinations were the Loyalist response to the Provisional IRA bombing campaign. Also, Loyalist paramilitaries began bombing public places frequented by Catholics in an effort to force them into rejecting the Provisionals. By the end of 1971, the situation was at an all-time low. Protestants and Catholics had become enemies and paramilitary activity, extensive on both sides, was taking a dreadful toll of lives and property.

The Catholic protest against the denial of civil rights by internment continued in spite of Faulkner's renewed ban on marches. On 23 January, demonstrators marched to Magilligan Camp in Co. Derry, where many local internees were held. There they were halted by the rubber bullets of the 1st Battalion of the Parachute Regiment.

The climax came one week later, on 30 January 1972, when several thousand people took part in an illegal Civil Rights march in Derry. The march was blocked by soldiers of this same Parachute Battalion, and rioting broke out in the Bogside area. The Paratroopers went into the rioting crowd and began shooting. They said they were returning fire. Thirteen Catholic males were shot dead during the course of the afternoon (see page 163).

This was the second 'Bloody Sunday' in Irish history. The world now began to question British methods of dealing with its gravest political problem. In the USA, several Senators, including Edward Kennedy, made speeches that were distinctly hostile to Britain. In Strasbourg, meanwhile, the European Human Rights Commission began to investigate complaints against Britain made by the Dublin Government. More directly, the day of the funeral of the 13 Bloody Sunday victims was made a day of mourning in the Republic, and enraged Dubliners burned the British Embassy to the ground whilst the police looked on.

Loyalist opinion hardened, and working-class pressure built up on the Right. Extremists called for more Bloody Sundays. A letter to the *UDA Bulletin* asked why not 'hit back in the only way these Nationalist bastards understand? That is, ruthless, indiscriminate killing.' A week after Bloody Sunday, former Home Affairs Minister William Craig launched a new Loyalist movement, the Ulster Vanguard. Vanguard was 'an association of associations' bringing together a number of Unionist, Orange and Loyalist groups, who demanded continued majority rule, an end to concessions, and the extermination of the IRA. In a series of rallies in February and March 1972, thousands of Loyalists came out to march in line behind Vanguard banners. They recalled Carson's resolve 'No Surrender'. Faulkner began to toughen his position in order to placate this Loyalist revival.

Westminster decided on a reappraisal. By the end of March 1972, the death-toll in Northern Ireland since 1969 stood at 761: 525 civilians, 166 soldiers, 33 UDR and 37 RUC and reservists. Nine hundred people were still interned, and the troubles were costing Britain millions of pounds. For several weeks, the Cabinet wrestled with its options before deciding to deliver to the Unionists a package of three main proposals as the price for continued devolved government in Northern Ireland. These were periodic plebiscites on the border; the gradual phasing out of internment; and the transfer of responsibility for law and order to Westminster.

On 22 March, Faulkner went to Downing Street to be told of the Government's proposals. With the Loyalists demanding greater security powers, he could hardly concur with the transfer of responsibility from them to London. Faulkner said that the Stormont Government would resign rather than accept the proposals. Heath said that if it resigned he would suspend Stormont and bring in Direct Rule.

Faulkner returned to Belfast, where his Cabinet agonised for two days before choosing resignation. On 24 March 1972, the British Government prorogued Stormont — discontinued their meetings — and announced Direct Rule from Westminster. The problem about the balance of political power once the British Army moved in to the streets, which had worried Wilson and Callaghan in the summer of 1969, had been confronted. Westminster, which had been in control of the army in Northern Ireland, now assumed political responsibility as well. Constitutionally, the province of Northern Ireland ceased to exist. The Catholic 'rebellion', which had begun with the Civil Rights campaign of the 1960s and had been met with unbending opposition until it had become the violent insurrection of the early 1970s, had succeeded.

5: DEADLOCK

Stormont had been the focus of the Roman Catholic resentment in the province of Northern Ireland, and now that it had been removed and replaced by Direct Rule from Westminster, the minority believed that reform could be achieved through constitutional politics. In this atmosphere of optimism, support for the Provisionals waned. Meanwhile, Protestant indignation was expressed in the growing support for William Craig's Vanguard Movement. Increasingly large rallies were organised through the early months of 1972, and at the end of March, a two-day Loyalist protest strike closed down the power, transport and other major industries.

Catholic opinion further hardened against the IRA in May 1972 when the Official IRA shot dead Ranger William Best, a Derry Catholic who had joined the British army and was home on leave. The revulsion against the killing led to a ceasefire, initially with the Officials, and in June with the Provisional IRA. On 7 July, Secretary of State William Whitelaw sat down to negotiate with Provisional IRA leaders.

The fragile ceasefire lasted only a few days more. In the Lenadoon estate of Belfast, the Housing Executive decided to house Catholics in homes recently vacated by Protestants. When the UDA objected to this, the army prevented the Catholic families from moving in, and it seemed to the Catholics that the army had taken sides in a sectarian housing dispute. A riot broke out accompanied by shooting, and the truce was over. On 21 July, or Bloody Friday, as it came to be known, Provisional bombs in the centre of Belfast killed nine civilians and injured more than a hundred. In the atmosphere of horror that this created, Whitelaw moved against the 'No-Go' areas of Derry. Four thousand extra troops were assembled, and on 31 July 'Operation Motorman' was launched. The troops went in and the barricades came down. This was followed by a conference at the end of the next month when moderate Catholic representatives and Unionists met Whitelaw at Darlington. The Irish Taoiseach, Lynch, had meetings with Prime Minister Heath. A Green Paper of October 1972 revealed Government thinking by announcing that there could be no change in the status of Northern Ireland without the consent of the majority, but that the minority must have a share in executive power, and the whole arrangement must be acceptable to the Republic. By bringing the moderates back together, the Government was hoping to outflank the extremists on both sides. Futhermore, it wanted to appease the Catholics, and during the latter months of 1972 the army's relations with the UDA became increasingly abrasive and resulted in a series of shooting incidents. The tension between the communities resulted in a welter of random sectarian killings; averaging by the end of 1972, three Catholics for every Protestant, killed for simply being in the wrong place at the wrong time.

In March, 1973, a White Paper announced the Government's plans for Northern Ireland. There was to be an elected Assembly of 78 members, but it would be given no authority until an executive coalition of both Catholics and Protestants, prepared to share power, had been formed. Control over law and order was to be retained by Westminster. To satisfy Nationalist aspirations for a United Ireland, the idea of a Council of Ireland, to discuss matters of mutual concern to North and South, was resurrected from the 1920 Government of Ireland Act. Thus, the Government was proposing a share in power for the Catholics and an Irish 'dimension', whilst at the same time guaranteeing the constitutional position of Northern Ireland. Moderates welcomed this ingenious proposal.

In June, elections for the Assembly took place. The SDLP took nearly all the votes from the minority, whilst the majority vote was split. Faulkner's moderates, who were in favour of power-sharing, won 22 seats, whilst the anti-power-sharing Loyalists of Craig's Vanguard and Paisley's Democratic Unionist Party took 27 seats. The first meetings of the Assembly were disrupted in July but agreement was tentatively reached later in the year and a power-sharing executive with a joint social and economic policy was set up, led by Brian Faulkner (leader of the Unionist Party) and Gerry Fitt (leader of the SDLP). Faulkner called this 'a new dawn' and Fitt declared, 'I have never felt such hope for the future.' But behind the optimism, the reality of politics was not so encouraging. The SDLP, in its enthusiasm for power-sharing, was going back on its previous stand over internment in which its members had refused to serve under Faulkner — the man who had been the hard-line advocate of internment. In any case, most Protestant opinion was hostile to the idea of sharing any power with the minority. At the beginning of December, Loyalist leaders, including Craig, Paisley and Harry West, came together to form the United Ulster Unionist Council with the express intention of bringing down the power-sharing executive.

In December 1973, the long-awaited London–Belfast–Dublin conference took place at Sunningdale in Berkshire, to formalise power-sharing and settle the details for a Council of Ireland. The conference lasted four days and was attended by Heath and the new Taoiseach of the Republic, Liam Cosgrave, along with their senior ministers. The South recognised that the position of Northern Ireland within the United Kingdom could not be changed without the agreement of the majority and agreed to co-operate over all security arrangements. A two-tier Council of Ireland was to have unspecified executive powers in relation to limited economic and social matters such as tourism. It legitimised the aspirations for a United Ireland without doing anything towards achieving it. Knowing that the substance would be too much for the majority, it was hoped that the symbol would be sufficient for the minority.

The British Government was walking a political tightrope with the skill acquired from handling complex colonial problems around the world for decades. On 1 January 1974, six Protestants and five Catholics took office in the Northern Ireland Executive. Faulkner, the head of the Executive, resigned as leader of the Unionist Party after it rejected the Sunningdale agreement, and was succeeded by Harry West, one of the founders of the UUUC, who was committed to bringing down the Executive which Faulkner still led. Then, in February 1974, a sudden General Election was called as a result of a miners' strike and the three-day week in Britain. The UUUC won 11 out of the 12 Northern Ireland seats at Westminster, a clear sign of no-confidence in Faulkner's leadership, and a massive rejection by Protestants of Whitelaw's cleverly balanced compromise solution to the Northern Ireland problem.

Events over the next few months moved quickly. Paisley called for 'drastic steps' to end the 'perfidious agreement', and demanded the restoration of a majority-rule Parliament at Stormont. Meanwhile, in the South, the Dail refused to implement proposals to extradite terrorists wanted in the North, and Cosgrave's acknowledgement of Northern Ireland's position in the UK was challenged. Both had been crucial to the Sunningdale agreement. Paisley and his supporters began to disrupt the meetings of the Assembly. Finally, grassroots Loyalism decided to take action. On 14 May, a motion rejecting Sunningdale was put before the Assembly. Various Loyalist groups declared that if the motion were defeated there would be a 'constitutional stoppage'. The motion was defeated and accordingly the Ulster Workers' Council called for a general strike (see page 176).

After two weeks, the province of Northern Ireland had been brought to a complete standstill. The resolution of the Protestant community was unyielding. The Executive resigned and with it collapsed the entire British initiative. The first administration in the history of Northern Ireland to contain representatives from the minority had lasted just five months. Paisley called this 'a triumph for traditional Unionism', and bonfires blazed in celebration up the Shankill Road. It was a sign that the Protestant community felt it had surrendered too much since 1969; that the Catholic Rebellion had been too successful. As Faulkner himself said later, 'People were showing that we had had five years of being kicked around.'

The impasse laid bare the contradictions within Northern Ireland. The majority had rejected Sunningdale because it conceded too much. The minority, however, could accept nothing less. Beyond the celebrations on the Shankill lay a political void. The failure of Sunningdale left little hope of finding a solution to the Northern Ireland crisis that relied on devolved government incorporating power-sharing. Meanwhile, opinion in the South was inclined to leave the North to sort out its own problems.

Nevertheless, the British Government persevered. In July 1974, a White Paper outlined a plan for a Constitutional Convention to provide a framework for Northern Ireland politicians to devise a settlement. Elections for the Convention took place in May 1975, with the main parties, the UUUC and the SDLP, taking 46 and 17 seats respectively. The UUUC felt that its position as the representative of the bulk of the Loyalist population was now consolidated, and it was forthright in its demands: there was to be no power-sharing, no Council of Ireland, and the Provisional IRA must be exterminated. It was surrendering nothing, and there seemed few prospects for real progress as the talks unfolded.

BOMBS IN ENGLAND

In February 1972, as a reprisal for Bloody Sunday, a bomb planted by the Official IRA went off at the Parachute Regiment's Headquarters in Aldershot. It was ominous. Frustrated by the lack of response to the Northern Ireland problem in mainland Britain, the Provisional IRA decided to open a new phase of its campaign in March 1973, on the day a border referendum was being held in Ulster. Two massive car bombs went off in London, at Great Scotland Yard and outside the Old Bailey, and 195 people were taken to hospital.

In August 1973, the assault started in earnest. Fire-bombs were left in Harrods and other West End stores and a Provisional IRA Press Officer told the Press Association ' . . . These operations will continue until the British Government states clearly its intention of allowing the Irish people to decide their own destiny.'

The Metropolitan Police already had a Bomb Squad, later renamed the Anti-Terrorist Squad, headed by Commander Bob Huntley. As letter bombs in the form of paperback books started to arrive on the desks of prominent men, he warned the public to be wary of their mail. By the end of August, the Bomb Squad had expanded, with the addition of extra explosives experts and Special Branch men, to 120. They appealed for public help against the terrorists by saying:

These people have come to London to kill and maim — and they could be living in your house. . . . If you have anybody lodging with you, or using your garage, that you are not happy about, let us know, and we will check them out.

The toll at the end of the year was two dead and 370 injured. The IRA operations continued, and on 4 February 1974, a 250-pound bomb blew the rear end off a coach carrying army personnel and their families on the M62. Twelve people were killed, nine of them soldiers. The explosion was heard five miles away.

People were searched going into shops, museums and places of work. Left-luggage offices in railway stations were closed, and packages left unattended were regarded with suspicion. For the first time, London had something of the feel of Belfast.

Bombs went off at Heathrow, the House of Commons and, in July at the Tower of London. In October, two bombs went off in pubs in Guildford, killing five more people and injuring another 65.

On 21 November, the anniversary of Dublin's Bloody Sunday in 1920, two bombs were left in pubs in Birmingham. They went off soon after 8 p.m., resulting in 21 dead and 162 injured. This led to a backlash against the Irish community in Britain: petrol bombs were thrown into Irish buildings in London. Four days later, the Home Secretary, Roy Jenkins, introduced the Prevention of Terrorism Act into Parliament. It banned the IRA, and made it an offence to belong to or support the organisation. It gave the police the power to bar suspected terrorists from Britain or to deport them back to Northern Ireland or the Republic. The Special Branch drew up a list of nearly a thousand IRA suspects or sympathisers, and moved in to expel those already in Britain.

The PHOTOGRAPH shows the aftermath of the Birmingham pub bombings.

The Ulster Workers' Council (UWC) grew out of the remnants of the Loyalist Association of Workers and, recognising the power of industrial action, set about recruiting shop stewards and key workers in essential industries. The idea of political power-sharing was anathema to the hard-line UWC. It threatened to strike if a motion to reject Sunningdale were thrown out by the Executive. At 6 p.m. on Tuesday 14 May 1974, the motion was defeated; minutes later, the UWC announced power cuts, and the strike was on.

The stoppage got off to a slow start but, backed by the Loyalist paramilitary organisations, especially the UDA, it soon gathered momentum. Road blocks were manned by masked men. People were intimidated as they tried to go to work by such actions as having their names taken or being 'photographed' with empty cameras. Transport was disrupted and Loyalist farmers blocked country roads with tractors. Petrol stations were closed to all but workers in essential services holding UWC passes. Catholics, trapped in their ghettos, could not get to work, and it was left to the Provisional IRA to supply milk, bread and petrol. The British Army was powerless, unable to force people to go to work. Within a week the Province was at a standstill.

Craig, although wary, had supported the strike, and now Paisley and West gave it their approval. They joined the UWC co-ordinating committee, chaired by Glen Barr. The Executive, led by Faulkner, was demoralised. It attempted to placate the strikers by announcing that the full Council of Ireland and the Consultative Assembly would not be given executive power until after the next Assembly election.

It was not enough for the extremists: they had the politicians on the run. The strike continued. On 23 May, Faulkner, Fitt and Napier (of the Alliance Party) flew to London to beg Prime Minister Harold Wilson to use the army to repress the strike and arrest the leaders. He refused and went on television to condemn the strikers as 'people who spend their lives sponging on Westminster and British democracy and then systematically assault democratic methods. Who do these people think they are?' It was an unfortunate speech and made the UWC even more determined to succeed. Loyalist workers pinned little sponges to their lapels. In desperation, the SDLP threatened to resign from the Executive on 27 May if the troops were not called in. That morning, the soldiers opened up 27 petrol stations in the Province.

Undaunted, the UWC threatened to close down all essential services if the troops intervened. Faulkner pleaded with Merlyn Rees, the Secretary of State, to negotiate with the UWC. Rees refused, and Faulkner resigned on the afternoon of 28 May saying: 'I have never experienced a sadder day in my life from the point of view of the country that I love.' The strike had been totally successful in achieving its objectives. The ideals of Sunningdale were in ruins.

The PHOTOGRAPH shows jubilant Loyalists welcoming the news of the fall of the Executive.

In the hope of encouraging the political dialogue to continue, and in an attempt to pull the Provisionals towards establishment politics, another truce was negotiated with them early in 1975. Again, the ceasefire was to prove precarious, and hostilities resumed in October. The Provisionals intensified their bombing campaign against commercial targets, and also stepped up their border campaign with the increasing use of sophisticated remote-controlled bombs. But they were aware that the deaths of innocent civilians only alienated public opinion in general and their own supporters in particular. So they turned their attacks on to the security forces — the army, the UDR and the prison officers, whom many Catholics saw as 'the enemy'. In July 1976, they widened their attacks to include members of the political establishment, when they assassinated the British Ambassador in Dublin, Christopher Ewart-Biggs (see page 167).

The Constitutional Convention, predictably, was unable to agree on the form of devolved government in Northern Ireland. Paisley's implacable hostility towards any form of power-sharing seemed to dominate the Loyalist side, and the Convention finally voted by 42 votes to 31 for a return to the Stormont system which had been rejected by Westminster in 1972. The second initiative since the imposition of Direct Rule expired at the beginning of November 1975.

By the end of the year, the last of the internees was released. This caused friction between the Government and the army who felt that the release of the internees was sabotaging its attempts to defeat the Provisionals. This, together with the failure of the truce and the collapse of the Convention, made for a change in British policy. Accordingly, Secretary of State Merlyn Rees announced the end of 'Special Category' (political) status in prisons. From March 1976, anyone convicted of a terrorist offence would be considered a common criminal and would have to obey the rules of a conventional prison regime. This led to a direct confrontation between the authorities and the prisoners, resulting first in the 'blanket' and then the 'dirty' protest in the H-Blocks of Long Kesh. This had now become a propaganda war to force the political issue out into the open and to generate condemnation of Britain's policy on the world stage (see page 182).

Militarily, the British had introduced the Special Air Service (SAS) into Northern Ireland at the beginning of 1976 following a spate of brutal sectarian killings in South Armagh. Its counter-insurgency operations since then have caused several civilian deaths, arousing great controversy about the nature of SAS tactics, and serving to increase further Catholic bitterness at the British military presence in Northern Ireland.

Roy Mason's appointment as Secretary of State in September 1976 coincided with a new phenomenon in Northern Ireland. When the army shot dead a Provisional as he tried to evade a road block, his car crashed into three small children who were killed. In a wave of grief over the deaths of the three innocent children, Betty Williams and Mairead Corrigan formed the Women's Peace Movement. The Movement succeeded in bringing together Protestants and Catholics, who, for a short period, united out of a sense of genuine despair before the continued violence. Although it attracted

GUERILLA WAR: MILITARY

The avowed aims of the IRA are to force the British out of Ireland, and the present confrontation is seen as merely the latest phase in a struggle that goes back over several centuries. The strategy and tactics of a modern guerilla war largely came out of the Anglo–Irish war of 1919–21. It has two facets: firstly, the military objective of making Ireland ungovernable and thereby sapping the will of British politicians, and secondly, a propaganda war in which the insurgents attempt to provoke the British into actions which would cause revulsion and war-weariness among the public at home, and censure from international opinion. The military battle is to be conducted on the streets and in the countryside: the propaganda war in the media, the courts and prisons. The British have to be persuaded that the game is not worth the playing.

On the military side, the war must be made to seem so vile and futile that it produces an upsurge of sentiment in Britain demanding that the troops should be brought home and the contending parties left to sort it out amongst themselves. But this strategy also runs the risk of alienating local support and of provoking official and unofficial reprisals. It was most successfully used against the British in Palestine by the Zionist groups, the Stern gang, and the Irgun under the direction of Menachem Begin. The bombing of the British administration offices in the King David Hotel, where 91 people were killed, and the hanging of two British sergeants whose bodies were then booby-trapped, so sickened public opinion in Britain that it was easy for the British to abandon Palestine, leaving Jew and Arab to fight over it. The IRA bombings over the years have not been as successful, perhaps because being nearer to home, they tend to produce outrage rather than revulsion. Having been schooled not only in Ireland and Palestine but also in Cyprus, East Africa, Aden and elsewhere in the Empire, the British Army is the most experienced in the world in dealing with insurgency. The major problem facing an army confronted with a civil insurrection is that it cannot behave like an army. The 'battlefield' contains homes, shops, factories and civilians, and traditional military methods would have the effect of totally alienating the civilian population. Indeed, measures that are too 'firm', like the reprisals of 1920–21 or internment in 1971, risk uniting the whole community behind those whom the army is seeking to destroy. In other words, the measures which are needed to defeat the terrorists are precisely those measures which ensure that the terrorists will get maximum support from their community. This leaves the army on the ground with the impossible task of not being able to hit back effectively at an unseen enemy that strikes and then melts back into the community. It puts great pressure upon the army, whether in Co. Cork in 1920 or Co. Armagh in 1980.

In 1975, a split emerged between the Official IRA and a breakaway group called the Irish Republican

Socialist Party. The latter organisation called for a more aggressive approach and subsequently became militarised when some of its members formed the Irish National Liberation Army. It was this group who carried out the murder of Airey Neave in April 1979, in the build up to the General Election. At the same time as this split, feuding recommenced between the Officials and the Provisional IRA, continuing intermittently until 1978.

Early in 1978, a development that had been taking place gradually inside the Provisional IRA for some time was formalised. The traditional command structure of Brigades, Battalions, Companies and Active Service Units, arranged on a geographical basis, was restructured around specialist cells, autonomous from each other. This reorganisation, thought by the army to be the work of Provisional leader Gerry Adams, put the IRA in line with the command structure of other guerilla armies throughout the world, and made it much more difficult to infiltrate.

Although the Provisional IRA has been repeatedly defeated in open elections, there is little doubt that part of the Catholic community, at least tacitly, supports it, and is willing to shelter its active service members. A senior officer in Defence Intelligence, Brigadier Glover, prepared a secret intelligence appraisal of the situation in Northern Ireland in 1978. This paper, known as Document 37, was later leaked to the Press. It said:

Although the Provisionals have lost much of the spontaneous backing they enjoyed early in the campaign, there is no sign of any equivalent upsurge of support for the Security Forces. There are still areas within the Province, both rural and urban, where the terrorists can base themselves with little risk of betrayal and can count on active support in emergency.

The military situation in the Province has reached stalemate. The IRA has not been able to make areas ungovernable, as it did with parts of the south and the west in 1920–21, but on the other hand, in Document 37, the army does not believe that it can defeat them. It concludes: 'The Provisionals' campaign of violence is likely to continue while the British remain in Northern Ireland.' Both sides are aware of the risks of escalating the situation. The army knows that it would alienate more of the Catholic community. The IRA, by stepping up the campaign to wholesale assaults on property, would risk innocent deaths and the abrogation of its own supporters.

The first PHOTOGRAPH expresses all the incongruity of the British army in its latest 'battlefield' — the housing estates of Northern Ireland. It shows troops in the Lenadoon estate of Belfast in July 1972. The second photograph shows an IRA gunman silhouetted against a burning vehicle, a result of the wave of protest which swept Belfast after the introduction of internment on 9 August 1971.

enormous media attention, particularly after the co-founders Williams and Corrigan were awarded the Nobel Peace Prize in 1976, the peace campaign was more of a spontaneous expression of a mood rather than a viable political movement. It seemed to offer an opportunity for the community to reject violence, but in fact there was no consensus within the community, except the revulsion from violence, on which they could build.

One of the causes of dissension in the minority community was the adoption of a new system of prison sentencing in 1976. In an effort to find a judicial process less crude than internment, but less susceptible to intimidation than the orthodox British system of witnesses and juries, the government had appointed a commission, back in 1972, under Lord Diplock, to examine 'legal procedures to deal with terrorist activities in Northern Ireland'. The recommendations of Lord Diplock made it possible to hold prisoners on remand for long periods and, more importantly, in all trials of terrorist offences the normal courts were replaced by courts with no juries and presided over by a single judge. This avoided the problem of the intimidation of jurors and inevitably, in such courts, the evidence of confessions proved especially important (see page 183). A large proportion of these confessions were obtained under interrogation at the RUC Castlereagh barracks outside Belfast. Between April 1972 and October 1974, over 600 complaints were made against the RUC interrogators, and in 1978 Britain was found guilty by the European Court of Human Rights at Strasbourg of 'inhuman and degrading treatment' of prisoners. In 1979, a government inquiry under Judge Bennett confirmed that there had been cases of ill-treatment. However, Secretary of State Mason, RUC Chief Constable Newman and GOC Army General Creasey decided to continue the interrogation of prisoners, confident that it was the only way they could ensure the conviction of the men they believed to be terrorists.

Towards the end of 1977, Mason instigated his own political initiative, the second since the failure of the power-sharing Executive. It was based on the idea of a devolved non-legislating 78-seat assembly from which sub-committees would be drawn to run non-contentious areas such as health, social services, transport and housing. Discussions on the plan dragged on for some months but never looked particularly hopeful, and in January 1978, Harry West said the official Unionist Party would not discuss the issue of interim devolution until Britain repudiated the idea of power-sharing. When the proposals were discussed in the House of Commons, a total of only 13 MPs sat right through the debate and attendance rarely exceeded 25 members at any one time.

By the summer of 1980, the deadlock in Northern Ireland looks no nearer to resolution. Over 2,000 people have been killed since the troubles began in August 1969. In the same period, there have been 6,500 explosions and over 27,000 shooting incidents; £325 million compensation has been paid on damage to property and £55 million to persons. It has been calculated that the total cost to the UK Exchequer of Northern Ireland, above taxes collected there, is now running at about a thousand million pounds annually. The growing military sophistication of the Provisional IRA has been secretly acknowledged by the army in Document 37 (see page 167), and was glaringly demonstrated in August 1979 when Lord Mountbatten and his family were blown up in his boat off Co. Sligo on the same day that 18 British soldiers were ambushed and killed at Warrenpoint near the border. Meanwhile, the Loyalists seem no more willing to accept any form of power-sharing, and in the European Parliamentary elections of 1979, Paisley was revealed as the most popular leader of the Protestant community. At the time of writing, the 1980 initiative of the Conservative Secretary of State, Humphrey Atkins, looks likely to founder on the same rocks as previous attempts. All Westminster initiatives, to a greater or lesser extent, come down to a form of institutionalised power-sharing, and whilst this remains unacceptable to the majority, there can be little hope of a settlement agreeable to the minority or to Dublin. Whilst the politicians carry on talking, sectarian killings by Loyalists continue to answer Provisional IRA assassinations of prison officers and UDR personnel, and in the H-blocks of Long Kesh, 380 men on the dirty protest, reinforced by over 30 women in Armagh jail and by 150 men on remand in Crumlin Road jail, highlight the continuing political impasse.

Sunningdale and the political initiatives that have followed it clearly spell out the intractable nature of the problem. Given the Protestant record in government, the Catholic community will not agree to majority rule because, as they rightly point out, this means Protestant rule. There must be Catholic participation in government from top to bottom, they argue, for the civil, social and political rights of the Catholics to be assured. On the other hand, the Unionists argue that, as in other societies, the majority party should have the natural right to govern. They find concessions particularly hard to make when they are demanded by the minority which has consistently shown itself to be disloyal, is committed to a United Ireland and in which some people give support to the Provisional IRA's military campaign against the state. Most Loyalists, therefore, favour a return to majority rule under a regime similar to Stormont, in which government is dominated by the majority political party — and in the case of Northern Ireland, this means one-party, Unionist government. But majority rule can only work when there is consensus and when there is the opportunity for an opposition to take power. Neither of these pre-conditions exists in Northern Ireland and devolved government is discredited by the evidence of its history.

The other obvious and traditionally pursued solution to the problem is unification. From the British point of view, a united Ireland, in the long term, could be a very acceptable solution, finally jettisoning the Irish problem that has plagued British politics for centuries. In 1971, Harold Wilson, albeit whilst in opposition, put forward a proposal for a United Ireland, preceded by a 15-year transitional period, and there is evidence that in private, politicians talk of reunification as the eventual resolution. In the South, according to a recent opinion poll, few people are prepared to give up the claim to a United Ireland as enshrined in the constitution of the Republic. With its long folk memory of British injustice, passions still run deep, as the anger of the crowds that burnt down the British Embassy in Dublin in the

GUERILLA WAR: PROPAGANDA

An essential part of guerilla war is the propaganda battle, a campaign to win over public opinion. In the context of Ireland, this involves forcing British politicians into actions that would discredit them at home and bring down censure on them from abroad. In the aftermath of the 1916 Rising, Republican prisoners in Mountjoy Jail, Dublin, demanded political status – that they should be treated as prisoners of war, not criminals. This was refused, and a hunger strike was called in protest. One prisoner, Thomas Ashe, deprived of his bed, bedding, prison uniform and boots, died as a result of injuries incurred during forced feeding. Massive popular support for Republican prisoners ensued, and the Government was forced to concede the prisoners' demands. Similarly in 1972, Republican prisoners interned in Long Kesh decided to challenge the British Government over the issue of political status. A hunger strike brought huge popular support, and faced with widespread civil disturbances, the Gov-

ernment once again gave way and granted 'Special Category' status. Prisoners were allowed to wear their own clothes, do no prison work, and were segregated from prisoners convicted of criminal offences. They were allowed free association with their colleagues, and unlimited mail. At the end of 1975, Secretary of State for Northern Ireland, Merlyn Rees, announced the end of political status. From March 1976 those found guilty of terrorist offences would be treated as criminals.

Nineteen-year-old Ciaran Nugent was the first prisoner to be denied political status. So, in September 1976, he refused to wear prison uniform, and wore only a blanket, having nothing else to cover himself with. Others followed Nugent and went on the 'blanket' protest. The prisoners were denied parcels, writing materials, newspapers, radio or television. Dr D. Deeny, a member of the Government-appointed Long Kesh Prison Visiting Committee, commented in March 1977:

I found they were, for all practical purposes, in the equivalent of solitary confinement. They had been allowed to wear a blanket in their cells, but are not allowed to wear a blanket outside their cells. This means that if they leave their cells they are naked: this they regard as degrading, and therefore, they refuse to go.

As the men were not allowed to leave their cells without wearing prison uniforms, the prison cells became lavatories. The filth accumulated, and the blanket demonstration now became the 'dirty' protest. By the summer of 1978, more than 300 prisoners were on the dirty protest at Long Kesh, mostly Provisionals, but some members of the Loyalist paramilitary groups. Such was the public concern over the health of the prisoners that the Primate of All Ireland, Cardinal O'Fiach, visited the H-Blocks. He was shocked by what he witnessed:

One would hardly allow an animal to remain in such conditions, let alone a human being. The nearest approach to it that I have seen was the spectacle of hundreds of homeless people living in sewer pipes in the slums of Calcutta . . . I was unable to speak for fear of vomiting.

During the late 1970s, just as in 1917 and in 1920, the issue of political status has become a trial of strength between the British Government and the IRA. Despite widespread support for the prisoners amongst the minority population in the North, the general media line on the H-Blocks has reflected the Government attitude that the men are convicted criminals and terrorists, and that their degradation is self-inflicted. The extensive publicity for the H-Block campaign that would provide the forum in which wider issues of British policy might be raised has not been, so far, forthcoming.

The refusal to accept criminal status presents problems for the police and courts as well. In Northern Ireland, convictions for terrorist offences are usually obtained in Diplock Courts on the basis of confessions extracted under interrogation (see page 180). Amnesty International has calculated that between 70% and 80% of convictions are based

wholly or mainly on admission of guilt (self-incriminating statements) made to the police during interrogation and only in a minority of cases is other evidence — forensic evidence, intelligence evidence or the testimony of witnesses — produced in court to secure a conviction.

In January 1978, the Court of Human Rights at

Strasbourg found a group of RUC officers guilty of using 'inhuman and degrading treatment', but not torture, in extracting confessions from 14 internees back in 1974. There is growing disquiet about police methods being used in Northern Ireland, and the classic guerilla stratagem of forcing the authorities to go beyond what civilised societies regard as acceptable in the war against terrorism, is being more successful.

The British authorities have been remarkably adept in keeping the issue of the H-Blocks and the interrogation centres at a very low level, even though there has been some criticism abroad, mostly in America, of the Government's policy. The sensitive nature of this subject and its ramifications in the propaganda battle helps to explain why reporting on these matters, particularly on television, has been so tentative and restrained.

The first PHOTOGRAPH shows women protesting over the treatment of Irish prisoners in Mountjoy Jail, Dublin in April 1920.

The second photograph shows women protesting in the Falls Road, Belfast, over the treatment of prisoners in Long Kesh in 1978.

CHURCH AND STATE

The Roman Catholic Church in Ireland is one of the most powerful and conservative in Europe. Its particular place in the hearts and minds of Irishmen stems from the Penal days, when the peasantry and the outlawed church drew close together in opposition to the alien Protestant state. The authority that many Irishmen and Irishwomen allow the priest at the local level, and the church hierarchy at the national level, has caused the Ulster Protestants to fear that Dublin Rule would mean Rome Rule. It was this desperate hostility to living in a Catholic state that helped to inspire the Protestants of the North from 1910 to 1914, and it is behind the implacable opposition to becoming a minority in a Catholic United Ireland many Protestants have today.

The record of the Catholic Church in the Free State has certainly confirmed some of the worst Ulster Protestant fears. The Catholic Church's attitude to mixed marriages and education, for example, has always been severe. The church blesses mixed marriages only when it is agreed that the children of the marriage will be brought up as Catholics, and it has long believed that exclusively Catholic education is all part of its duty.

Many Protestant fears were realised when the new constitution for the Republic was drawn up in 1935–6

(see page 109). The Catholic flavour of this constitution is unmistakable, and marks it apart from the constitutions of other western states. Not only was the Catholic Church assured a 'special position' in the state (Article 44) but Catholic teachings on the family are strongly reflected in the constitution. Article 41 states that the family is 'the natural primary and fundamental unit group of society' and as a 'moral institution' possesses 'inalienable and imprescriptible rights, antecedent and superior to all positive law.' It specifically forbids divorce and guarantees that 'mothers shall not be obliged by economic necessity to engage in labour to the neglect of their duties in the home'. This was backed up with the 1935 Criminal Law Amendment Act which forbade the sale and the import of contraceptives. Article 42 of the constitution acknowledges the family to be 'the primary and natural educator' of children (although it goes on to say that the state will provide 'a certain minimum education'). Added to all this, the government established a Censorship Board with the responsibility to recommend that any indecent or obscene books should be banned (including any publication that advocated birth control). The Board has banned many of the great works of modern literature, and during the early 1960s, as many as thirty books a

184

month were still being banned. Similarly, a government Film Censor has prevented many of the masterpieces of the modern cinema from being seen in Ireland, at least in their full versions.

The most obvious manifestations of the power of the Catholic Church came in 1951, when the bishops objected to the Mother and Child Scheme of the Health Minister, Dr Noel Browne. He planned to introduce a national health scheme for maternity and child welfare which was to include the education of women 'in respect of motherhood', that is, some form of sex education by state medical officers. This was thought to impinge upon the primacy of the family, and it provoked a decisive confrontation between the Catholic bishops and Dr Browne. It resulted in Browne's resignation and a victory for the ecclesiastical defenders of the Irish people's faith and morals.

Much of this emphasis on Catholicism must be put in the context of a long and distinctive tradition of Catholic Christianity in Ireland. In a country where 90% of the population go to mass on a Sunday, the Irish identity has become indelibly associated with a Catholic identity. The popular affirmation of Catholic values has to some extent been an affirmation of the 'Irishness' of the state, a statement of the independence and integrity of a people whose national identity and religion have been denied for centuries. However, no country exists in a vacuum, and the attempt to preserve values from outside 'corrupting' influences has become impossible over the recent decades. The Catholic Church itself has been under attack for its attitude towards contraception and abortion, and there is considerable evidence of a change in attitude towards these emotive issues in Ireland. Furthermore, views on censorship have become markedly more liberal today than fifteen years ago. The country's membership of the EEC has brought further re-assessment, and in a referendum at the end of 1972, the people of Ireland voted to remove from the constitution Article 44 which had given the Catholic Church its 'special position' in the state. In the spring of 1980, the Taoiseach, Charles Haughey, hinted that the Republic would be prepared to repeal for the six counties of the North in a united Irish Republic those Articles of the constitution which most grated on Protestant sensibilities. As a gesture to attract the Ulster Protestants into a United Ireland, this is clearly of the utmost significance, as it could remove at a stroke many of the Protestant fears about Dublin Rule.

The Protestants too, in Northern Ireland, have striven to assert their religious convictions. The attitude of the Orange Order towards segregated education, for instance, has been no less strict than

that of the Catholic Church (see page 122). Religious fundamentalism has often been close to the surface in Northern Ireland, with religious leaders frequently in the vanguard of political movements. Ian Paisley is the most spectacular example of recent times. His loathing of Romanism has encouraged him to look for the best safeguards against being dragged into a Catholic state. Indeed, to fundamentalist Protestants like Paisley, liberty is reliant upon people being able to pursue their *own* understanding of the scriptures. So it is logical that to preserve freedom itself, it is necessary to resist the authoritarian strictures of the Roman Catholic Church. It is no coincidence that church attendance in Northern Ireland is very high and that the more puritanical counsels have prevailed in, for instance, legislation on Sunday Observance and drinking and gambling. Northern Ireland is today the only part of the United Kingdom where pubs are closed on Sundays.

The PHOTOGRAPHS illustrate two aspects of Irish Catholicism. The public face — when over a million people turned up to see the Pope in Phoenix Park, Dublin, September 1979; the private face — an old man comforted by crucifix and madonna at home.

wake of Bloody Sunday bears witness. But for some people in the Republic, a United Ireland has become more of a symbolic gesture necessitated by Ireland's past than a desirable political objective. This is reflected in the ambivalence of the Republic's government towards the IRA, the traditional weapon in the battle for unity. The government claims to be totally opposed to its tactics of terrorism, yet refuses to implement fully extradition; it is known that in 1969 Cabinet members colluded in gun-running for the Provisionals. Politicians in the Republic are required to support the ideal of a United Ireland, but are aware that should the Provisionals achieve a unified state, they would redirect their struggle against Dublin in order to attain a socialist Republic in Ireland. In the end, however, the need to realise the Republican dream and to honour the debt to the past would, probably, outweigh the anxieties of those who are fearful of the problems that the North would present to Dublin in a united Ireland. Such a solution remains, of course, totally unacceptable to the Protestants in the North. Ulster, they argue, is different by religion, birth, economic interest and in its feelings of national identity, that it contains a people who are emphatically different from the rest of the country and in a united Ireland their identity would be lost. While the Irish Catholic Church remains so authoritarian, and with its unique status in Irish society and government, unity is unthinkable (see page 184). There can be no doubt that they would fight to prevent it and that, as in 1912, they would find allies amongst British conservatives. The core of the problem comes down to whether the Catholics should be a minority in Northern Ireland or the Protestants should be a minority in a United Ireland. For, whoever is the minority, both sides are convinced that they will suffer discrimination and exploitation. So, a Federal Ireland or a British–Irish Condominium Rule are rejected by Loyalists on the grounds that each represents a small but significant step towards drawing Northern Ireland out of the UK and pushing it towards the Republic.

Meanwhile, total integration into the United Kingdom is no more admissible to Republicans today than it was to the Irish Nationalists in 1800, at the time of the Act of Union. There are, of course, more radical proposals, among them the idea of an independent Ulster put forward by the New Ulster Political Research Group, closely associated with the Loyalist paramilitary group, the UDA. This move towards independence is coming from working-class Loyalists who are shifting away from traditional Unionist politics and traditional Loyalism to Britain, because they believe both have betrayed them and they are left with no alternative but to opt for an independent Northern Ireland. They argue in their paper 'Beyond the Religious Divide' that 'any proposal which involved London would be rejected by the minority community and any proposal which involved Dublin would be rejected by the majority community.' The logic of this, they conclude, is that Ulster must be independent from both London and Dublin. Reaching beyond the religious divide, a constitution for their independent Ulster would seek to establish 'consensus politics' and to 'develop a common identity between the communities'. The rights of all the citizens of this mini-state would be protected by the Bill of Rights, and its supporters insist that an independent Ulster would not be 'the creation of a Protestant-dominated state, nor a stepping stone to a United Ireland.' However, whilst these ideas are gaining ground in some Protestant districts, the Catholic community remains unconvinced that such promises would not just mean, at best, a return to Stormont government or, at worst, rule by the paramilitary Loyalists of the UDA. Also, it is difficult to see that such a state could never be an economically viable proposition without some kind of international support.

The unilateral withdrawal from Northern Ireland of British troops, would be likely to spark off sectarian warfare more severe than anything the Province has yet suffered. The scale of fighting would be likely to result in a flight of Catholics from Protestant districts and vice versa throughout the Province. The situation in Belfast would be particularly serious, as the Catholic ghettos are not only scattered in a predominantly Protestant city, but surrounded by an overwhelmingly Protestant countryside. The Republic could hardly be expected to stand idly by and watch the slaughter, and no doubt would be tempted to intervene on behalf of the isolated Catholic communities. A war would probably result in a smaller Protestant state, with the Catholic border areas seceding to the South. This is the sort of solution that Britain has finally resorted to, in the past, when faced with apparently intractable problems such as India or Palestine. But the blood-letting that would be inevitable in a part of the United Kingdom, the international ramifications that a unilateral withdrawal would bring, along with the damage to Anglo–Irish relations, preclude it as a viable solution in Northern Ireland. The withdrawal of troops, unless accompanied by a longer-term political programme that is acceptable to all sides in the dispute, would result in a blood bath.

What seems plain is that given the position of the contending political factions in Northern Ireland at present, there *is* no political solution to the problem. No proposals, however sophisticated, can bring together or satisfy parties which fundamentally disagree. Interestingly, many of the historians we spoke to in the preparation and making of *The Troubles* took the view that the problem was, in the short run at least, insoluble. No matter how unpalatable it may be to politicians, there is no reason to believe that there are political solutions to *all* problems. If the political parameters defy solution, the only approach is to begin to change, in the context of a society that has agreed to disagree, those parameters themselves. Politics in Northern Ireland is not about solutions, but about how to change the situation sufficiently to make talk of solutions realistic.

The historian, Patrick O'Farrell, has noted that: 'No other of England's historical relationships has generated such protracted and intense difficulties nor produced such emotion, exasperation and bewilderment, nor so many differing plans for some solution.' This is partly due to the length of the relationship, stretching across nine troubled centuries. Ireland has frequently been called England's first colony, and will probably turn out to be her last. But Ireland itself possesses several important characteristics that make its

LOYALTY AND DISLOYALTY

One of the paradoxes of the Unionist position is that they express a loyalty to the crown and country which, by English standards, is wildly exaggerated, yet at the same time they have shown themselves willing to challenge the authority of the state with insurrection. They fly the Union Jack above platforms from which they preach sedition. This they did before the First World War, and again in the mid-1970s, in their resistance to power-sharing.

Ulster Protestants have never experienced the nationalist phase of European development. Nationalism is the cohesive force which holds most nations together. People in society accept the authority of the state because they believe themselves to be a 'nation', a group of people of like ideas, and usually of common culture, religion and ethnic origin. Nationalism as a nineteenth-century notion superceded a contractual view of society which is still largely held by Ulster Protestants. This espouses a concept of society in which there is a contract between ruler and ruled and each side takes up certain obligations towards the other. If this trust is broken by one side, the other side is released from its obligations. Ian Paisley pointed this out to the Secretary of State in 1977 when he said: 'Government is not a one-way street. It is a civil contract in which each party has a duty.' The people of Ulster choose to remain British, not because they are like Britons (a survey of 1968 showed that Protestants in Northern Ireland regard the English, and not the Irish, as 'different') but because the British connection is a guarantee to them against being drawn into a Catholic Ireland. Thus, a pamphlet issued by the Loyalist group, Vanguard, after Direct Rule in 1972, argued that Ulster Loyalists are 'an old and historic community' and saw the British connection as 'a means of preserving Ulster's British traditions and the identity of her Loyalist people.' Vanguard described the Whitelaw administration as 'the government of usurpation set up in flagrant breach of a constitutional compact made with our ancestors in 1920 and accepted by them for their posterity after a generation and more of political struggle.' If Britain abrogated its responsibilities, then the people of

Ulster had a right to resist the policies of the Ministers of the Crown. This they were prepared to do in 1912 in the Covenant, which affirmed loyalty to the British Crown whilst giving notice of the intention to resist Home Rule although that was the will of the Westminster Parliament. The same happened in 1974 when they brought down the power-sharing Executive, which had been democratically elected, in a general strike. In other words, their loyalty to the British Crown and Government was conditional; conditional upon the British Government carrying out its part of the contract by wholehearted support for the Union in 1912, or the maintainance of Northern Ireland as part of the United Kingdom in the 1970s. So the Loyalists can be rebels against the very institution to which they give loyalty.

This view also has ramifications for the Catholic community in Northern Ireland. In their refusal to accept the legitimacy of the State, they refused to take up the contract and thereby, in Loyalist eyes, put themselves outside the State and the protection and benefits it was obliged to provide. The State had no obligations to those who have not taken up their responsibilities.

Furthermore, for that part of the community who refuse to recognise the right of the State to exist, the institutions to which the Loyalists swear their loyalty have become the symbols of their opposition and hatred. Just as the Loyalists applaud and rejoice in

the monarchy, so it represents to Republicans all that they despise and reject about the Northern Ireland State.

In August 1977, the Queen visited Northern Ireland as part of her Jubilee celebrations. It was her first visit since 1966, and a huge influx of extra security forces was needed to keep order in the Republican ghettos: 30,000 security forces were deployed to contain potential Republican protests. The visit illustrated the divide in the community. As a cause for Loyalist jubilation, it became an opportunity for Republican animosity. Widespread rioting punctuated the week of celebrations, although this was generally ignored in the British media, which created an impression of calm and stability in the Province.

The British Government faces a situation in Northern Ireland where the ultra-Loyalists are prepared to fight it, if it breaks the contract on which their loyalty is dependent, and where the institutions of government are themselves the object of hostility from the minority who resent the existence of the state.

The first PHOTOGRAPH illustrates the excess of loyalty that can be seen amongst the Ulster Protestants; two women take part in the 1970 Orange Parade. The second photograph shows a wall daubed with the colours of the Irish tricolour and anti-Jubilee graffiti, in 1977.

situation unique. Firstly, the people of the island do not share a single national identity; secondly, religion and economics have further broadened these divisions; thirdly, there has never been a time when all the people of Ireland have been effectively governed by an authority that they fully accepted as legitimate. Moreover, Britain and Ireland were two nations with deep cultural differences that were never as obvious as the difference between Britain and her colonies. After all, the Irish are the same colour, speak the same language and are in such close proximity that they could be thought of as part of the British nation. In fact, the differences between Ireland and Britain, particularly over the last 200 years, are more striking than the similarities. Ireland was poor, rural, Catholic and Gaelic. Britain was rich, industrial, Protestant and outward-looking. But when the Irish failed to behave in the way the British predicted, they were characterised as backward, irrational, superstitious and treacherous. As early as 1807, Sydney Smith pointed out that 'The moment the very name of Ireland is mentioned, the English seem to bid adieu to common feeling, common prudence and common sense and to act with the barbarity of tyrants and the fatuity of idiots.' Indeed, the British have thought it essential to control Ireland from at least the sixteenth century, not only for reasons of strategy and imperial pride, but also because of the need for a convenient source of agricultural goods, land, rent and cheap labour. In this context of colonial exploitation, it has been helpful for the British to regard the Irish as their inferiors — for they could hardly have had the same relationship with their equals. Hence, the myth of the Paddy has grown up, the drunken, happy-go-lucky labourer with the clay pipe and the *Punch* magazine ape-face, which is still strong in English culture, in different forms, today.

Britain always found it easier to subjugate Ireland than to understand the Irish. Ireland was close enough to be a constant irritation, but distant enough to prevent familiarity. So the British, bedazzled by a righteous belief in the virtues of their own civilisation, had neither the inclination nor the modesty to understand the culture of the Irish. On the Irish side, it was the effect of the imperial relationship that was most pernicious, both in its economic exploitation and in its denial of political independence. So, English rule was blamed for being the cause of every Irish grievance. It was even said that England's principal motivation for being in Ireland was to destroy the Irish. This Irish view of the English became so virulent that John Mitchel wrote of the Famine that a 'million and a half men, women and children were carefully, prudently and peacefully *slain* by the English government.' Just as Ireland became integral to the spirit of Empire in Britain, so for many Irishmen the conflict with Britain became an anti-imperialist struggle, and it is salutory to reflect that the Provisional IRA today regard themselves as the heirs to this campaign to oust British colonial rule from Ireland.

Irish history does not loom large in the English experience, yet the English dominate Irish history, and from the beginning of the nineteenth century the Irish issue was always discussed in a British setting — it became '*England's* Irish problem'. *The Times* was driven to write in 1867 that 'the Englishman's view of the question is that which must prevail in the end, whatever

TWO COMMUNITIES

In Northern Ireland, religion is a badge for the political divisions of the community. Church attendance is not only a religious but also a political act, an outward expression of sectarian solidarity. Both communities find strength and security by remaining inside their own clearly defined territories. The two ways in which a community is likely to come together through non-sectarian education and mixed marriages, are taboo. In both communities, the church and the school are the focal points around which people gather, thus creating and sustaining the ghetto.

These tribal areas are not confined to the cities. The social anthropologist Rosemary Harris studied a mixed country area near the border and found the community divided in many aspects of day to day life, not just religion and schooling. With sport, for instance, one group played hockey, rugby and football whilst the other side played hurling, camogie and gaelic football. Each group had its own pub, grocer, chemist and doctor. Dances were nearly always segregated and held in halls with religious or political connections. When members of the two communities did meet, there was hardly any discussion on religious or political matters or, significantly, any subject that might lead up to them.

Harris, an English Protestant, stayed with a Catholic family. She wrote:

I was invited into the house of Protestant neighbours whom I had not previously met — the wife saying to me, 'Do come in and have a cup of tea; the people you're staying with are very nice, but it's not like being with your own, is it?' The assumption was that I would be able to relax and feel at home only in a Protestant household.

Sociologist F.W. Boal studied the two adjoining Belfast districts of the Clonard (98% Catholic) and the Shankill (99% Protestant). Without exception, they supported different football teams. Of the Clonard families, 83% read the Catholic *Irish News*, but only 3% of the Shankill. In both districts, 90% supported the shops of their own community, even when they were not the most convenient. In an area of less than 5,000 people, there were two distinct communities where people felt secure amongst their own kind.

This geography of sectarianism cannot be seen, except perhaps from the graffiti, but every local person knows the sectarian area and its boundaries. In Belfast, there are many Catholics who have not walked down the Shankill Road and Protestants who have never visited the Falls, even though they are only a few hundred yards apart. These sectarian divides are often a cause of puzzlement to outsiders, and when the army has been called in to keep the peace between the two communities, its response on many occasions (in 1872, 1935 and 1969) has been to erect 'peace lines', or barricades, down the divide between the two groups.

The PHOTOGRAPH shows the peace line running between the Catholic Clonard and the Protestant Shankill in 1979.

In the evening of the next day, the two parties met for a pitched battle, to the number of several thousands, in the brickfields between the Shankill and Falls Roads. The police tried in vain to separate them and the military were sent for . . . [they] forced the combatant mobs apart, but showers of stones were thrown over the heads of the line of soldiery, and fierce howls of mutual execration were exchanged by hostile bands of Irishmen, who were prevented from slaughtering each other. The houses . . . on the Shankill Road and in adjoining streets have been gutted by mobs who took the furniture out and burnt it in the street . . . It was pitiable to see families leaving their houses as though going into captivity or exile, and hear the lamentations of the women and children. Protestants living in Roman Catholic districts and Catholics living in Protestant districts have found it necessary to change their quarters and go to their respective friends for protection.

This account of a Belfast riot does not come from the 1970s or even 1920. It is taken from a report in the *Illustrated London News* on the Lady Day riots in Belfast in 1872.

There are patterns in Irish history which are repeated throughout the centuries. The Woodkerne of the sixteenth century, the rural gangs of the late eighteenth and early nineteenth centuries, the IRA of the 1920s and the Provisionals of the 1970s; all have a common lineage.

They have been known as the 'Boys' since Elizabethan times, and they have all been renowned for their attacks on the magistrates and the police. Even the language used by the 'Boys' for these killings, suggesting execution rather than murder, remains similar: 'put out of the way' in the nineteenth century, as against 'getting the message' or being 'blown away' in the twentieth. The methods of maintaining discipline amongst these groups are consistent also: tarring, placarding, and knee-capping. Now, as then, figures appear out of the shadows, strike and then disappear again into the community. Now, as then, the silence of the community is met by the suspension of juries in order to obtain convictions, the Diplock courts being only the latest in a line of such courts throughout the history.

These consistent patterns of violence can be seen in the detail of riots and rioting. Today, the images of soldiers behind their perspex shields have become familiar, but they have a long pedigree going back to the sectarian rioting of the nineteenth century. The armament of the rioter, over and over again, has been the paving stone and the cobblestone. So

regularly were they torn up in Belfast in the latter decades of the nineteenth century that the city corporation decided to lay down 'a more prehensile system of paving in all the argumentative localities of the town'. During periods of tension, the same phenomena spark the riots: the flying of a flag or banner, the singing of a song or, most commonly, an Orange March either through or across the boundary of a Catholic district. The Commission on the disturbances in Londonderry in 1869 remarked 'that it is difficult to say what is not a party tune in Derry; for the most innocent airs, if played by a particular band, assume, at once, for another section of the people, a party character.'

All the phenomena of the current troubles are to be found in the accounts of the nineteenth-century riots: the destruction of the street lighting, the barricades, the accusations that the police sided with the Protestants, police complaints of the wall of silence, and so on. In 1872, the army erected a peaceline after rioting, burning and looting, in the same streets between the Falls Road and the Shankill Road as they were to do in 1935 and 1969. In 1886, there was a 'No-Go' area in the Protestant area of West Belfast, policed by vigilantes, lasting for two months. In 1935, it was several months after the rioting had died down before the barricades were removed.

In England, where this tradition is not understood, violence in Northern Ireland is described by politicians and by the media as 'mindless'. It is not so. It is,

in fact, highly ritualised and structured, and carefully executed. The tactics of a riot, right down to the details of how to set fire to a building or bus, are learned from a long folk memory that is passed on from one generation to the next.

Frankfurt Moore witnessed the riots of 1869 and wrote:

Every boy and girl in the crowd understood the art thoroughly. When the police charged in military fashion, they hurried to one side or the other, refraining from obstructing them in the least, but returning immediately afterward to the place they had occupied before the 'charge'.

Such behaviour can be seen in the film of any minor riot of the last ten years. As the historian A.T.Q. Stewart has written of this re-emergence of the rituals of violence in the late 1960s:

Men and women who had grown to maturity in a Northern Ireland at peace now saw for the first time the monsters which inhabited the depths of the community's unconscious mind. It was as if a storm at sea had brought to the surface creatures thought to have been long extinct.

The ILLUSTRATION left is an *Illustrated London News* drawing of the 1886 riots in Belfast. The photograph shows British troops 'under fire' in the Bogside of Derry, during the recent phase of the troubles.

DEPRIVATION

'Northern Ireland has a higher proportion of low-paid men than any other region in the UK' according to a report published in June 1980, by the Low Pay Unit, an independent research and campaigning body. In April 1979, 20.5% of full-time manual working men earned less than £60 a week (in Great Britain the figure was 9.6%). On average, hours are longer and earnings are lower in Northern Ireland than anywhere else in the United Kingdom. Average hourly earnings for men represented only 89% of the UK average in 1979.

Yet these lower incomes are not offset by lower living costs. In fact, the reverse is the case. Fuel costs, for instance, are much higher: electricity costs 22% more than in Britain and gas charges are nearly three times the national average. Food costs more: a typical Northern Ireland family would have to spend 8% more on basic foodstuffs than one in the UK as a whole.

A generally lower level of income combines with higher costs of many basic requirements to produce the lowest living standards in the whole of the United Kingdom. This is shown in the lower expenditure on consumer durable goods. In 1977, the figures were:

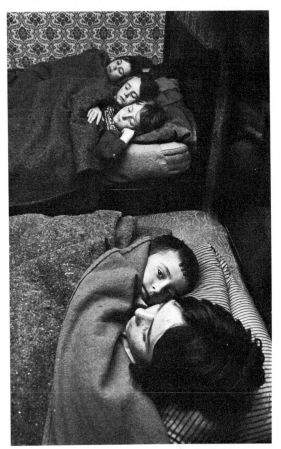

Proportion of households with

	%NI	%UK
washing machines	62	75
refrigerators	75	90
television	89	96

The percentage of the population in public housing and the rate of infant mortality are by far the highest in the United Kingdom. According to an official housing survey of 1974, 20% of all housing in Northern Ireland was classified as unfit, but in Belfast the figure was 50%.

Unemployment in Northern Ireland is on average about double the rate in Great Britain. In the summer of 1980, unemployment was running at about 12% in Northern Ireland which means that 70,000 workers were idle out of a total workforce of about 550,000. To make up for this, the Government spends about 50% more per person in Northern Ireland than in England. Despite enormous subsidies and job creation projects, the prospects for the economy seem bleak.

These figures conceal even higher pockets of unemployment. Since 1976, the Government's Northern Ireland Fair Employment Agency has kept tabs on any form of discrimination in employment. Although to discriminate is illegal, sectarian discrimination still exists despite all the advances of the last decade. In some of the Catholic ghettos of Belfast, unemployment now stands at about 50% of the male workforce. Unequal opportunities have been one of the deepest causes of resentment and grievance amongst the Catholic minority. The Fair Employment Agency has recently found that unemployment amongst Catholics is about two and a half times as great as among Protestants, and that, furthermore, Catholics are often found in the least desirable and least remunerative menial jobs. The Low Pay Unit report draws the conclusion:

. . . the high incidence of low pay and unemployment in Northern Ireland has brought with it poverty and deprivation without parallel in the rest of the United Kingdom.

The PHOTOGRAPHS on these pages are a reminder of what this means in human terms. The first photograph, taken by Don McCullin, shows a man and his daughter in the backyard of their home in Derry's Bogside district. The children are bathed in the tub once a week. The second, a family lunch of bread and tea. The third photograph shows the overcrowding common in Belfast. These photographs were taken by Chris Steele-Perkins.

temporary and partial expedients may be applied.' The British failed to redress the wrongs of the Irish peasant for so long largely because it was assumed that the Irish peasant was like his English counterpart. To the British, emigration was seen as a healthy, practical way to relieve some of the problems on the land; to the Irish it was an inhuman de-population of the countryside and a tragic disembodiment of the Irish way of life. Reforms for Ireland became dependent upon party politics at Westminster — Home Rule was conditional upon the determination of the Liberal Party and the curbing of the powers of the House of Lords. It was in this context that the Irish Parliamentary party under Parnell was able to exploit the electoral vicissitudes in Britain in the 1880s and for once exert real political muscle. To the Irish, matters of life and death in their country depended on the whim of distant English politicians. For the British, Ireland was a relentless irritant that ignored all benign attempts to improve its lot and succeeded in bringing down eleven ministries and ruining the careers of some of the ablest ministers. Few politicians had any deep interest in Ireland, fewer still actually visited the country, and at times when real progress might have been made in Ireland, after the Act of Union, in the wake of the Famine, or (in the context of the North) between 1922 and 1968, Britain turned her back, preoccupied with other issues. As O'Farrell has written 'Anglo-Irish relations were analagous to the story of the leaking roof. When storms made attention imperative, the climate was against anything more than temporary repairs; when the weather cleared, the problem could be forgotten.'

This has led the Irish, throughout their history, to resort to violence to ensure that their grievances receive a hearing. Before the unreasonable or the unyielding, even moderation has to resort to violence to be heard. However unpalatable, the fact is that violence, and often only violence, has been effective in achieving progress in Ireland. It was the violence of the Fenians that drove Gladstone to declare his mission to 'pacify Ireland'. It was the violence that accompanied the Land War that forced land reform. It was the threat of violence by Ulster Protestants from 1912–14 that kept them out of a United Ireland. It was the violence of the IRA campaign in 1920–21 that obtained the independence of the 26 counties. It was violence that brought down the Stormont government in 1972. It was the threat of Loyalist violence that led to the collapse of power-sharing in 1974. Resorting to violence is a symptom of the failure of politics, for when the statesmen fail to accommodate the great issues of their day, it is the 'men of violence' who take over. British governments have always reacted with outrage to deeds of violence, asserting that once the men of violence have been defeated, the problem can be solved. But this is to forget that the men of violence are themselves living proof of the problem, and of the failure of politics. As the historian T.W. Moody remarked, 'Both Northern Ireland and the Irish Free State owe their origin not to the force of argument . . . but to the argument of force.' If there is one lesson to be drawn from the history of Anglo–Irish relations, it is this tragic but inescapable fact.

Map of Ireland Showing the Principal Places Referred to in the Text

PROVINCES OF IRELAND

ULSTER

CONNACHT

LEINSTER

MUNSTER

Partition Boundary of NORTHERN IRELAND

PROVINCIAL BOUNDARIES

COUNTY BOUNDARIES

SITES OF BATTLES

DUBLIN LARGE CITIES

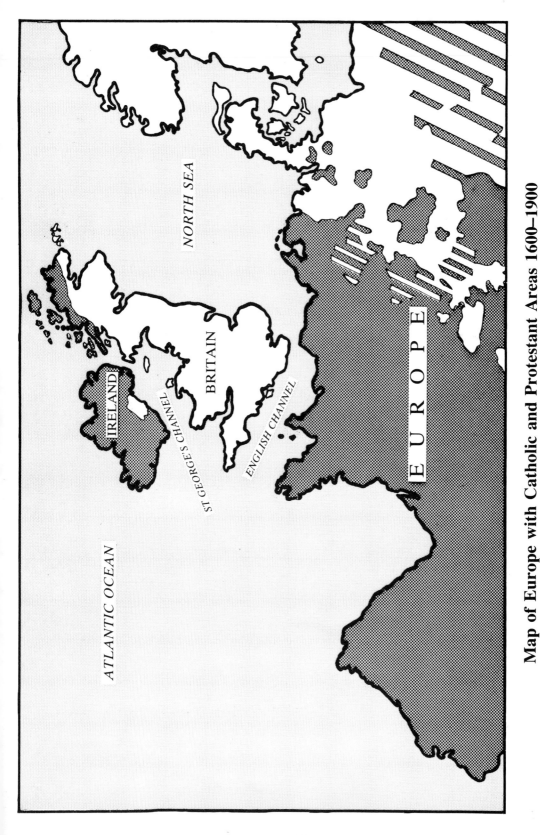

Map of Europe with Catholic and Protestant Areas 1600–1900

ATLANTIC OCEAN

NORTH SEA

IRELAND

BRITAIN

ST GEORGE'S CHANNEL

ENGLISH CHANNEL

E U R O P E

PROTESTANT

CATHOLIC

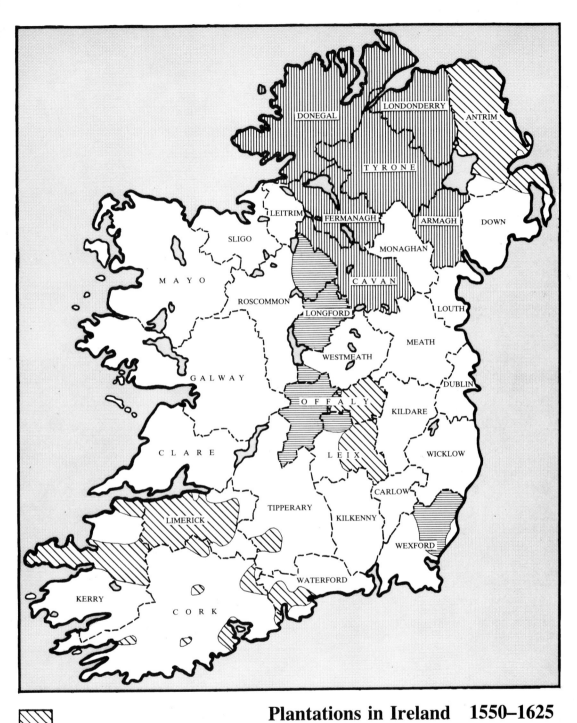

Plantations in Ireland   1550–1625

TUDOR   1550–1603

STUART   1609–1625

OTHER
STUART   1609–1625

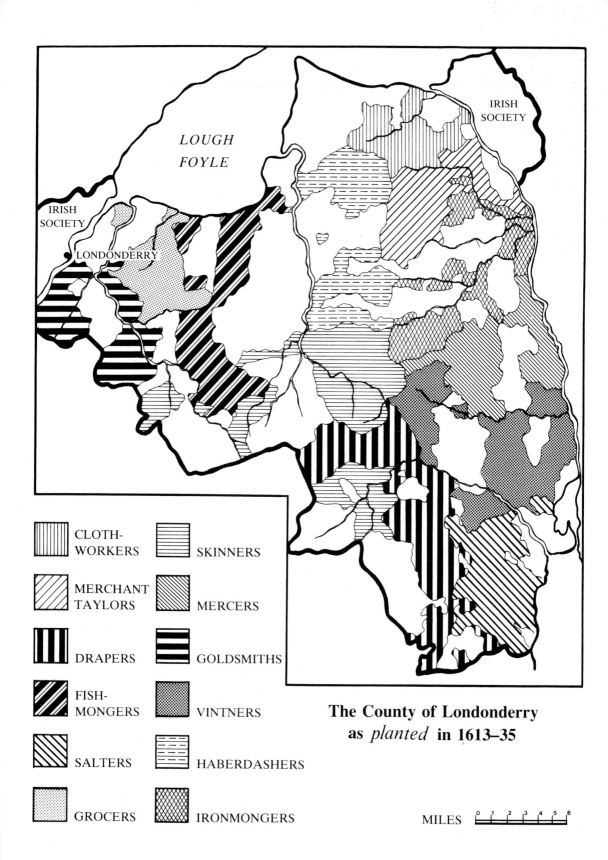

LOUGH FOYLE

IRISH SOCIETY

IRISH SOCIETY

LONDONDERRY

CLOTH-WORKERS

SKINNERS

MERCHANT TAYLORS

MERCERS

DRAPERS

GOLDSMITHS

FISH-MONGERS

VINTNERS

SALTERS

HABERDASHERS

GROCERS

IRONMONGERS

The County of Londonderry
as *planted* in **1613–35**

MILES 0 1 2 3 4 5 6

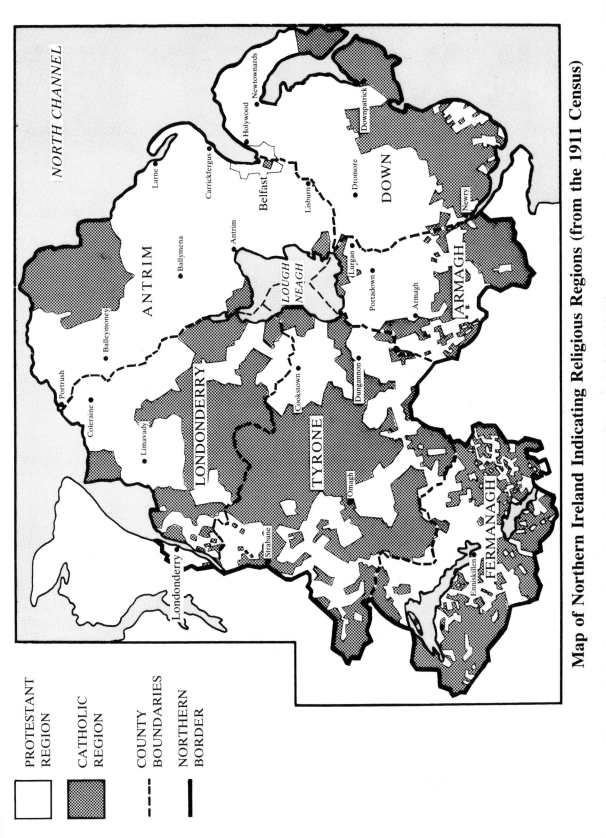

Map of Northern Ireland Indicating Religious Regions (from the 1911 Census)

NORTH CHANNEL

ANTRIM

Larne

Carrickfergus

Belfast

Holywood

Newtownards

Downpatrick

Dromore

DOWN

Lisburn

Newry

Ballymena

Antrim

LOUGH NEAGH

Lurgan

Portadown

Armagh

ARMAGH

Balleymoney

Portrush

Coleraine

LONDONDERRY

Cookstown

Dungannon

Limavady

TYRONE

Omagh

Londonderry

Strabane

FERMANAGH

Enniskillen

PROTESTANT REGION

CATHOLIC REGION

COUNTY BOUNDARIES

NORTHERN BORDER

BELFAST RIOTS

- **A** 1980
- **B** 1979
- **C** 1978
- **D** 1977
- **E** 1976
- **F** 1975
- **G** 1974
- **H** 1973

- **1** 1972
- **2** 1971
- **3** 1970
- **4** 1969
- **5** 1966
- **6** 1964
- **7** 1935
- **8** 1932

- **9** 1920–22
- **10** 1912
- **11** 1898
- **12** 1893
- **13** 1886
- **14** 1872
- **15** 1867
- **16** 1857

CATHOLIC REGION

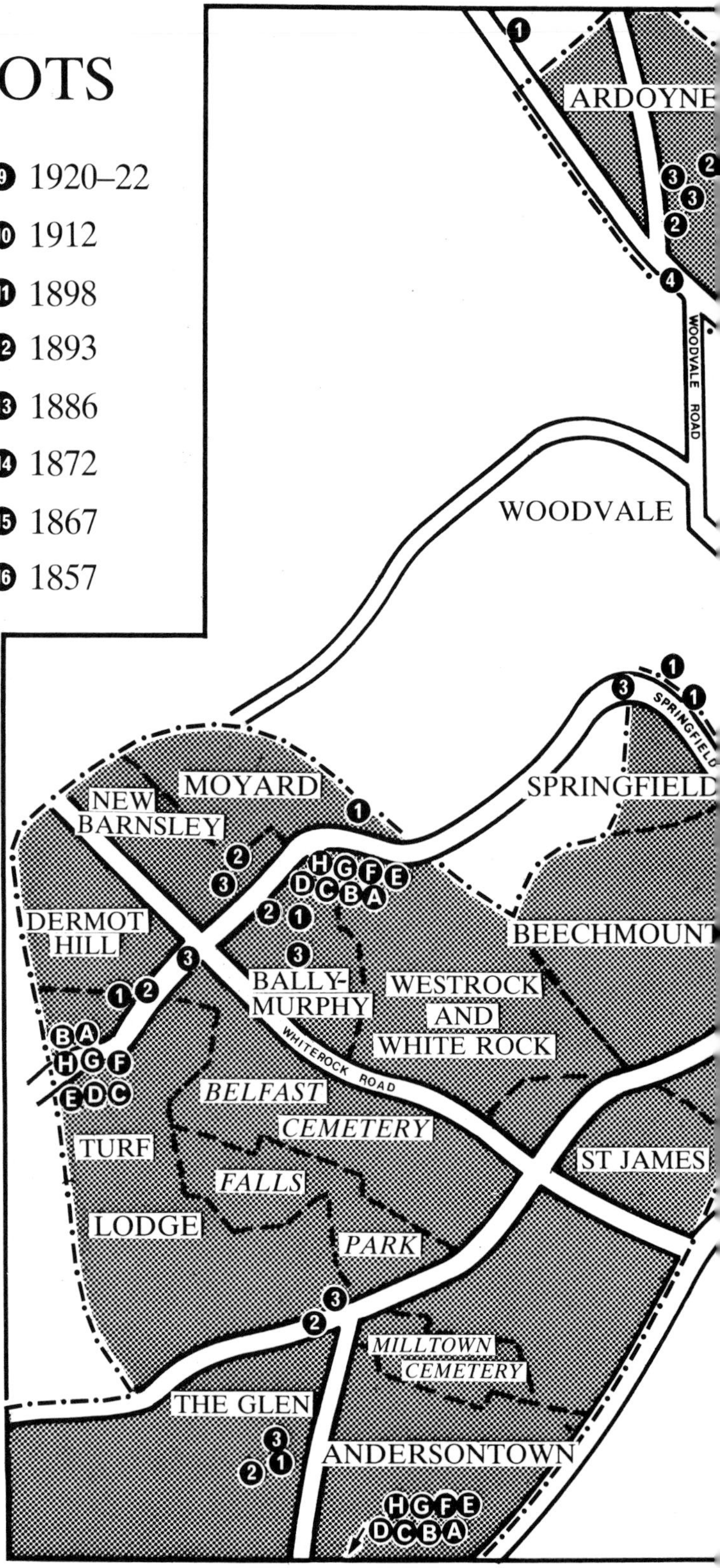

ARDOYNE

WOODVALE ROAD

WOODVALE

SPRINGFIELD

NEW BARNSLEY

MOYARD

SPRINGFIELD

DERMOT HILL

BEECHMOUNT

BALLY-MURPHY

WESTROCK AND WHITE ROCK

WHITEROCK ROAD

BELFAST CEMETERY

TURF

FALLS

LODGE

PARK

ST JAMES

MILLTOWN CEMETERY

THE GLEN

ANDERSONTOWN

The map shows that the principal Sectarian conflicts for well over a Century have all concentrated in the same areas of the City.

202

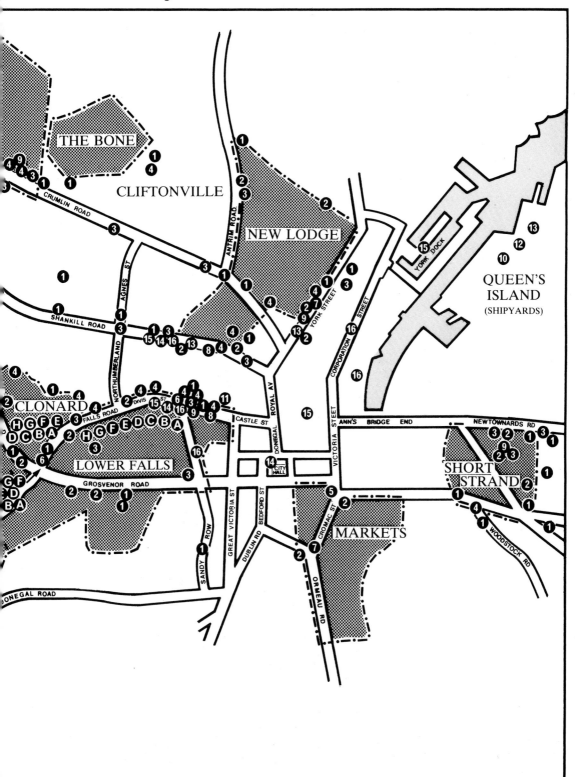

BIBLIOGRAPHY

The following is a list of the books which we have found most helpful in making *The Troubles* series and in writing this book. There is an enormous amount published on Anglo–Irish history and this recommended reading list is, of course, very selective. We hope that anyone whose interest is aroused by the book or series will find the following works useful. All these books are readily available at the moment. The publisher listed is that of the most easily available edition, usually a paperback if there is one. The date is that of publication of *this* edition.

MAIN SOURCES

Michael Farrell. *Northern Ireland: the Orange State*. Pluto, 1976. Critique of the Orange state, 1921–75.

F.S.L. Lyons. *Ireland since the Famine*. Fontana, 1973. The authoritative account of Irish history, 1840s to 1970s.

Patrick O'Farrell. *England and Ireland since 1800*. Oxford University Press, 1975. Fascinating analysis of English and Irish ideologies about each other.

A.T.Q. Stewart. *The Narrow Ground*. Faber 1977. Brilliantly thought-provoking analysis of key episodes in Ulster history.

Charles Townshend. *The British Campaign in Ireland 1919–21*. Oxford University Press, 1978. By far the best account of the Anglo–Irish War.

SUBSIDIARY SOURCES

J.C. Beckett. *The Making of Modern Ireland*. Faber, 1969.

Paul Bew, Peter Gibbon and Henry Patterson. *The State in Northern Ireland*. Manchester University Press, 1979.

J. Bowyer Bell. *The Secret Army*. Academy, Dublin, 1979.

Andrew Boyd. *Holy War in Belfast*. Anvil, 1970.

Patrick Buckland. *The Factory of Grievances*. Gill and Macmillan, 1979.

James Callaghan. *A House Divided*. Collins, 1973.

L.P. Curtis. *Apes and Angels*. David and Charles, 1971.

Liam De Paor. *Divided Ulster*. Penguin, 1971.

E. Estyn Evans and Brian Turner. *Ireland's Eye*. Blackstaff, 1977. Some of the photographs of Robert Welch.

R. Dudley Edwards and T. Desmond Williams (ed.). *The Great Famine*. Browne and Nolan, Dublin, 1956.

Rosemary Harris. *Prejudice and Tolerance in Ulster*. Manchester University Press, 1972.

Kieran Hickey. *The Light of Other Days*. Allen Lane, 1973. Some of the photographs of Robert French.

Christopher Hill. *God's Englishman*. Pelican, 1972. Oliver Cromwell.

Robert Kee. *The Green Flag* (in 3 vols.). Quartet, 1976.

Frank Kitson. *Low Intensity Operations*. Faber, 1975.

Joseph Lee. *The Modernisation of Irish Society 1848–1918*. Gill and Macmillan, 1979.

Eamonn McCann. *War and an Irish Town*. Pluto, 1980.

Oliver MacDonagh. *Ireland: the Union and its Aftermath*. George Allen and Unwin, 1977.

John McGuffin. *Internment*. Anvil, 1973.

David Miller. *Queen's Rebels*. Gill and Macmillan, 1978.

Dervla Murphy. *A Place Apart*. Penguin, 1979. Travel book which provides penetrating insight into Ulster attitudes.

Gearoid O'Tuathaigh. *Ireland before the Famine 1798–1848*. Gill and Macmillan, 1972.

Richard Rose. *Governing without Consensus*. Faber, 1971.

A.T.Q. Stewart. *The Ulster Crisis*. Faber, 1969.

Sunday Times Insight Team. *Ulster*. Penguin, 1972.

David Thomson. *Woodbrook*. Penguin, 1976. Autobiography of an Englishman's discovery of Ireland and her past.

Brian Walker. *Shadows on Glass*. Appletree, 1977. Portfolio of early Ulster photography.

Cecil Woodham-Smith. *The Great Hunger*. New English Library, 1968.

EDUCATIONAL PACKAGES

The Northern Ireland Public Record Office (66 Balmoral Avenue, Belfast 9) produces a series called *Educational Facsimilies* on different episodes of Irish history. They consist of a package of documents, maps and photographs and a brief introduction to the subject. They cover several topics ranging from 'Plantation in Ulster' to 'Steps to Partition' and would be invaluable to teachers. All very reasonably priced, they are available from the NIPRO and all Government Bookshops.

The National Library of Ireland (Kildare Street, Dublin 2) also produce a similar series called *Facsimile Documents*. They cover a slightly different range of topics and again would be useful to teachers of almost any aspect of Irish history. The National Library also sells 35mm slides of many of the key documents of Irish history.

FILMOGRAPHY

The following list of films in no sense purports to be a comprehensive list of films on Ireland, but is designed to cover the situation in Northern Ireland from as many perspectives as are available on film. The capital letter indicates the distributor, where there is one. The key is at the end. p = Production company d = producer/director r = reporter

1959. *Mise Eire*. p. Gael Linn. d. George Morrison. (A). Compilation of archive film and photographs; the first film account of Irish history, up to 1919. Sadly, only available in Gaelic.

1962. *Saoirse?* p. Gael Linn. d. George Morrison. (A). Continues the film history up to 1922. The third part of this planned trilogy, dealing with the Civil War, has never been made because of the sensitivity about the subject. In Gaelic only.

1962. *Ulster Covenant*. p. RHR Prod. for Govt. of N. Ireland. d. R. Riley. (B). Made on 50th anniversary of the signing of the Covenant, to show how partition created an 'anti-Home Rule' state in the North.

1966 *The Irish Rising, 1916*. p. Dept. of External Affairs, Govt. of Ireland. d. George Morrison. (C). Made to celebrate the 50th anniversary of the Rising; covers the period 1913 to release of the internees in 1917.

1968 *World in Action: Backs to the Wall*. p. Granada TV. d. John Sheppard and Mike Ryan. Report on the campaign for civil rights in Derry.

1969 *World in Action: All Change at Newry*. p. Granada TV. d. Charlie Nairn and Mike Ryan. (D). Report on the violence during civil rights march at Newry.

1969 *World in Action: No Surrender*. p. Granada TV. d. Brian Armstrong and David Boulton. Profile of the Protestant working class in N. Ireland.

1969 *This Week: Men in the Middle*. p. Thames TV. d. Chris Goddard. r. John Edwards. Report on British Army's construction of the Peace Line in Belfast.

1969 *World in Action: Crack o' the Whip*. p. Granada TV. d. Brian Armstrong and David Boulton. Profile of the Catholic working class in N. Ireland.

1970 *Bernadette Devlin*. p. ATV Network. d. John Goldschmidt. Biography of Westminster's 22-year-old MP, focusing on her role in the Battle of the Bogside.

1971 *This Week: Whatever Happened to the Moderates?* p. Thames TV. d. Mike Ruggins. r. John Edwards. Profile of John Hume.

1972 *A Sense of Loss*. d. Marcel Ophuls. (F). Portrait of the people of N. Ireland by distinguished French documentary maker.

1972 *World in Action: In Search of Gusty Spence*. p. Granada TV. d. David Boulton. Profile of Loyalist folk-hero, inc. clandestine interview after jumping bail.

1972 *World in Action: A Question of Torture*. p. Granada TV. d. Stephen Clarke. (D). Allegations of ill-treatment which led to Parker inquiry and to European Court of Human Rights in Strasbourg.

1972 *Price of Violence*. p. BBC TV. d. Tony Broughton. r. Harold Williamson. (D) and (E). Report on those maimed, widowed and orphaned by the violence.

1973 *Last Night Another Soldier*. p. BBC TV. d. Eric Davidson. (E). Investigation of feelings of British soldiers serving or about to serve in N. Ireland.

1974 *Ireland Behind the Wire*. p. Berwick Street Film Collective. (D). Intended to help English working-class families understand the violence stemming from the Catholic working-class communities in N. Ireland.

1974 *Five Years — A Thousand Deaths*. p. BBC TV. d. Bill Cran. r. Martin Bell. (E). Analysis of five years of the army in N. Ireland.

1974. *This Week Special: Five Long Years*. p. Thames TV. d. David Elstein. r. Peter Taylor. Survey of events in N. Ireland since troops went in.

1975. *This Week: Hands Across the Sea*. p. Thames TV. d. Ian Stuttard. r. Peter Taylor. Fund-raising for the IRA amongst Irish-Americans.

1977. *This Week: In Friendship and Forgiveness*. p. Thames TV. d. Ian Stuttard. r. Peter Taylor. Whilst the Queen was given by some 'a right, royal welcome', to others in N. Ireland, her Jubilee visit was not popular.

1977. *This Week: Life Behind the Wire*. p. Thames TV. d. Ian Stuttard. r. Peter Taylor. Using film smuggled out of the Protestant H-Blocks, an impression of life in Long Kesh.

1978. *Home, Soldier, Home*. d. Chris Reeves. (G). A film that strongly expresses the dissatisfaction that some soldiers feel after serving in N. Ireland.

1979. *The Patriot Game*. d. Arthur MacCaig. (G). Compilational history of events from late 1960s to late 1970s by Irish–Canadian with heavy Republican interpretation.

1979. *Creggan*. p. Thames TV. d. Michael Whyte and Mary Holland. (H). A portrait of the people who live in the Catholic housing estate in Derry looking back over events of the past few years.

DISTRIBUTORS

A. Gael Linn. 26 Cearnog Mhuirfean, Dublin 2. Dublin 767283.

B. N. Ireland Educational Film Library, Belfast Education and Library Board, Academy Street, Belfast 1. Belfast (0232) 29211.

C. Irish Embassy (Cultural Attaché), 17 Grosvenor Place, London SW1. 01-235 2171.

D. Concord Films Council Ltd, Nacton, Ipswich, Suffolk. Ipswich (0437) 76012.

E. BBC Enterprises Film Hire Library, Woodsten House, Oundle Road, Peterborough. Peterborough (0733) 52257/8.

F. Contemporary Films Ltd, 55 Greek Street, London W1. 01-734 4901.

G. The Other Cinema, 12–13 Little Newport Street, London WC2. 01-734 8508.

H. Film Forum (DBW) Ltd, 56 Brewer Street, London W1. 01-437 6487.

Note: Not all the films listed above are in distribution. Television companies are not always able to make films available for non-theatrical distribution but even when they are able, sometimes do not do so. The National Film Archive holds some of the above films for preservation purposes, but does not allow access to them.

ACKNOWLEDGEMENTS

The authors and publishers would like to thank the following for the use of copyright illustrations. The key to abbreviations is:

BTN	Belfast Telegraph Newspapers	Pace	Pacemaker Press Agency, Belfast
CSP	Chris Steele-Perkins, London	RTE	Radio Telefis Eireann
Hulton	BBC Hulton Picture Library	SI	Syndication International
ILN	Illustrated London News	UFTM	Ulster Folk and Transport Museum
IWM	Imperial War Museum	UM	Ulster Museum
NLI	National Library of Ireland	UTV	Ulster Television Ltd

r indicates right; **l**, left; **t**, top; **b**, bottom. All numbers refer to pages.

11l, 11r NLI. **12** NLI. **16-17** National Gallery of Ireland. **18** Popperfoto. **22** NLI. **24** NLI. **28** UM. **30** UM. **34, 35, 36** NLI. **40, 41** NLI. **46, 47** NLI. **50** Popperfoto. **51** NLI. **56** UFTM. **57t** Taylor Downing. **57b** UFTM. **58** Hulton. **59** NLI. **62, 63** UM. **66** NLI. **67** UM. **68, 69** UM. **72** Central Press Photos Ltd. **73** Independent Newspapers Ltd, Dublin. **74** EMI-Pathé. **78** IWM. **79** Ian Stuttard. **81l, 81r** NLI. **84, 85** IWM. **88, 89** Cork Public Museum. **90** J. Cashman, Dublin. **93** UM. **99** SI. **103** BTN. **104** J. Cashman, Dublin. **105** BTN. **107t** Public Record Office of Northern Ireland. **107b** BTN. **110** Central Press Photos. **112, 113** British Movietone News. **115** ILN. **118, 119** Hulton. **121** IWM. **123** Terence McDonald and David Bigger Collection, Londonderry. **126** Fox Photos. **127** BTN. **131** Barnaby's Picture Library. **135** BTN. **136, 137** BTN. **141t** Press Association. **141b** Central Press Photos Ltd. **143** RTE, except Frames 5, 6: UTV. **146** Associated Newspapers. **147l** Clive Limpkin, London. **147r** Central Press Photos Ltd. **150** SI. **151t** SI. **151b** Colman Doyle, Camera Press, London. **152** Pace. **153t** Popperfoto. **153b** Fox Photos. **158** Camera Press, London. **159** Pace. **161** Pace. **162** Independent Television News Ltd, except Frames 1, 4: RTE. **167** Camera Press, London. **169** SI. **175** Press Association. **176** Express Newspapers. **178** SI. **179** Pace. **182** J. Cashman, Dublin. **183** CSP. **184** CSP. **185** Associated Press. **188** Popperfoto. **191** Ian Stuttard. **192** NLI. **193** Clive Limpkin, London. **194t** Don McCullin, Camera Press, London. **194b** CSP. **195** CSP.

The maps are drawn by Leszek J. Majtas of Ray Moore Animation. Jacket design by Lester Halhed.

INDEX